PRAISE FOR THIS BOOK

»Were Per Albin Hansson, the father of Swedish Social Democracy, to see the state of Sweden today, he would almost certainly turn in his grave. Daniel Hammarberg has comprehensively assembled a representative sample of information about the true condition of contemporary Sweden. Many, including homeschoolers like myself, know first hand the unpleasant truths of Swedish totalitarianism that the government is desperately trying to hide from the world. This book needs to be read by everyone who wants to know what's really going on behind the scenes and past the glossy media image of Sweden's 'Social Paradise'.«

C.C.M.Warren, M.A. Educator, Lecturer, Writer and Homeschooling Activist and Consultant - www.FreeSweden.net

»Daniel Hammarberg goes into great detail to describe the specific details of how life is like in Sweden. I have heard many who think that Scandinavian Socialism is the way to go. For those who are interested in the facts, then "The Madhouse" is a must. Thought the use of government to enrich peoples' lives was a good idea, read "The Madhouse" first!«

Christopher R. Butler, U.S. Army Sergeant, Constitutional Advocate and a supporter of free people everywhere

The author has also worked with the Nordic Committee for Human Rights in bringing to the world's attention the state of child seizures in Sweden, such as the recent Domenic Johansson case, which along with a couple of others are covered in the book. Recently Domenic's father was jailed for withholding his son from the social services, and a married Christian couple was sentenced to nine months in prison this November for having used spanking as part of their child-rearing. Countries that ratify and implement the UN Convention on the Rights of the Child may suffer the same sort of tragedies as the ones that have taken place in this country.

The Madhouse

—

A critical study of Swedish society

Published by Daniel Hammarberg
http://www.danielhammarberg.com/

ISBN-10: 9197936219
ISBN-13 978-91-979362-1-7

To my late mother Agnetha

-

alas, all your effort to salvage our family was for naught.

Table of contents

"THE WORLD'S BEST COUNTRY"

... because its own government says so.

I mean, what can you say about a country whose state TV even has a running show called *Världens modernaste land*, "The world's most modern country?" A country that since 1945 has had a government propaganda agency called *the Swedish Institute*, with a yearly budget of $30 million, with one of its stated goals being to "within the framework of public diplomacy create an interest and confidence in Sweden along with continuously evaluating Sweden's image abroad." A country that for the last half a century has thrown out accusations of human rights abuses against just about the whole world; as one British writer put it - "Internationally, Sweden is known for its main export being unsolicited advice."

The other year, an organization connected to the United Nations called *The Institute for Economics and Peace* started to publish something called the Global Peace Index, a statistic said to measure how peaceful countries are. It joined other dubious statistics such as the Press Freedom Index by *Reporters Without Borders* in presenting Socialist European states as success stories, while the USA is pretty much portrayed as a failed state. In the PFI, Sweden is ranked #1 in spite of laws criminalizing 'hate

1

speech,' while the USA in 2007 was ranked #48 in spite of probably being the only country in the world where the government is completely unable to imprison its citizens over political speech.

Just as in the so-called "Press Freedom Index," in the Global Peace Index, Sweden is ranked very high as well, #10 out of 149 countries in 2010. The USA is #85 this year. In 2007, the index gave an even larger difference - Sweden ranked #7 out of 121 countries, while the USA was at #96, beaten by such countries as Cuba at #59, China at #60, Mexico at #79 and crime-ridden Brazil at #83.

The value of the Global Peace Index was quickly endorsed by such men as CNN head Ted Turner, former President Jimmy Carter and former U.N. general secretary Kofi Annan. Endorsements by globalists and left-wing sympathizers make you a bit curious why the index is portraying the USA in such an unfavourable light - could it simply be because of an inherent anti-American bias in the index? Among the listed 'peace indicators' in the index are these:

Security officers & police - the fewer per population, the better ranking. Hence a country with no police force at all would be ideal.

Military expenditure - the less, the better ranking. Of course you'll have peace if you dismantle your military, everyone knows that.

Military capability/sophistication - the worse, the better ranking.

UN Peacekeeping Funding - if you're late paying your dues to the U.N., you lose ranking here. Now who would have guessed that the U.N. would favour an index containing such a post?

Access to weapons - the more disarmed the population is, the better ranking. 9 out of 10 dictators agree with this one.

Jailed Population - the more criminals locked up, the worse ranking. Of course it's good if the murderers and rapists are out in the streets killing and raping people.

When taking into consideration just what the index is made up of, it's no wonder Sweden ranks high - the country has nearly dismantled its military and severely hampered its law enforcement, while gun laws are very restrictive.

As of 7 July 2010, one of the indicators is "Potential for terriorist[sic] acts." Now who can dispute that they must have done a good job with the index when there's even a typo in there?

Well, enough of these globalist indexes praising Socialist countries. Will you let the likes of Ted Turner, Jimmy Carter and Kofi Annan claim that Sweden is a much better country than the USA - that the USA is indeed one of the worst countries in the world? Or will you learn from this book what really hides behind the facade of the supposedly successful Socialist utopia? By reading this book, you'll learn just why Sweden has such a need of coming up with development indexes such as these - it's because of the simple fact that Sweden isn't a good country to live in.

To paraphrase American Socialist Lincoln Steffens: I have been over to the future of American society, and it doesn't work.

THE JUSTICE SYSTEM

"Grabbarna som har snott en öl
de blir värstingar
bovarna i regeringen
blir landshövdingar
Sveriges lag har ju varit sån
ända sen den kom
att den gäller för dig och mig
men inte för dem"

"The boys that snatched beers
they become juvenile delinquents
the crooks in the Government
become governors
Sweden's law has been that way
ever since it came
that it applies to you and me
but not to them"

Eddie Meduza, vulgar Swedish folk singer

To commence this work on the utter madness of contemporary Swedish society, I will first describe the justice system, the foundation upon which a civilized society rests, without which nothing exists but *might makes right*. Sweden's justice system never fully assimilated the Western thought that gave rise to the English common law in Great Britain and the USA, or the system of civil law with its roots in The Roman Empire. Instead it's an idiosyncratic hybrid partially consisting of the remains of the legal system from the days of the rule of kings; and as many debaters hint at but are somewhat afraid of putting in explicit terms - partially the kind of socialist law that was practised in the Soviet Union, where political aims defined a subservient legal system.

Sweden never became a constitutional republic unlike most other Western countries, and it has managed to shield its basic philosophy of government from the influence of the

4

Enlightenment. The last serious popular uprising in Sweden was *Dalaupproret* in 1743, consisting of farmers marching to the capital of Stockholm, upset over the large numbers of their countrymen that had died during the recent wars. The uprising lacked leadership, however, and was struck down at Stockholm. Hence Swedish government power has never been overthrown since independence was achieved in 1523, the last half a millennium being an unbroken cycle of peaceful transitions of power.

One could say executive power has managed to stay in control of society by appeasing the masses when needed through political reform, but never actually surrendering the reins to the people. Up until a decade or so ago, the history of the Western world has for the last couple of centuries been one of liberation through the establishment of individual rights, with America setting the example for the rest of the world to follow. This process has had an impact on Sweden as well, when the people wanted the same rights and liberty that Americans enjoyed.

Somewhere along the line, however, the socialists appeared to learn a truly successful propaganda scheme; instead of the reactive responses to Western influences, they started aggressively marketing the country as a role model instead, ignoring traditional Western thought in favour of a socialist "third way." The world heard all about such concepts as an *ombudsman* as a watchman for the interests of the people, and later about the sexual radicalism that Sweden succumbed to during the 1960's, which made the country a positive example in the eyes of Western left-wingers.

So, how meaningful is it that a country can boast being the origin of the *ombudsmän*? And what are these *ombudsmän* like? Judging by their jurisdiction and their verdicts, not very reasonable at all, as we will see in the following sections, to be followed by a more serious discussion of the legal system.

5

HomO, the Ombudsman against discrimination on grounds of sexual orientation

Sweden actually had a special ombudsman for this kind of discrimination for a decade or so, mostly so complainants could apply for damages for the discrimination they felt they had been through. These are excerpts from some of the complaints sent to this ombudsman.

I was suspended for being gay

Day-book number 408-2007[1]

"A man filed a complaint to HomO that his membership of a so called Internet community had been suspended because he had threatened another member. According to the man, no threat had been expressed, but a conflict had arisen between him and the other member because of his homosexual orientation. The suspension meant that he couldn't keep in touch with his homosexual friends which comprised an encroachment of his sexual identity and his personal life. Because of the suspension, the man demanded damages for expenses, loss of income and mental anguish.

In his decision, the Ombudsman established that the man in his complaint had not accounted for any circumstances that pointed to that the decision to suspend his account had any connection to his sexual orientation. Hence there was no reason for HomO to go through with the man's complaint and the case was closed without any further action by HomO."

Damages for expenses, loss of income and mental anguish. Can you say... GAY? Sure would be interesting hearing the other guy's version too.

---

1   http://www.homo.se/o.o.i.s/3853

The library won't let me watch gay porn!

Day-book number 23-2007[1]

"A man filed a complaint to Homo that the municipality library in his town had put in a block in their computers which made it impossible for him to visit a certain so called Internet community for homo, bi, trans and queer people. In his complaint the man explained among other things that he had been told by a librarian that other visitors felt sick when he was watching naked pictures. He had then attempted to explain that the website in question wasn't pornographic but a so called "dating site." According to the view of the complainant it wasn't his fault that other people wanted to present themselves naked and he himself kept only appropriate pictures on the site.

In a statement to HomO, the municipality explained that for the use of the municipality's public computers there is a general ban on visiting websites with pornographic content or content that for other reasons may be found offensive. When the complainant had visited the site in question, on several occasions there had been other visitors reacting to images they found offensive. The library staff had then asked him to click away the images but he didn't comply with the wishes of the staff. After this had been repeated on several occasions, the municipality blocked the site in question. The block was lifted two weeks later, when they had found a technical solution that made it possible to automatically remove the images when the site was frequented from the municipality's public computers."

Homo's response:

"[...]Hence there is no reason to assume that the municipality's decision to temporarily block the website constituted discrimination."

Well... What could possibly be said about the case?

---

1 http://www.homo.se/o.o.i.s/3848

7

Better watch what you say about homosexuality

Day-book number 124-2005[1]

"Three students at a college filed a complaint to HomO that a teacher during a class had made derogatory statements about homosexuality and homosexuals. When the students then visited the teacher to discuss his statements he didn't appear interested in their opinions and how his statements had affected them. During these conversations as well, the teacher expressed discomfort and disgust towards homosexual relationships.

During contacts with HomO, the college declared among other things that the teacher in question mostly denied having expressed himself in the way claimed by the complainants. The college did however concede that the teacher through his actions outside the time of the lecture had subjected the students to a violation.

During deliberations between HomO and the college, there was an agreement according to which the college would pay 30,000 crowns ($4,000) each to the three complainants. In the agreement, the college also regretted that it, through one of its employees, had behaved in an offensive manner. The matter was closed through the agreement."

This teacher was subsequently fired from his job, in spite of the complaint filed by the students having been a gross overexaggeration of the views he had really expressed.

---

1   http://www.homo.se/o.o.i.s/3690

I'm not a transsexual, I'm a bisexual!

Day-book number 160-2006[1]

"A bisexual man sentenced to involuntary psychiatric care filed a complaint to HomO that the physician in charge of him at the institution treated him based on the diagnosis of transsexuality, in spite of this being at odds with both his own opinion and a statement by forensic psychiatry. He felt discriminated against since his bisexual orientation wasn't respected and because he wasn't provided access to the same benefits given to other patients."

"HomO found that in what remained, no circumstances had been accounted for that made it appear that the treatment the complainant was subjected to, and that he felt was to his disadvantage, had anything to do with his bisexuality. HomO therefore found no reason to take any further measures in the matter."

So even in a psych ward, an LGBT person feels he's being discriminated against. Now if only the delusions of persecution entertained by gay activists out in society were exposed as equally baseless. And if all homosexuals and bisexuals were properly sentenced to involuntarily psychiatric care just like this man, the way they should...

Kidding, of course... That would be a huge waste of taxpayer money.

---

1   http://www.homo.se/o.o.i.s/2540

Want a gay blow job as a tip?

Day-book number 470-2007[1]

"A man filed a complaint that he had been subjected to harassment by a taxi driver after a taxi ride, who had made derogatory comments towards him, his girlfriend and another man. The complainant stated in the report that both he and the other man are transvestites and that they had been dressed in women's clothes at the time. According to the complainant, the taxi driver had at the end of the trip explained that he didn't want any tips from them and among other things yelled "f***ing fags" at them. During contacts with HomO, the taxi driver denied having expressed himself in the stated way. The driver also stated that the third passenger in the car had offered him tips in the form of a specific sexual service, and that he thereafter had said "I'm not gay, you f**k!

In his decision, the Ombudsman established that contradictory information had been provided about what had taken place during the taxi ride in question. Considering that the other man who had taken part in the trip hadn't wanted to participate in the investigation, and with the information provided by the taxi driver as background, there was according to the Ombudsman insufficient prerequisites for HomO to file charges in the errand that was therefore closed."

The cases where people file complaints even though it becomes evident that they might be guilty of criminal offences themselves (sexual harassment) are truly amusing.

---

1   http://www.homo.se/o.o.i.s/4095

Sometimes truth is stranger than fiction

Day-book number 180-2008[1]

"A man filed a complaint that a lottery required everyone who wanted to take part in the lottery to have access to direct debit. According to the man he lacked employment because of his sexual orientation which led to him not having a personal bank account or access to direct debit. With this background, the complainant felt that the lottery's requirement to have access to direct debit constituted discrimination because of sexual orientation.

HomO established in his decision that for a refusal to make available a product or service to an individual to constitute direct discrimination because of sexual orientation, a causal relationship must exist between the decision to not make available the product in question, and the sexual orientation of the individual. The circumstances the complainant has brought up - that it was impossible for him to satisfy the lottery's requirement for access to direct debit because of his lack of employment, and that his lack of employment in turn was due to his sexual orientation - could according to the view of the Ombudsman not be considered sufficient for the requirement that such a relationship exists to have been met.

Referring to what was brought up in the complaint there was no reason to assume that the man had been subjected to discrimination based on sexual orientation, the errand was closed without any further action on the part of the Ombudsman."

I actually feel a bit of sympathy for the HomO ombudsman over this one... How do people come up with these cases?

Some 320 complaints were sent to HomO between 1999 and 2009, when it was merged into DO, the Ombudsman against Discrimination, or at least that's the number that can be accessed

---

1   http://www.homo.se/o.o.i.s/4041

11

online.

On top of the mentioned ones, no less than six complaints were about welfare application forms, how these only let you enter husband/wife or man/woman as the residents of one's household, not the more 'modern' forms of cohabitation. And LGBT activists always tell you that they're paying taxes just like everyone else...

(Day-book numbers 297-2007, 149-2007, 371-2006, 499-2003, 248-2003 and 30-2001. All of the involved parties agreed to change the forms in the requested manner as a consequence of these complaints.)

The parliamentary Ombudsman (JO) – A convict's best friend

In Swedish called *Justitieombudsmannen* (JO), which directly translates into the Ombudsman of Justice, this institution was established as part of the new constitution in 1809; its role being to monitor the exercising of power by the government and receive complaints by people who feel their rights have been violated. The idea was to provide the people with a counterbalance to the king's natural unconstitutional influence over government.

Though the institution itself has been lauded internationally as proof of how progressive and protective of human rights Swedish society is, very few citizens find they can get justice here, with plenty of expressions of dissatisfaction surfacing on the Internet. Other countries have introduced similar authorities in their own countries, inspired by the appearance of what the Swedish JO supposedly is. Earlier, the JO would prosecute authority figures who had neglected to abide by the law, but today it produces admonishments at best.

A particular demographic has however found the JO very obliging towards its requests - namely convicted felons. On the webpage for the Swedish Prison Service, *www.kvv.se*, there's even a link to the JO's webpage, with instructions on how to file a complaint. It doesn't cost any money to file a complaint, and you can even do it through E-mail. The JO webpage provides a form to use for complaints, but that's optional, you can write one freely too. The pdf document the form is in includes a "send" button that automatically sends the complaint to the JO. And can you believe it - the pdf document is available in English as well! And so are the instructions. To quote the instructions on the webpage www.jo.se:

"Who can complain?

Anyone can complain to the Parliamentary Ombudsmen (JO), you do not need to be a Swedish citizen or even live in Sweden

You do not have to reach a certain age before you can complain

Your complaint does not have to be about something that affects you personally"

"What information should a complaint contain?"

(Whom it's against, what's happened etc. No requirements on being specific concerning involved parties or such information, and no requirements on just what it should contain.)

"Attach **copies** if possible of any documents that help to show that the authority and/or the public official acted improperly"

(That's their bold emphasis, not mine. I guess they had a problem with people sending in original documents. Notice that it's not a requirement to send in any.)

"a written complaint should be **signed**"

Notice the absence of a "have to." I guess the bold emphasis of the word "signed" means that it's supposed to be a signature and not just some funny drawing you want to end your complaint with.

What follows here is just two days' worth of complaints by prison inmates, the two days before the initial draft of this section of the book:

I don't deserve to be in solitary confinement

Date of the adjudication: 2010-04-09

Registration numbers: 488-2009, 1830-2009[1]

"Complaints against the Prison Service, Hällby institution, concerning solitary confinement of an inmate."

"In a complaint, arriving at the JO on the 29th of January 2009, A.M. complained about the way he's been treated and thereby expressed his dissatisfaction with having been placed in solitary confinement for four months."

Statement by the prison service:

"On 16 February 2009, A.M. was reported for threatening and assaulting an officer. From a written report concerning suspected mismanagement, it's clear from among other things two accounts that A.M. has requested to talk to a specific keeper. It's also stated that the keeper comes to the prison block to talk to him. By one account, it's stated that A.M. rushes into the guard room, where the specific keeper is residing, but that he's stopped at the door by another keeper. As this happens, A.M. is instructed to go into a dialogue room to sit down and talk. It's also stated that he attempts to pass the keeper, but fails. At the time of the failed attempt, A.M. asks "whose c**k are you sucking?" to then spit the sought-after keeper right in the face and exclaim "f***ing gypsy whore!" It's also stated that staff intervene and move A.M. back to his living quarters.

"The 12th of March 2009 at around 8:05, an inmate from the prison block requests solitary confinement for his own safety. The staff establishes that the inmate had visible injuries in the form of a knocked out tooth along with a thick lip. For forensic investigations, all inmates are solitarily confined. It's also stated

---

1   http://www.jo.se/Page.aspx?
MenuId=106&ObjectClass=DynamX_SFS_Decision&Id=4753

15

that upon inspection of A.M.'s quarters, the staff find a pair of blood-stained pants, and the knuckles on his right hand are swollen and turned red."

JO's response:

"What's now been said means in my opinion that the institution on the 28th of September 2008 placed A.M. in solitary confinement without in the decision in any way relating to the legal requirements for the measure, something I consider very serious."

"I am very critical of the institution's handling in mentioned respects."

"The matter is closed with the serious criticism contained in what's been stated."

But doesn't this guy sound like someone who should indeed be in solitary confinement?

I need my mail on time!

Date of the adjudication: 2010-04-08

Registration number: 2344-2009[1]

"Complaint against the prison service, Ystad jail, about the handling of mail to an inmate.

In a complaint to the JO, J.B. complained that Ystad jail had stalled in delivering a letter to him. The letter contained sound recordings from the trial in the district court which he was going to listen to with his attorney before the negotiations in the appeals court."

Statement by the prison service:

"Shift Officer Monika Eriksson states that she remembers the package addressed to J.B."

"She remembers that the package was addressed to his home address and that there was no sender."

"Unfortunately the electronics didn't work and the material couldn't be viewed in the newly acquired DVD player that had been purchased to manage most disc formats and USB memory cards. After the visit, Monika Eriksson followed J.B. to his room to see if the disc worked in his CD player."

Sounds like a pretty comfortable life in there, having your own CD player, as well as having the Shift Officer run errands for you.

"That none of the packages were forwarded to J.B. before the visit of the attorney appears to have been due to the communication between staff not functioning adequately, which is regrettable."

---

1   http://www.jo.se/Page.aspx?
MenuId=106&ObjectClass=DynamX_SFS_Decision&Id=4747

JO's response:

"The prison service is under criticism for its handling of the mail in question."

How dare the prison chief tell an inmate to shut up?

Date of the adjudication: 2010-04-08

Registration number: 6741-2009[1]

"Complaints against the prison service, Västervik Norra institution, about the treatment of an inmate.

In a complaint that arrived at the JO's office on December 1, 2009, T.B. expressed complaints about the institution and had among other things this to say. One time, Prison chief Richard Göransson told him he "wasn't wanted" and told him to "shut up."

Statement by the prison service:

"Prison chief Richard Göransson has stated the following, among other things. On the morning of November 26, 2009, T.B. was brought into his quarters to be interrogated, since T.B. had been behaving badly in the prison block. T.B. didn't seem the least bit interested in participating in this interrogation on the institution's terms but chose time and time again to interrupt him when a report etc. was to be read.

After the interrogation was over, Richard Göransson explained that it wasn't in question that T.B. would return to the prison block he was placed at before he was moved to Karlskoga institution. The reason for this was that T.B. himself had applied to leave since he didn't feel comfortable and wanted to be moved to a treatment centre. T.B. was placed back into Västervik Norra institution since it had available regular rooms which the placement unit thought was what benefited T.B. the most. T.B. didn't want to accept this but kept going over injustices and misfortunes that he had suffered at society's hands and by Västervik Norra institution.

---

1   http://www.jo.se/Page.aspx?
MenuId=106&ObjectClass=DynamX_SFS_Decision&Id=4742

When he time and time again started over and tried to get T.B. to listen and be quiet, he uttered, somewhat annoyed, the following line: "T.B., how about you shut up for a moment and listen instead, so we can get this done."

T.B. immediately responded "Shut up yourself, you old f***!"

JO's response:

"Hence I share the opinion of the prison service about the unsuitability of Richard Göransson telling T.B. to 'shut up' and Richard Göransson can't escape criticism."

I can imagine what this response did to T.B.'s attitude.

Don't you dare messing up my dental care!

Date of the adjudication: 2010-04-08

Registration number: 4750-2009,4751-2009[1]

"Complaints against the prison service, Västervik Norra institution, concerning the handling of requests for dental care etc."

"In two complaints, that arrived at the JO's office on 27 August 2009, T.B. expressed complaints about the institution and had among other things this to say."

Yes... This is the same T.B. as above. Adults who are not clients of the prison service are not entitled to the free dental care that convicts are. It requires quite a bit of audacity on the part of an inmate to send a complaint to the JO just because the routines for arranging dentist appointments outside the institution had left the inmate not informed about the scheduled time. The prison service explains when asked about the matter that the inmates can't be informed in advance when they have their appointments, since they might then coordinate escape attempts.

JO's response:

"I take seriously what has taken place, and the institution is under criticism."

This T.B. filed at least seven complaints (some other complaints on his part are referred to as well in these complaints, but these aren't to be found on the JO website) between June 2008 and November 2009, on such matters as a late food serving, a request for more furloughs, having to pay money for xerox copies

---

1   http://www.jo.se/Page.aspx?
MenuId=106&ObjectClass=DynamX_SFS_Decision&Id=4744

inside prison and being assigned to work when he instead wanted to study. On top of this, in one footnote he complains about having to take part in a treatment program for convicted sex offenders when he maintains he's innocent. (Apart from mentioned ones, registration numbers 5451-2009, 4435-2009, 5754-2008, 3108-2008. Every single complaint led to the JO criticizing the hotel... oops, I mean prison T.B. stayed at at the time.)

Though these next three complaints weren't produced the two days in question, their silliness make them worth mentioning still.

You kept me locked up during breakfast!

Date of the adjudication: 2010-06-16

Registration number: 964-2010[1]

"In a complaint arriving at the JO on 18 February 2010, inmates at section A of the Hall institution generally stated the following. On the morning of 12 February 2010 the institution staff forgot to unlock M.S.'s cell. First during breakfast at 8:20 his fellow inmates noticed he was missing. The institution staff then unlocked his cell. Because of what took place, M.S. didn't get breakfast that day."

Statement by the prison service:

"From the statements it's become known that the keeper started the unlocking at 7:45 in section 2. It only takes a couple of minutes since the section only has eight rooms. At 8:15, the staff is contacted by M.S. through the signal device in his cell, who then states he's still locked up. The keeper immediately heads there to unlock. She assures herself that M.S. is all right and apologizes to him.

Because of what has taken place a report has been made and an interrogation has been held with the keeper. The keeper can't state exactly what took place before the missed unlocking. Someone possibly initiated a conversation with her or she got distracted in some other way."

Response by the JO:

".... inmates at a closed prison may be locked up in their cells for at most twelve hours per day. Incarceration may take place at 19:00 at the earliest and 20:00 at the latest. Unlocking may take place at 6:30 at the earliest and 8:00 at the latest.

---

1   http://www.jo.se/Page.aspx?
MenuId=106&ObjectClass=DynamX_SFS_Decision&Id=4948

The investigation shows that the unlocking of M.S.'s cell that day took place at 8:15 and therefore too late. It's obvious that it was an individual mistake that caused the delayed unlocking. Even if it is that way, it's not acceptable that the staff forget to unlock the door to an inmate's living quarters. The institution can't escape criticism for what has taken place."

Hall is one of Sweden's two highest security prisons. My, the inmates there seem to have it rough, occasionally not being served breakfast and having to complain to the JO because of it.

Male convict scared of female keeper

Date of the adjudication: 2008-09-25

Registration number: 900-2008[1]

"V.S. has in a complaint, arriving at the JO on 19 February 2008, lodged a complaint against Kumla institution and stated the following. When he woke up one morning there was no yoghurt, and therefore he called keeper Ann-Sofie Karlsson and asked if she could contact the kitchen and request a litre of yoghurt. After the call the keeper forgot to turn off the communications equipment, and then she said "what a f***ing idiot, I could kill him" so that both he and other inmates heard it. He feels threatened and scared because of this event."

Statement by the prison service:

"When A-S.K realized that the communications equipment wasn't turned off, she went to V.S. to explain to him that the statement wasn't about him."

"No matter whom the statement was made about, the prison service considers it very serious that an employee states that she feels like killing someone. This is completely unacceptable and is in direct violation of the ethics and values of the prison service. This regional manager is therefore considering reporting the event to the staff disciplinary board of the prison service."

"A-S.K. has naturally been reprimanded and reminded over how highly inappropriate the statement was."

Statement by the JO:

"In my opinion it's still completely unacceptable that an employee in the prison service at all expresses herself in the way Ann-Sofie

_____

1   http://www.jo.se/Page.aspx?
MenuId=106&ObjectClass=DynamX_SFS_Decision&Id=3244

Karlsson has done. The conduct warrants especially serious criticism.

The Prison Service is currently investigating whether the event shall be reported to the staff disciplinary board at the Prison Service."

And Kumla is Sweden's toughest prison... I'm also appalled at the JO for not recognizing that the convict is harassing the keeper. In a sane society, a male inmate harassing a female employee would result in sanctions against the inmate, not the other way around. Though the text in the case doesn't give that many details, I'm inclined to think in terms of the kind of psychological terror rape convict Max Cady waged in the movie Cape Fear. The convict both told the keeper to get him yoghurt in a manner that seems to have stressed her out, and also filed a complaint with the JO against her. It's baffling how the identity of the convict is hidden, while the shamed keeper is explicitly named.

Cop killer crying about being transported by police officers

Date of the adjudication: 2006-06-30

Registration number: 2345-2005[1]

I found this entry while looking for T.B.'s complaints, but this is obviously not the same person.

> "T.B. complained that the correctional facilities Hall and Kumla on two occasions had handed the responsibility of transporting him between prisons to the police and that there during the transports hadn't been any staff from the prison service present. He also complained that the police officers, during one of the transports, had expressed themselves in a threatening manner towards him. He thereby stated among other things the following. At the end of January 2004, he received information that he was going to be transported from the Hall institution to the Kumla institution. He was therefore handcuffed and led to the transport car. To his surprise he discovered that there was only a police van present. When he had entered the van he also realized that there were only police officers in the van and no staff from the prison service. During the transport, the police officers told him that one of their colleagues had attended a course with **one of the police officers** he's convicted of having killed. They explained that he was lucky that this police officer wasn't present during this transport and that there was nothing that stopped them from beating him up if they wanted to."

Oh, poor multiple cop killer... Is there no justice in Sweden? A man who has killed several police officers has to be transported by angry police who threaten him, even though they never actually lay a finger on him.

---

1   http://www.jo.se/Page.aspx?
MenuId=106&ObjectClass=DynamX_SFS_Decision&Id=2576

Statement by the prison service:

(Lots of quotes on the responsibilities of the prison service towards inmates cut.)

"It can be established that the handling of the transports in question haven't been carried out in accordance with the directions of the prison service."

"The execution of the transports was handed to the police even though there was no constitutional support for such an action."

"No matter the formal deficiencies in the handling of the transports it was in this case according to the prison service suitable for them to be catered for by the police. It was a matter of transports of an inmate for which it requires an extensive security arrangement to avoid rescue attempts and similar. It's only the police that has adequate resources to secure that such high risk-transports can be carried out in a secure manner. The prison service should therefore have the option to request that the police take over the execution of a transport."

Statement by the JO:

"By they themselves having planned the transports, the staff in charge at the Hall and Kumla institutions have neglected [legal] framework in force. For this they can't escape criticism."

"Furthermore, in accordance with the regulation of the prison service, at every transport a transport leader in charge from the prison service's transport service has to accompany [the transport]. From the investigation into the matter it becomes clear that this hasn't been the case, but the responsibility for T.B. was handed completely to the police. This procedure as well is in violation of the framework in force and deserves criticism."

I wonder whom the families of the killed police officers can complain to... Instead of criticizing the prison service over mere nonsense, how about calling out this man T.B. for murdering these men?

The Supreme Court - Den of indecency

"Muriel," she said, "read me the Fourth Commandment. Does it not say something about never sleeping in a bed?"

With some difficulty Muriel spelt it out.

"It says, 'No animal shall sleep in a bed *with sheets*,' she announced finally.

Curiously enough, Clover had not remembered that the Fourth Commandment mentioned sheets; but as it was there on the wall, it must have done so.

George Orwell - Animal farm

The highest legal organ in Sweden is *Högsta domstolen*, The Supreme Court, whose members are appointed by the incumbent government for an indefinite period, without public discussion or scrutiny, unlike what is the case for the American counterpart. Though the Justices on this court have the highly important task of setting legal precedents on whose basis future criminal cases will be judged, their members are quite anonymous to the broad public, and the average Swede can be expected to name at most one of its currently 16 members. One would assume that the men and women on this court are devoted judges with impeccable morals, since their job is such a critical one, and until a couple of years ago, few Swedes would have thought otherwise.

This was a bubble that burst in March of 2005, as Supreme Court Justice Leif Thorsson pleaded guilty to having bought sexual services from a young man still attending high school. Justice Thorsson had spent time on the Internet chat of the Swedish gay lobby RFSL, where he had come into contact with this young man. The RFSL chat is a well-known nexus for homosexual prostitution, and the business that's made here rarely results in any legal consequences, but as it would turn out, Thorsson had run into a bit of bad luck.

The young man, 19 years old at the time of his hookups with 59-year-old Thorsson, had amassed personal debts and decided to go into prostitution to sort out his financial calamity. The RFSL chat provided plenty of opportunity for a man in his predicament - customers weren't hard to find. On the chat, he used the nickname *STHLMung* - short for "Stockholm young," and this is the name he'll go by here. *STHLMung* had met up with Thorsson in January of that year. This is the chat log from the first time they hooked up:

(Thorsson was using the name *Leif 59 Gamla Stan* - "Leif 59 Old Town" (a district of Stockholm).)

(Text somewhat filtered by me. The entirety of the log was unfortunately not available to yours truly - using the one quoted by tabloid Expressen.)

"STHLMung: YOUNG F***ING H*RNY GUY WANTS TO HOOK UP NOW IN STHLM
Leif 59 Gamla Stan: want h*rny now
S: i charge money
L: yeah
S: ok i'll do anything except [anal intercourse]... charge 500 crowns you can go at it for as long as you want!
L: where are you and how do you look?
L: sounds fine, where are you now?
L: do you like to [give head]?
S: i'm in xxxxxxx look cuuuute 170 cm tall 65 kg and xx xx xxx... i've got car so i can quickly go to you but only if you're really serious....
S: i like to [give head].
S: we can hook up if you want, would be nice... at Järntorget
L: i like to [be given head] 500 ok

S: call me on 07xxxxxxxx but only if you're serious i don't want
to go to you and then you're not there...."

The next two months, according to the testimony of
STHLMung, he and Thorsson meet up at Thorsson's home five
times, with STHLMung selling his body to Thorsson for cash.
STHLMung doesn't go about his affairs in a very orderly manner,
however - as a way of gaining faster money, he starts to rob his
wealthy clients. Although he never puts Thorsson through this, a
man in Tyresö whose home he had gone to as part of the same
business, instead finds himself robbed; this becomes a legal
matter, and when the police investigate STHLMung's affairs, they
discover that his many clients included an actual Supreme Court
Justice.

On STHLMung's cell phone, they find Leif Thorsson's
number as well as SMS messages he has sent to this young man.
Thorsson contacted STHLMung quite frequently, and one of the
messages had been:

"Let me know when we can hook up. It felt so good the last time
we hooked up."

The police also find the session log from the RFSL chat,
where STHLMung had talked to Thorsson. STHLMung is quickly
sentenced to 14 months in prison for the robbery, but since buying
(although not selling) sexual services is a crime, now an
investigation is initiated against Justice Thorsson. During an
interrogation, STHLMung had told police he met up with
Thorsson on five different occasions, but this doesn't have
Thorsson worried.

At first when the police question Thorsson in early March of
2005, he denies any responsibility, yet when the police present
their 55-page investigation, he pleads guilty to a single count of
sex purchase. The matter is settled without a trial through an order

31

of summary punishment, charging Thorsson a 42,500 crown fine, or about $6,000. The misdemeanour had only resulted in 50 *dagsböter* [a fine based on daily income], but due to Thorsson's two million crowns a year personal income, the fine becomes quite heavy. Thorsson was also spared the usually mandatory house search that follows a criminal investigation, which most likely would have uncovered evidence of a large range of sex purchases.

As a Supreme Court Justice, Thorsson had been tasked with delivering the final verdict on a number of sex crimes cases, and setting future precedents. One of these cases was *NJA 2003:45*, where a young man had been charged with distributing child pornography over the Internet.

To quote the court documents:

"M.F. has on 14 June 2000 in a computer in his residence in Uppsala municipality been in possession of 2195 data files, including 74 movie clips, containing depictions of children in pornographic imagery."

"In the pictures, the district court has been able to witness how young boys have both been penetrated by older [ones], as well as masturbating themselves and/or others. The participants in the pictures have, as far as the district court has been able to tell, not been subjected to other violence than the violence that the participation in the sexual acts and the posing has constituted. In a number of pictures, it has however been possible to see how badly the participants have felt about the excesses."

"M.F. has during a period from the autumn of 1999 to June of 2000 communicated on ICQ, a so called chat program on the Internet, with 15 to 20 people, among others a person calling himself Kaninhövdingen [The rabbit chieftain]. In this circle, the people have amongst themselves traded child-pornographic pictures and movie clips."

When this case had reached the Supreme Court in 2003, the prosecutor wanted to sentence M.F. to prison. Two of the five Supreme Court Justices judging that case wanted to go with the prosecutor, but on the other side, Thorsson and two other Justices determined through a majority vote the sentence to be a fine of 18,000 crowns. The two Justices with the minority opinion had based their view that prison was the proper punishment on the precedent set in *NJA 2002 s. 265*, where a man had been sentenced to six months in prison for *gross child pornography crime*. This man, in the online version of the legal documents referred to as A.Å., had hosted a server to distribute child pornography, sending a total of 8299 pictures to 881 different users. To quote this case:

> "In the case, the following has been stated concerning A.Å.'s dealing with child-pornographic pictures. He had two computers for which he used a software that provides the opportunity to "chat" with other Internet users. By this means, people with certain interests can communicate with each other on special "channels." A.Å. was connected to such a one under the name "Preteen." As an additional service he had at his disposal space for storing material. To this, visitors could "upload" files onto A.Å.'s computer equipment and from there also "download" files to computers of their own. A.Å. used a space named "Emma" from 12 Dec. 1999 to 2 Jan. 2000 and another, "Anna," from 3 Jan. 2000. There was a form of "advertisement" that was meant to attract visitors. To be able to "download" three files to his own computer, a visitor had to "upload" one file to A.Å."

Since M.F. had acted in a similar way, the two Justices had a good case for sending him to prison, but thanks to Thorsson and the two others, he was left with only a fine and parole. In general, Swedish courts appear very reluctant to take child pornography seriously, with only four prison sentences delivered in 2009 out of a total of 44 such convictions, most of which led to fines; 345

cases were reported to the police that year.[1] A stunning verdict that year was delivered on the 28th of may - the one in *RH 2009:78*, where a man on several occasions had taken pictures of the genitalia of children (girls), whose underwear he had personally removed. In Svea court of appeal, all he's sentenced to is a fine of 15,000 crowns, or $2,000. The man also got to keep the hard drive on which he had stored the images even though it had been in state custody as evidence.

But to return to Thorsson; as it became publicly known at the end of March 2005 that he had been found guilty of this offence, his position as a Supreme Court Justice was brought into question - there were calls for his dismissal. Chancellor of Justice (JK) Göran Lambertz, a personal acquaintance of Thorsson, is then tasked with determining whether a dismissal trial is to be brought before the Supreme Court. Delivered at the end of May that year, this was the JK's verdict:

> "Question concerning the possible measures of the Chancellor of Justice due to a Supreme Court Justice having been found guilty of a crime.
>
> Date of decision: 2005-05-25
> Registration number: 2495-05-22"[2]
>
> "Assessment by the Chancellor of Justice
>
> LT is in possession of a regular judge office as a Supreme Court Justice. He's now been handed an order of summary punishment. It can be questioned whether at the side of the sanction under criminal law, a procedure shall be initiated for the purpose of separating him from his office. I've agreed with the head parliamentary ombudsman that the matter shall be managed by

---

1   Kriminalstatistik 2009, Brottsförebyggande rådet

2   http://www.jk.se/Beslut/Tillsynsarenden/2495-05-22.aspx

me."

You have to love a justice system where people are allowed to step in and and act as judges for their personal friends. Lambertz has also used his JK office to prosecute tabloid Expressen after it had portrayed his friend Mikael Persbrandt as an alcoholic.

"My position in the case in question will be based on the crime for which LT has been handed an order of summary punishment. Hence he will not be charged with the suspicion having included additional crimes.

Hence, that the suspicion includes additional crimes will not be held against him during the assessment I'm making."

Lambertz would later state in mass media the line, *en gång är ingen gång*, perhaps translated as "one time is no time at all." Except that as was evident, the matter wasn't fully investigated, the one charge wasn't the only highly probable one.

"LT has been handed an order of summary punishment for one count of violating *sexköpslagen*, the sex purchase law. The crime has resulted in a relatively limited fine, 50 *dagsböter*. It's clear that the confidence in him as a judge has been damaged. But he can't through the crime - its sentencing guideline, the extent or the form - be considered to have proven himself to be obviously unfit to hold his office."

"The Chancellor of Justice doesn't take any action in the matter and hence will not raise a suit in the Supreme Court."

Due to the media publicity, Thorsson did however go on sick leave, and after returning to work he made an agreement with the Supreme Court that he would not preside as a judge for the next two years, but work in *Lagrådet*, the Council on Legislation, instead. This judicial body is tasked with previewing proposed law before it becomes actual law, determining whether the legislation

35

is in agreement with the constitution and if the proposal in general is a valid and functional piece of legislation.

One of Thorsson's sharpest critics at this time is district prosecutor Hans Ihrman, who had found his attempt to get two men guilty of *gross procuring* sent to prison for a long time hampered by Thorsson, who had presided over the case when it reached the Supreme Court.[1] Two men around 40 years of age had in 2003 trafficked women from Hungary to be used as prostitutes in Sweden, and in the district court, they're found guilty of *gross procuring* and sentenced to 2.5 and two years, respectively. By the time the case reaches the Supreme Court, the charge has been changed to *procuring*, and the sentences are reduced from 2.5 years to one year and 10 months; and from two years to one year and two months.

Due to Thorsson's conviction, Ihrman now felt that that made the precedents set by this Justice invalid. Something else had also angered him in this matter; the then chairman of the Supreme Court, Bo Svensson, had ridiculed the criticism against Thorsson over his conviction and the relevance that it had to him judging sex crime cases. Interviewed by *Dagens Nyheter*, Svensson had expressed his view that Thorsson's familiarity with prostitution needn't be held against him. "On the contrary, one could say he's got deep knowledge on the subject." Svensson said that he found the Swedish reaction to sex purchases peculiar - he felt that paying for sexual services might be the only option widowers have, hence a big deal shouldn't be made out of it. It appeared as if he would have had abolished *Sexköpslagen* if he had been able to, but felt he had to respect it now that it was actual law.

Ihrman and other lawyers blast Svensson over this comment, and a proposal is made for judges, including Supreme Court

---

1   NJA 2004 s. 646

Justices, to be required to attend education on *Sexköpslagen* and the nature of sex trafficking. Svensson is very dismissive towards this proposal, however, stating that there's no need for instruction since they learn so much from the cases they judge and study as a part of their offices anyway.

In May of 2007, Thorsson returned to presiding as a judge on the Supreme Court in spite of plenty of resentment towards him in the justice system, and in 2009 he was joined by Göran Lambertz as well, who becomes a Supreme Court Justice after his days as the Chancellor of Justice are over. Today they both serve on this judicial body, while 70-year-old Svensson has gone into retirement. It appears as if there's a huge gap between the sense of justice in society at large, and the one of the elite clique on the Supreme Court.

Politics trumping law

One of the ways in which the Swedish legal system contrasts itself in a more obvious manner from Anglo-saxon tradition is that an independent judicial body never really evolved. Whether during the old days of formal monarchy, or the present day of parliamentary democracy, the legal system has always in practice been a lap-dog of executive power. The concept of *natural rights*, the idea that man is born with unalienable rights that aren't granted by the state, was never introduced to Sweden. In the religious tyranny that was in place before late 19th century, the right of the king and the established order to rule was founded on the belief that this was the leadership ordained by God; today's order is founded on the concept of *legal positivism*, the idea that man can make his own laws, and they are what majority rule determine them to be. Hence, if you find yourself outmanoeuvered within the realm of politics, your interests aren't relevant and you have no rights.

Carl Lidbom and "Lidbommery"

More than anyone else, Carl Lidbom has been associated with legal positivism within Swedish politics, and he's even given rise to a term called *lidbomeri* - "Lidbommery" - for the view on law as merely a tool in achieving political aims. In the mid 20th century, Lidbom was employed as a regular judge, when he was invited to come to work with the Social Democrats as a legal expert. In 1969, he becomes a Minister without Portfolio in Olof Palme's Government, and sets to work enacting laws on a scale that has never been done in Sweden before. The spirit of the 60's had been one of radically different values than before, and in Sweden, these values had unfortunately come to dominate the Government. Hence, when Lidbom set out to transform society through law, he met little resistance, and he also didn't bother granting much protection for individuals and businesses whose lives the new legislation might intrude upon.

Natural rights didn't exist at all to Lidbom - as he put it in a speech to the congress of the union of paper-workers in 1974:

> "We must rid ourselves of the view of past days of laws as expressions of some kind of unchangeable justice. Law shouldn't be viewed with subservient respect. The laws are instruments to achieve our political aims."

From his perspective, what mattered to legislation was the needs of society today; some time later, the laws could be replaced with other ones that better fit the new situation. His stance is perhaps the most radical one that has ever reached the highest level of government in the Western world, since traditionally the backing the law has through state force has been reserved for the basic structure of society - basic rights and so on. In a society governed by the rule of law, you don't just arbitrarily decide something should be changed in a certain way and then have the police make it so. In the 1970's, exactly this became the case in Sweden.

To the socialist government, naturally the 'capitalists' became targets to go after. The goals of the 'capitalists' were seen as diametrically opposite to one's own, and therefore law should be used to get at them. As taxes had drastically shot up from 1970 and onwards, businesses had turned to tax-planning to salvage their profits, to the frustration of the government. Carl Lidbom happily wrote applicable law on demand that would make these attempts impossible and secure this money for government spending. Critics on the other side of the political aisle felt there was now almost an environment of persecution against entrepreneurs, whose businesses were broken into in search of untaxed income.

The general clauses that he became known for put ever more power into the hands of bureaucrats, and their numbers swelled as a consequence. This sort of law didn't specify the exact conditions under which state force could be used to intervene, but was put in broader terms that put the decision in the hand of government officials, who were given extensive mandates. Not only were anti-business laws introduced, but anti-family legislation as well, which would later result in international criticism as it became known that the police were dragging crying children from the arms of their parents, due to some unsubstantiated charge of child neglect.

Society can be divided into the government, and the governed. In the modern world, we've grown accustomed to fairly predictable government that lets us plan our own lives even as governed, since the response of government to our actions is known in advance. In such a society, the citizen is the subject (as relating to an object), and the opportunities provided by society are objects in his hand. What if the government is dissatisfied with the governed and starts directing our lives for us? Well, then the governed have no choice but to become mere objects in the hands of the government, since their own initiatives are stifled. What confidence can there be in society and what faith in the idea that we're all in the same boat, when people watch other people arbitrarily rewarded or punished? Obviously the belief in justice is lost, and personal responsibility as well. When your own constructive behaviour doesn't matter, what's the point of it? What really matters are your political connections, and life in society is transformed from the natural mutual cooperation found under the rule of law, to ruthless suspicion and selfishness under this new form of government. All under the guise of the *public good*, of course. The favoured parties get to present their perspective, one gloryifying the role they themselves play.

Though Lidbom was out of the Government in 1976 after

the Social Democrats lost the election, a decade later he would be at the centre of a new controversy. In 1987, he had been tasked by Prime Minister Ingvar Carlsson to investigate the routines of the security police SÄPO in recent errands. He's given full authorization to go through the SÄPO records, but blatantly defies the law as he invites his acquaintance, publisher Ebbe Carlsson, to share in this information. Carlsson is also given access to eavesdropping equipment which he puts to good use against individuals residing in Sweden. Carlsson quickly becomes quite critical of SÄPO, alleging that it could have prevented the assassination of Palme in 1986, and as he's disseminating his theories left and right, in May of 1988 some people start to ask themselves why he has access to this information.

On 1 June 1988, the story that would later be referred to as the Ebbe Carlsson affair becomes public as tabloid *Expressen* describes the role Lidbom has given Carlsson. The opposition parties press for a parliamentary investigation of the affair, and in March of 1989, Carl Lidbom stands before *Konstitutionsutskottet*, the Committee on the Constitution. Vice chairman Anders Björck of the Moderates, one of Sweden's few outspoken conservatives, leads the interrogation of Lidbom, and a portion of their verbal exchange is remembered to this day; Björck demands to know the details of Lidbom's management of his assignment, but Lidbom hasn't kept a diary and has discarded his written notes. Lidbom is displaying outright contempt at the proceedings as his actions are questioned by a political opponent.

> "Yes, but isn't it really strange, Carl Lidbom, that sometimes you remember and sometimes you don't remember, here when it suits you?"
> "No, it isn't that way."
> "Yes it is."
> "No it isn't."
> [...]

"That question is mere nonsense... You're not getting any answer, because that's just nonsense."
"You have let your wife read secret documents?"
"You're not getting any answer because what you're doing is nonsense."
"I do not feel it's appropriate for Carl Lidbom to make such remarks here. You will know your place when you're here, and that's that!"

His role in politics was diminished after this, and he spent the last of his days womanising in spite of being married, especially when his wife contracted polio. His wife is aware of his sexual affairs, but reluctantly accepts them. In 2004, he passes away at the age of 78, but alas many of his laws still stand. In spite of the temporary nature of his sort of law, they've stayed on for decades in the madhouse that is Sweden.

Political appointment of judges

"The essay compiles material that shows that 44 of the 56 reviewed judges of the Supreme Court and the Supreme Administrative Court have a background in the Government Offices. This means that for eight out of ten judges, the career to the most esteemed judge offices has gone through acting as lawyers at different ministries, mainly as legal advisers at the ministry of justice and the ministry of finance."[1]

"9 § A position at a court or at an administrative authority that is under the jurisdiction of the Government is appointed by the Government or by an authority decided on by the Government."

11th chapter, Swedish Instrument of Government

4:2 of *Rättegångsbalken* also specifies that all positions as judges at criminal courts are appointed by the Government. The

---

1   Henrik von Sydow, *Rättsstatens rötter*, 2007

procedure of appointing a judge in Sweden doesn't involve any elections, and no parliamentary examination either; the constitution grants the Government the supreme authority to fill these offices without any public scrutiny possible. It's a well-known fact that when it comes to the higher offices, the only lawyers that have a fair shot at being able to attain them are the ones that have performed legal work for the political parties, mainly the Social Democrats. The higher positions aren't even announced to the public when they need to be filled, but merely picked by the Government at will.

If anyone is curious as to why a certain person was appointed as a Supreme Court Justice, he's got no legal way of finding out; but if he suspects personal connections, nepotism or political loyalty as the person's way in, he's probably close to the truth. Nevertheless, the appointment proceedings are confidential, and the public has to be content with judges even on the Supreme Court being there without having their value systems disclosed or their personal affairs investigated.

Even when it comes to interpreting law, the justice system is somewhat handcuffed. Though just as in other countries, the Supreme Court sets precedents for further cases through its verdicts, albeit as a not very independent judicial body, there is one thing that is fairly unique to Swedish law: The foundation on not only these precedents, but on preparatory work by the legislators as well, giving them yet more control over the verdicts, apart from what's stated in the law text.

Hence, a law could on the surface appear quite harmless and not any infringement on liberty to speak of, yet when the judges apply this law based on the preparatory work, it becomes an horrendous tool of oppression. One example: On the surface, Sweden enjoys freedom of speech, with far-reaching guarantees granted in the documents that make up the constitution. Yet in the preparatory work to the Swedish "hate law" - *hets mot folkgrupp*, you can find statements such as these:

> "Outside this private sphere it should in my view not be permitted to disseminate statements that express threats or disrespect against an ethnic group because of race or similar."[1]

Hence you can be imprisoned in practice if you express yourself in a derogatory manner about other races. One can hint at a tactical advantage for the government in this approach. The perceived respect for liberty and democracy will be based on the formal law, while preparatory work and political appointment of judges make sure the verdicts are of a completely different nature. The government won't have to worry about being judged for its trampling of free speech - after all, the constitution claims Swedes enjoy freedom of speech, and that is what's referred to.

Another thing that's different about the Swedish legal system is that lawyers are quite silent, expected to hush up and fill only a subservient role. It's rare to see lawyers participate in society's debate, and consequently, constitutional matters are hardly ever brought up. Then again, it's understandable that they keep this approach, since if they were to speak "truth to power," they'd most certainly find themselves with little prospect in the way of a career.

Even Russia has a constitutional court

... but Sweden doesn't. Yet another deficiency of the Swedish system is the lack of a constitutional court, where the constitutionality of laws can be tried. In this country, judicial review is unheard of, and citizens often find themselves in Kafka-like situations, suddenly being charged with something that you'd never think was possible given the rights granted by the central document of the constitution - the Instrument of Government. The

---

1   Proposition 1986/87:151

current constitution, enacted in 1974, wasn't even voted through in a referendum, but merely a product of legislation like any other law. Though no surveys have been made, it's this author's belief that most Swedes don't know what year our constitution arrived, or even what the name is of its central document (*Regeringsformen* in Swedish); this is of how little significance the Swedish constitution is.

Some Swedes have attempted to establish a constitutional court; more on this later.

Rättshaverister - the ones who can't find justice

"the right of the people[...]to petition the Government for a redress of grievances."

United States Constitution, First Amendment.

Ok, that's the USA, most definitely not Sweden. If a truthful account of the option Swedish citizens have to complain to their government is to be given, I propose it worded this way:

"The right of the people to be mocked and laughed in the face as well as publicly humiliated if they ever get the idea that they're going to get any justice after having been stepped on by the government."

The word *rättshaverist*, an expression taken from the German word Rechthaber signifying a know-it-all, has in its Swedish form been given the meaning a person who maintains his own right even when the authorities are unwilling to acknowledge this alleged right. Its most common use is a derogatory one, for people who keep a legal fight going when the one using the word feels he should just give it up.

In a society such as the Swedish one, with extensive government administration and politics governing all possible spheres of life, there's a great need of legal protection for the individual against possible miscarriages of justice. Yet when an individual is dissatisfied with the decisions the government makes that affect his life, he can find little justice, sooner or later being denounced as a *rättshaverist* as he struggles to make his government admit its wrongdoing. By the time that word comes out, he knows he's outside the boundaries of what society is willing to accommodate, and that the authorities have sensed his weak and marginalized position.

The concept of a *rättshaverist* is discussed a lot; there are no less than 33,000 hits on Google at the time of writing, as well as 813 on the media search engine *Mediearkivet*. Sometimes personal stories of the sort "I almost became a *rättshaverist*, but then..." etc. The message is usually that you shouldn't believe there is any objective justice. If the authorities don't recognize you being right, then you're simply wrong. Other stories relate some individual's failed fight for justice that resulted in that individual's loss of everything he had.

The *rättshaverist* is often discussed within the legal establishment, and in August of 2010, former Chancellor of Justice and current Supreme Court Justice Göran Lambertz is invited to comment in the journal *Jusektidningen*. In an article entitled "That's how to deal with the *haverist*," he has this to say:

> "I don't know. I don't have the faintest idea. But I suspect that when it's gone that far it's too late. What the *rättshaverist*s have cost society I don't know, don't care either. But what I do know is that they've ruined their own existence, that they live in a hell that eventually in a way costs them their life."[1]

It's a bit shocking that a man who's held these very high positions in the justice system can claim that the *rättshaverist* has ruined his own life. It's a kind of bullying... "See how you've ruined your own life in your search for justice!" One can't help but

---

1   Jusektidningen 6/10

to notice a bit of gloating.

In 2005, during his time as the JK, Lambertz wrote a 16 page report called "*Rättshaverist*s - problems or challenges?." In it, he proposes the idea that the origin of the *rättshaverist* is more to be found in the psychological make-up of the individual, than any actual wrongdoings committed by the system.

> "Many of the *rättshaverist*s most definitely have a mental disorder at the core, but not all of them."

He then goes on to categorize them based on their perceived psychological problems, into six types, A to F: (his cursive for the type names)

> "A. The most common *rättshaverist*s are people who have suffered one or more setbacks and who - often because of a mental disorder or a particularly stubborn or frail temperament - have had a hard time putting what's happened behind them. We can call these *the setback cases*."

> "B. Relatively common as well are people who at the core appear to have a mental illness or serious mental disorder and whose behaviour to a large extent is defined by this. (*the illness cases*)"

Then he goes on with *the projection cases*, *the bullying cases*, *the crisis cases* and *the* [human] *contact cases*. It's simply appalling what prejudice he establishes through these definitions, reading mental illness into people's search for justice. Is this a proper role for the head of the justice system in a decent and civilized society?

Judging by the discussion in legal journals and forums, it appears as if the emerging generation of lawyers convince themselves that anyone referring to any objective form of justice that the government doesn't want to accommodate is a *rättshaverist*; hence their cases aren't the concern of the lawyers. A newly graduated female lawyer made an insulting blog post with the explicit title "*Rättshaverist*s need psychiatric care."

A psychiatrist by the name of Susanne Bejerot, chief physician at St Göran hospital and highly influential in Swedish research concerning psychiatric disorders, has expressed the view that some people are more or less born to become *rättshaverist*s; people born with 'autism spectrum disorders' often become *rättshaverist*s according to her. As she put it in the medical journal *Läkartidningen*:

> "*Rättshaveri* is remarkably common within the Asperger group, which can be explained by a personality defined by lacking common sense, pedantic adherence to rules, pronounced stubbornness and verbal aptitude."[1]

Oh, the joy of doctors as well offering their services to a politically controlled justice system in order to dismiss people wanting their grievances redressed, as pathological. And correct me if I'm wrong, but didn't both the USA and France go through revolutions at the end of the 18th century declaring all citizens to be born equal under the law? To be treated equally? Sweden appears to be a couple of centuries behind these countries in this regard, when expectations on people with certain genetic traits affect how they're regarded by the government.

In the same article, she also has this "wisdom" to share about how some people are born to fail in life (my bold emphasis):

> "Crime is common among people with ADHD."

> "Women with ADHD have a hard time dealing with family responsibilities."

> "Substance abuse is frequent within the whole group."

> "paranoid, schizoid, schizotypal, obsessive-compulsive, borderline and phobic personality disorder can be **expected** for

---

1   Läkartidningen, No 42 2004

[people with] autism spectrum disorders, sometimes also narcissistic. For [people with] ADHD, borderline, antisocial, obsessive-compulsive and histrionic personality disorder can be **expected**."

It's a bit bizarre that a person in her position can express herself in this way. If her words are taken at face value, people born with these traits would have no hope of avoiding developing these personality disorders? This is of course nonsense, and rarely do you see such statements outside Sweden. Then again, Sweden is the madhouse of the world.

Maybe this depiction of the *rättshaverist* in pathological terms is a whip in the hands of political power with which to subjugate the individual insisting on his objective justice into accepting the subjective one agreed upon by society in large. What's right is here not determined by any God-given standards or natural rights, but only by what the majority vote of the parliamentary system has determined it to be.

Or in other words - might is right.

The Civil rights movement... of Sweden

The deficiencies in the 1974 constitution didn't go unnoticed. Lawyer Gustaf Petrén had in the late 1940's after graduation started work at the parliament as a secretary working with legislation. Unlike most lawyers, Petrén takes a stand in the political debate and stresses the need for judicial power to be able to overturn political decisions, when society was moving in the completely opposite direction. As a man who more than anyone else would symbolize politics, Olof Palme, made his presence known in the 60's, these two were naturally on a collision course.

Right-wing Petrén was apart from his legal work also active within politics, which in 1974 would eventually result in him founding *Medborgarrättsrörelsen* (MRR), the Civil rights movement. Mostly founded in protest of the new 1974 constitution, *Medborgarrättsrörelsen* attempted to establish individual rights of the Western sort in an era when Sweden was its most prominent position internationally; it appeared from the Swedish example that politics could trump everything - there was no need for any separation of powers. Petrén and his cohorts still alerted society that all was not well, however, and one thing annoyed them more than anything else: That a new constitution was being enacted just like any other Government bill, without even a referendum. One could ask oneself what the point is of having a constitution, if politicians can just go ahead and write their own? Another of the criticized properties of this constitution was that it didn't include any protection for rights given by it to not simply be abolished through mere legislation.

Little appeared to have been achieved for the MRR during the 70's, however, though without the organization still around today, you wonder how many today would be told the story of deceased Gustaf Petrén. In the early 80's, the new politics gone amok had resulted in numerous complaints by citizens sent to the European Court of Human Rights (ECHR). People who found themselves stepped on as the government implemented its new aims wanted their right, and more than anyone else - families whose children had been taken from them as the government had branded the parents unfit under the newly expanded foster care laws. At this time, Sweden dwarfed all other countries with the number of complaints sent to the ECHR, and Petrén was very active in this area.

Olof Palme derided this legal activism, even going so far as to slam the ECHR as "Petréns playhouse." Though little resistance was met within the country to the newly inflated government, Sweden met criticism internationally, especially following the publication by German magazine *Der Spiegel* of an article entitled *"Children's gulag in the Swedish welfare state."* Palme himself had to hold a personal press conference to answer this criticism, but this is pretty much forgotten today, and established media rarely reminds people about what transpired back then.

In 1990, Gustaf Petrén died and leadership of the MRR passed on, though the organization is still very much active today. Alas, it appears as if the judicial fight is back on square one. The European justice that was going to be a salvation to Sweden appears to have caught up with it; in *Council Framework Decision 2008/913/JHA* of 28 November 2008, the EU council imposed upon the member states to criminalize "publicly inciting hatred directed against a group of persons or a member of such a group defined by reference to race, colour, religion, descent or national or ethnic origin," as well as "publicly condoning, denying or grossly trivialising crimes of genocide etc." The suggested punishment is incarceration. Goodbye, European freedom of speech. It seems as if the EU has learned from Sweden instead of the other way around.

And when it comes to child custody errands, where the social authorities have seized children, the ECHR has today ceased being a refuge for the citizen that's been stepped on by his government. This court has been swamped with errands of all sorts, and simply can't deal with them all. In its 2008 annual report, the ECHR stated that it declared about 95% of its complaints inadmissible or simply struck them out. Almost 100,000 applications were pending in the beginning of that year, and the legal proceedings can these days take up to five years. Hence the complainant can't expect much of a restoration for himself, but only hope a verdict will set precedent for similar cases in the future. Unfortunately, the EU itself is hard at work drafting ever more legislation that will limit individual rights at a much faster pace than one can hope to reaffirm them through legal precedents.

Olof Palme must be laughing from his grave.

THE NANNY STATE

"Snart kan man väl inte knulla sin kärring
förrän man hör ett jävla liv utanför
det brakar till i fönstret, och i nästa sekund
så står det en långnäst myndighetsperson och ska mäta hur djupt
man kör"

"Soon you won't be able to f**k your b***h
before you hear a f**king commotion outside
there's a crash in the window, and the next moment
there's a long-nosed authority person there to see how deep you
penetrate."

Eddie Meduza

The population registration (Folkbokföringen)

There's a saying in Sweden that goes *ingenting är privat*, "nothing is personal/private;" It's quite a pun in that *privat* can mean both "personal" and "privately owned." The population registration is a good example of this, with all the personal information it contains. All residents of the country are covered, and are required by law to inform the government whenever they move to a new location or leave the country.

Among pieces of information contained are these: Full name, personal identity number (used to look you up in national registers), civil status, the names of all family members as well as address (including the exact property or apartment you reside in).

In early January of 2010, after I had moved to a new apartment and had filled out the mandatory form to the authorities, being meticulous in getting everything right to keep them off my back, they still called me up. It seems they had recently introduced a new system for the property information - the old apartment code I had entered for my new residence wasn't the correct one.

I glance around in my house at the papers I had been given, the apartment lease and similar documents, trying to find the information the woman on the phone requested, when she interrupts me within seconds, apparently trying to save time.

"Never mind that, I can look up the code from here anyway... You say the address is XXX," she says.

"Yep," I respond.

"What floor?

"The ground floor."

"It's **the** 1-room apartment?"

At this point I'm taken somewhat aback as I realize she's sitting there with a file on all the apartments in the block, with information on the number of rooms in each one of them.

"Yep, that's the one."

"Ok, I'll enter code YYY for you then... Good we could get this sorted."

Why don't they just implant a GPS locator under my skin while they're at it?

The County Administrative Board (Länsstyrelsen) ... and my cats.

The authorities must love me for some reason. During the first week of August of 2010, my half-sister dumped her cats on me since she was going to be 'preoccupied' during the next couple of months. I like cats, so that's no problem - I get her litter box and buy some cat food and sand, expecting care-free temporary ownership of these cats, cuddling them a bit now and then and keeping them fed. I don't like having my night's sleep disturbed, however, so when I go to bed I lure them outside and place the food bowls there, then locking the balcony door. My apartment is on the ground floor, and the cats can run out freely through a hole in the balcony, hence it seems just fine in my eyes. Sometimes the cat meow a little when I leave them outside, but I figure this might be a good opportunity for them to go catch rats or something.

Now on the 19th of August, I get this woman from the County Administrative Board paying a visit to me in my apartment, saying she's from the pet supervision section of this public authority and that they've learned that the cats might be **neglected**(!) in my house. She asks if she can come into my apartment and inspect. I let her do that, being hospitable and all, and show her both the litter box and the bowls the cats usually eat from. She also wants to see the cats, so I show them to her - when she enters, only the female is inside, so I step out on the balcony and look for the male too, and thankfully he shows up as well, so I can let the woman inspect the two cats that I keep in my home. She asks about their age and whether the male is castrated. I've not checked myself - to be honest, I've never taken too great an interest in cat genitalia and don't know how castrated cats look. So I lift him up and show that part of his body to her to inspect, and she tells me he doesn't appear castrated.

She's pleased to see that they appear to be just fine, but still asks me about how I keep them. I tell her I usually give them dry food since that's cheaper and that I give them milk since they don't seem very interested in drinking water. Once a day I give them a bit of wet food, but sometimes I find that the bowl out on the balcony attracts flies when they've not finished eating it - the dry food doesn't on the other hand. She now tells me that the cats are still required to have access to water, but that it's possible that they might still find that if they can walk outside. The woman also tells me that if I keep cats, I'm required to check on them at least twice a day, and I console her by telling her I do that.

This is not quite over yet though; she's also concerned about how it will be during the winter if I keep two cats in my 1-room apartment and I can't keep the door open to let them run out as they please. Then I tell her that I'm only keeping the cats temporarily for my half-sister and that I'll return them to her long before the snow is here. Now she wants the name and phone number of my half-sister, so I tell her that, and she also hands me her contact information, telling me I'm supposed to inform the County Administrative Board when I return the cats to my half-sister. Naturally I'll be such a vigilant servant of the state as to do that... Finally, she asks for my phone number as well and I hand her that too. Bureaucrats sure can make it a hassle keeping pets... I wonder if I made the right move in telling her that the reason my half-sister couldn't take care of the cats was because she's incarcerated.

Life in Sweden... Is there any wonder I daydream about another life? I guess if you lack company, it's not very hard to get government employees to come visit you though.

Two cats too lazy to be catching rats.

Why chase rats when you can sleep in your master's bed all day until you get up and meow a bit to be fed?

I think there must be some essential difference between country cats and city cats. When I grew up in our cottage out in the country, we had several generations of cats, and though we generally provided them with food when they were kittens, as they grew up they went outside and caught rats on their own, securing their food supply that way. They usually came back to our house for the company, or we'd call on them to give them special treats such as perhaps some herring. Our first cat, called Missan, who became the ancestor of all subsequent cats, once even caught a white hare that she brought back to the house in her mouth. If any cat that wasn't her offspring snuck into the house, she'd make them sorry. I even remember once when a male did just that, and she went after him with such a fury, chasing him across floors and window seats until he got the message that he had to get out.

The two cats I have now have not caught a single rat during the four weeks or so I've had them, they rely on me exclusively for food even though I let them go outside. And naturally the food I give them isn't good enough for them, they keep meowing and I have to figure out just what they want now. Every morning I wake up, they're sleeping on the quilt out on the balcony, waking up and rushing inside as I open the door. Now and then other male cats in the neighbourhood walk up to the balcony when they see my female cat. When my male cat spots one of them approaching, he runs for safety instead of chasing them away. The cats sleep for 20 hours a day and spend at least an hour each of the remaining time washing themselves or eating the food I serve them.

I want country cats instead...

31 August 2010 update

Well, what do you know. This morning the female actually ran into my apartment with a bird in her mouth, as if she's sensed my dissatisfaction in the two. It managed to get loose from her jaws and fly around a little inside before the male cornered it and took it instead, without the female noticing. Now she's meowing and searching for it in my apartment, poor girl. Maybe I should give the male less food so he'll learn to catch his own prey... But then I guess I'll get *Länsstyrelsen* on me again.

7 September 2010 update

Today I received a written confirmation in the mail of the inspection two weeks ago. To quote:

"Inspection in accordance with *djurskyddslagen* [the law on the prevention of cruelty to animals]

Date   2010-09-02

Day-book number   xxx-xxxx-2010"

The bastards actually made an official document out of the inspection...

Två katter, en hona och en hane, 2 år gamla hölls i en lägenhet med möjlighet att gå ut via balkongen. Torrfoder och burkfoder fanns, vatten saknades dock vid kontrolltillfället. Katterna var i normalhull och verkade pigga och harmoniska. Daniel Hammarberg tog över katterna från sin syster för ett par veckor sedan, katterna ska tillbaka till henne om ca två månader.

The cats have come right in from outside and already one week after have managed to soil the paper to this state where it was lying. Sometimes I think they can read, and that they're simply showing the authorities proper respect.

"Two cats, one female and one male, 2 years old were kept in an apartment with the option to walk outside through the balcony. There was dry food and canned food, water was however missing at the time of the inspection. The cats were in normal shape and appeared alert and harmonious. Daniel Hammarberg took over the cats from his sister a couple of weeks ago, the cats will return to her in about two months."

Maybe the government should put the cats up on Facebook

so everyone can follow in detail the events of their lives. What kind of government business is it just when I return the cats?

"The cats should have free access to drinking water. There may be deficiencies that weren't noticed during the inspection. No fee is charged during this inspection."

Thanks for the suspicion... Just because you see that the cats are all-right doesn't mean that you can't bee too sure. I guess I was lucky not to be charged for the unannounced inspection.

I was also given a printed 14-page colour brochure from the Board of Agriculture (*Jordbruksverket*).

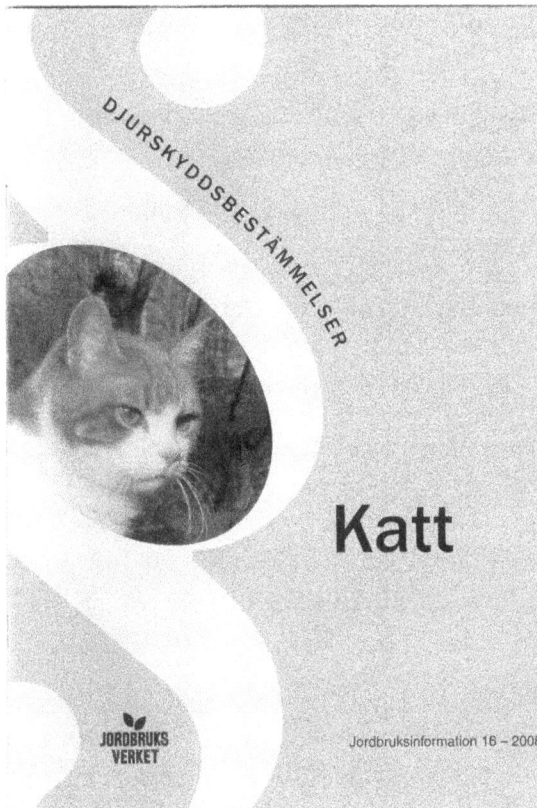

To quote:

"In this brochure you can read about how to keep and take care of your cat."

Oh, and I didn't know how to do that until the government told me.

"Your animals depend on you to follow the rules on animal protection. The regulations establish a minimum level and declare what has to be at least fulfilled for your cat to feel well and act in a natural way."

Man has kept cats for thousands of years with their enthusiasm intact. Now in 2008, the Swedish government decides this must be regulated under law.

Ok, the bold emphasis of the words "you will" in the following quotes isn't present in the brochure, but is simply me highlighting the outrageous language.

"From 1 May 2008, several new rules apply to keeping a cat, among others the following:

* You or someone else **will** look after your animals at least twice a day. Young, sick or injured animals shall be looked after more often.

* Cats **will** have their need for social interplay met."

Etc, etc...

"If several cats are kept indoors without the possibility to go outside, **you have to make sure** that there's at least 1 litter box per 2 cats."

"**You will also make sure** that your cat doesn't become obese or underweight. If several animals are fed together, **you will make sure** that they all are able to eat in peace and quiet, without disturbing each other."

These rules and this trust in me on the part of the

government makes it so much fun keeping cats...

> "The Swedish regulation on breeding makes clear what is acceptable as far as animal protection goes when it comes to breeding cats. It also supports the means of controlling genetic deficiencies that today take place within many race [breeding] clubs.
>
> Breeding that can bring about suffering to a cat is forbidden. The cat may not be used for breeding if it among other things
>
> * has a disease or a disability that may be inherited
>
> * is carrying or can be assumed to be carrying certain dispositions for disease
>
> * has behavioural disorders such as exaggerated fear and unprovoked aggression"

Eugenics for cats... Maybe this is why the country cats I grew up with seem gone these days - some government planner decided that cats weren't allowed to be self-sufficient. If they had been, these pet inspectors wouldn't have jobs. Maybe the mere existence of cats is a thorn in the eye of bureaucrats, not needing any supervision or government. You just can't let anything go unregulated...

> "A permit is required for whoever"
>
> " * breeds 3 or more litters per year"
>
> " * stores or feeds 4 or more cats"
>
> "Whoever hasn't applied for a permit is in violation of the *law on the prevention of cruelty to animals* and risks facing criminal charges."
>
> "If you intentionally **or inadvertently** violate the rules on animal protection, you can be sentenced to a fine or prison for up to two years."

On the last page under the heading "legislation," the brochure refers to eight laws and regulations that contain the full ordinances on keeping cats, with this brochure being only a summary.

Lagstiftning

Broschyren är en sammanfattning av djurskyddslagen, djur-skyddsförordningen samt föreskrifter och allmänna råd för hund och katt. Vill du läsa de fullständiga reglerna hittar du dem i:

- Djurskyddslagen (SFS 1988:534)
- Djurskyddsförordningen (SFS 1988:539)
- Lagen (2007:1150) om tillsyn över hundar och katter
- Statens jordbruksverks föreskrifter och allmänna råd (SJVFS 2008:5) om hållande av hund och katt
- Djurskyddsmyndighetens föreskrifter och allmänna råd (DFS 2004:10) om transport av levande djur
- Djurskyddsmyndighetens föreskrifter (DFS 2004:5) om kravet på tillstånd enligt 16 § djurskyddslagen
- Djurskyddsmyndighetens föreskrifter (DFS 2004:14) om operativa ingrepp på eller injektioner till djur
- Djurskyddsmyndighetens föreskrifter (DFS 2004:6) om märkning och registrering av hundar

Du hittar föreskrifterna på Jordbruksverkets webbplats (www.sjv.se).

Reading *The ordinances and general advice of the Board of Agriculture on the keeping of dog and cat*, SJVFS 2008:5, I start to wonder if these legislators have even seen a cat with their own eyes. Is it any surprise that most of the pictures of cats in the brochure are from the free stock footage website www.sxc.hu?

They're actually tagged as such... I guess whatever cats the government workers had must have run away. To quote said legislation:

> "17 § Dogs and cats shall have their need of social contact catered for."

> "Contact with people should take place **a couple of hours every day** through activation, exercising or other occupation."

What if I don't have three to four hours available every day for petting my cat? And what if I simply don't want to spend that much time with him or her? Does that mean I'm not allowed to keep a cat?

> "19 § Dogs and cats shall be kept sufficiently clean and their fur shall be attended to."

I know dogs are quite helpless animals and can't take care of their own hygiene... But cats? Haven't you seen them clean themselves all the time? Some of the rules are quite silly, such as for example:

> "7 § Indoor spaces for dogs and cats shall be equipped with lighting. The lighting mountings shall be placed and the lighting amplitude regulated and aimed so that the animals that reside in the space are not subjected to discomfort."

> "13 § Breastfeeding bitches and breastfeeding female cats shall have access to a calm and undisturbed location for themselves and their kids."

To think that this would never have occurred to me on my own... It's my experience that the cats take care of this themselves too, usually finding an open closet or something similar.

> "3 CHAP. SPECIAL REGULATIONS FOR KEEPING OF CAT"

> "3 § Breastfeeding female cats shall have access to a special sleeping place that's inaccessible to the kittens."

I guess they project their parenting styles onto the cats... "I can't stand having my children around me all the time, so surely the cats can't either." Feminism for cats... "Cat mum needs her night out!" I wonder how long it takes until they introduce mandatory public daycare for kittens?

6 §:

"Cats with low rank in their group shall have the opportunity to eat and drink without stress."

"There should be food and water bowls in different places and different heights so that cats with low rank have the opportunity to eat and drink undisturbed."

I think these legislators ought to take the personal integrity of the cats into account too... Don't you think it's insulting to them assuming that they can't fend for themselves just because they're of "low rank?" Typical socialist condescension.

On a related note, the wording of some of the legislation under "2 CHAP. SPECIAL REGULATIONS FOR KEEPING OF DOG" becomes really funny when translated into English (my apologies if women find it offensive):

"17 § Forced mating of bitches may not occur.

With forced mating is meant forcing the bitch to mate by holding on to the bitch in spite of the bitch expressing discomfort or attempting to get away."

If anyone wants to inspect this insane document for himself, search for "SJVFS 2008:5" and enter that URL into translate.google.com.

But, back to cats. I think it's a valuable experience for kittens fighting over the food, it teaches them to grow up and become real hunters. When I was a child, I was delighted to see some of the cats hogging all the food and not letting anyone else

66

have any until they were done. I guess that makes me cruel towards animals by today's Swedish standards. "Grow some balls, or go hungry!" Some cats have such cute ways of establishing their position in their litter... I once had a kitten who defied both other kittens and adults when it came time to be fed, by not confining himself to only stand outside the bowl when he ate, like the rest of them; although his back paws were outside the bowl, he had half his body inside it, eating from the centre and effectively covering the rest of the hard food with his front paws extended to his sides, to send the message that no one else could eat while he was doing it. Oh, I wish I had taken a picture. I could have sent it to the legislators now and written something like: "Watch me follow your regulations, bureaucrats!" Hmm, that might be a bit corny I suppose.

I can't stress just how grateful I am to my esteemed government for blessing me with its enlightened and important legislation... What would I do without you?

I propose a class action lawsuit on behalf of all cats. Self-sufficient and proud cats just don't want to be subject to the same legislation as stupid and helpless dogs. I suggest a suitable compensation would be for the cats to be given the legal right to dispose of their excrement on the lawns of these legislators, to atone for the psychological harm the cats have been subjected to due to this association. Let no one compare noble cats to puny dogs again.

I'm called Mimmi and I support this motion. I can be so hyperactive at times that my master found it hard getting a clean shot of me today.

Gun laws

Background and legislation

If you go back a couple of centuries in time, it was a nearly universal right for people to own weapons, with only subjugated and conquered peoples being deprived of theirs. Then again, the weaponry ordinary citizens had sometimes didn't make much of a difference when a foreign army decided to ransack their property for food or valuables, which was often the case. Modern day man naturally understands that these days, governments are benevolent and would never tread on their citizens, hence there is supposedly no need for private ownership of weapons. You often hear lines such as "only criminals ever need guns."

A case for private gun ownership could become quite a long essay in itself, hence I will here restrain myself from spending too much time reminding people about the atrocities committed by governments that have taken away their citizens' guns. Worth noting is however that one of the most quoted examples of governments taking away people's guns, Nazi Germany, had far more lenient legislation than Sweden does today. Perhaps reading the following examples of law enforcement dealing with people's attempts at owning guns will allow you as a reader to decide whether the government's apparent paranoia when it comes to gun ownership is a cause for concern.

1 § 1 of the weapons law (*Vapenlagen*) reads

"This law applies to firearms and ammunition along with certain objects that in the law are made equivalent to firearms."

1 § 2

"With firearms is in this law understood weapons by which bullets, cartridges, harpoons or other projectiles may be fired through the use of gunpowder loads, carbon-dioxide loads, compressed air or other similar means of launching."

Then paragraph 3 also lists start and signal weapons, crossbows, mace sprays, tasers and various other devices.

All is not doom and gloom in this law, however; even though old medieval cannons are illegal under the weapons law, salute cannons that can't be put to use in a military manner are exempt. So, you can fire that old cannon you inherited if you want to pay tribute to your precious monarchy.

2 § 1

"A permit is required to
a) possess firearms or ammunition
b) trade with firearms
c) in a professional manner receive firearms for reparation or overhaul, or
d) import firearms or ammunition to Sweden."

2 § 4

"An individual may be given a permit to own a firearm only if the individual needs the weapon for an acceptable purpose."

This intended purpose then has to be approved of by the government. As you'll see from the coming examples, well-justified fear of attack from neither man nor animal is a valid reason.

2 § 5

"A permit to own a firearm may be granted only if it can be reasonably assumed that the weapon will not be misused. A permit may be granted only for specifically noted purposes. A permit to possess a firearm for firing may be granted only if the weapon is suited for the purpose the permit is intended for."

So if the police disagrees with you in what type of gun is

suitable for your intended purpose, you get no permit.

2 § 6

"A permit to own fully automatic weapons or handguns may be granted only if there are exceptional reasons."

Or in other words, it's nearly impossible to get a permit even for a revolver.

2 § 18

"The National Police Board shall through the use of automated processing maintain separate central registries over

1. individuals and organizations that under this law have been granted permits to own firearms or ammunition or a permit to borrow firearms as well as individuals who belong to the staff of the home defence and whom by the military have been allocated firearms for storage in their residence. (*vapeninnehavarregistret*, the registry of weapon owners)

2. the firearms for which permits to own [them] have been granted under this law as well as firearms that have been found or reported stolen or lost (*vapenregistret*, the weapons registry) and

3. individuals and organizations that have been granted permits under this law to trade with firearms or receive firearms for overhaul or reparation (*vapenhandlarregistret*, the registry of weapon traders)."

Hence you as a gun owner are registered along with an individual entry for every single gun you own.

5 § 2

"When firearms are not in use, they shall be stored in a safety locker or in some other form of equally safe storage compartment."

5 § 7

"The one who has a permit to own firearms is required to grant the police authority access to check that the storage requirements are adhered to."

6 § 1

"A permit to own firearms or to import firearms to Sweden will be recalled by the police authority if
a) the permit owner has proven unfit to own firearms,
b) the permit owner without an acceptable reason has refused the police authority access to check that the storage directions are adhered to,
c) the conditions for the permit no longer exist, or
d) there is otherwise some reasonable reason to recall the permit."

So in other words, if you want to own a gun, you have to open up your home to the police whenever they want to inspect how you take care of it. And you're never safe from the police making an arbitrary decision that you're not allowed to own guns any more and invade your home to take them.

9 § 1

"An individual who is deliberately in possession of a firearm without having the right to do so or turns over or lends a firearm to someone who doesn't have the right to own the weapon is sentenced to prison for at most a year for weapons crime. [*vapenbrott*]

If the crime is serious [the individual] is sentenced to prison for at least six months and at most four years for major weapons crime. [*grovt vapenbrott*]"

A term such as 'major weapons crime' might have you think that it's at least a matter of automatic rifles, but quite often it's nothing more than a mere pistol.

Cases of *major weapons crime*

(Bold emphasis by me in this section.)

"Couple arrested for major weapons crime

A man and a woman in their 30's were arrested the night before Wednesday in Falun, suspected of major weapons crime. It was when the police searched the couple's apartment in another errand that **a loaded hunting rifle** was found."[1]

"Six people arrested for major weapons crime

First **a pistol** was thrown out of a car that the police attempted to pull over on Kymlingelänken in Kista in western Stockholm the night before Tuesday. Then the vehicle hit the car of the police patrol.

Now the driver and five passengers are suspected of major weapons crime. Björn Knutsson at Västerortspolisen offered no hypothesis on what the pistol would be used for. According to the police, several of the involved are also suspected of traffic offences. Knutsson however doesn't think that the six arrestees attempted to ram the police car but is more leaning towards it being an accident."[2]

It's pretty obvious that people are in great fear of being caught by the police with a gun in their possession.

RH 2001:74 (a criminal case in the Court of Appeal for Western Sweden)

"The prosecutor charged N.B. with major weapons crime, additionally for complicity in major weapons crime"

---

1   dn.se, 08-12-31

2   svd.se, 08-12-23

"[...] N.B. by owning and carrying a loaded pistol, although with no bullet in the barrel, of the brand Titanic, caliber 7.65 mm"

The district court sentences N.B. to six months in spite of him not actually having used this pistol and having a clean criminal record. N.B. appeals the sentence and the appeals court changes the charge to weapons crime instead and reduces the sentence to four months.

RH 1998:76 (a criminal case in the Court of Appeal for Skåne and Blekinge)

"Possession of a Magnum revolver has been deemed to be a major weapons crime."

"M.A. has 1 May 1997 in Helsingborg been in possession of a revolver of the brand Smith & Wesson loaded with six cartridges without having the right to do so. The offence should be considered a major one because of the potential of danger of the weapon and special qualities such as force of impact and calibre."

The revolver in question is a Magnum 357. The district court sentences him to eight months for major weapons crime even though he hadn't used it. This in spite of his great cover story which as quoted by the court went this way:

"He found the weapon in the flower bed near where he was sitting down to eat at McDonald's on Hävertgatan. He didn't see if it was a toy weapon or if it was a real weapon. He didn't have time to examine the weapon. He put the weapon into his bullet-proof vest. On top of the bullet-proof vest he wore a sports jacket and a skiing jacket. He didn't reflect on what kind of weapon it was or what he was going to use it for; it should not lie the way it did considering the crowd - including children - at McDonald's. He saw that the police arrived and immediately he was frisked. Therefore he didn't have time to spontaneously say anything about him having found the weapon just then."

In some cases you actually feel a defendant should be

awarded a reduction in his sentence due to a great and very believable cover story, but this guy had no such luck.

Both parties appeal the sentence, and in the appeals court he's sentenced to six months instead, under the same charge.

RH 2004:97 (a criminal case in Svea Court of Appeal)

"The deed: K.K. has 7 February 2004 inside a restaurant without having the right to do so deliberately been in possession of a loaded revolver. The district court found that the deed in accordance with the charges was to be considered a major weapons crime and stated in the justification among other things the following: From the investigation it's clear that K.K. has been in possession of a loaded and lethal handgun. The legal field of application for the weapon ought to be quite limited. That the weapon was lethal is supported by the fact that during test shooting at the police it has proven to work flawlessly. From the investigation it's also clear that K.K. has been aware of having been in possession of a loaded weapon."

"In the section on sanction, the court established that K.K was 59 years old and earlier only convicted for traffic offences as well as living under orderly conditions and was suitable for community service."

The district court still sentences him to six months for major weapons crime. K.K. appeals the verdict and he's instead sentenced to five months for regular weapons crime. The appeals court states that the revolver in question couldn't be considered a very dangerous one and that there was no reason to assume that K.K. would use the weapon.

"Four men charged with major weapons crime

Four men are being prosecuted at Norrköping district court suspected of major weapons crime. The weapon, a German revolver of the brand Arminius, has since 2007 been buried at a summer cottage in Åby until 26 May this year."[1]

The errand started with one of the men attempting to run from a police road block, after which the police caught up with him in his car. He then makes a run for it and attempts to hide a revolver. After he's taken by the police, they discover that no less than four men have been involved in a criminal deal:

> "The 25-year-old man contacted the 29-year-old and asked for help in getting a gun. The 29-year-old in turn contacted a 46-year-old man who had a gun for sale. The 25-year-old decides to buy the weapon and finances the purchase through a loan from a 33-year-old man."

Oh dear, merely lending someone money so he can buy a gun gets you charged with the same crime. With the way the authorities deal with guns, you'd think they were kryptonite or something.

> "A 17-year-old man has been charged with major weapons crime since he at the end of February was caught carrying **a loaded starter pistol** in central Malmö.
>
> The pistol was found when the police frisked the 17-year-old man after an alarm. It was then ready to fire with a bullet in the barrel, six in the magazine and the pistol cocked. The 17-year-old man according to the charges carried the pistol tucked into his underpants in front of his body."[2]

Someone ought to tell the guy it's quite dangerous carrying a cocked gun in your pants, it just might go off and hit something else with the same name, and you'd be a triumph for Darwinism - a walking example of someone whose lack of mental fitness prevented him from having children.

---

1   folkbladet.se, 10-06-17

2   sydsvenskan.se, 10-05-24

"21-year-old arrested for major weapons crime"[1]

"A 21-year-old man is in custody for major weapons crime. In his residence **one of the greatest confiscations of guns ever** was made in Sundsvall."

"The 21-year-old is a roomer with another man in a house in Haga, Sundsvall. And it was the landlord that found the guns.

- He contacted the police during Tuesday evening and told them he had found no less than **six guns** under the bed of the 21-year-old, says Jan-Erik Nilsson, preliminary investigation head at the Sundsvall local police.

The man came in with the guns himself and it proved to be no less than **three pistols and the same number of revolvers**. As well as **a major stash of ammunition**, roughly **50 cartridges** that according to the police appear to be **live rounds**."

It's funny how phrases such as "greatest confiscations of guns ever" and "a major stash of ammunition" can mean so little.

"24-year-old detained for major weapons crime[2]

Early June, the 24-year-old was pulled over on route 61 in Spekekorset with **a loaded pistol** in his car."

"Two people arrested for major weapons crime[3]

Two men have been arrested suspected of major weapons crime. **The gun** was found during a house search this Monday in an apartment in a residential block in Skellefteå."

---

1   dagbladet.se, 10-05-27

2   nwt.se, 09-10-17

3   folkbladet.nu, 09-11-04

"- At present we don't want to discuss what kind of a gun it is, but it is **a real gun**."

Oh no... A REAL GUN!

"Two people arrested for weapons crime[1]

Two men are in police custody suspected of major weapons crime

At around 19:00 on Monday, police checked two men in the Kristineholm area. During the check **a pistol** was found. The men, who are in their 20's, were arrested suspected of major weapons crime. They were later taken into custody by the prosecutor."

"33-year-old arrested for major weapons crime[2]

A 33-year-old man was arrested this Wednesday and was later taken into custody following the prosecutor's decision after a house search of the man's residence in Katrineholm. The police had through tips and surveillance received information that the man kept guns in his residence. Two complete rifles that had been manipulated were found during the house search along with ammunition. The 33-year-old is suspected of major offence against the weapons law."

"Nazi leader Klas Lund charged with major weapons crime"[3]

Oh no... This must be truly serious. Hey, wait a minute... Why does everyone else get to be anonymous in the media, even 'suspected' killers caught in the act, but not this guy? Normally they never even provide a description of the suspect, but here they provide a brief biography.

"Lund was arrested in his residence in Synnerby outside Skara in

---

1 alingsastidning.se, 10-05-25

2 kkuriren.se, 10-04-15

3 expressen.se, 04-03-23

connection with police raids at several locations in the country in November of 2003. Then **a loaded Norwegian army pistol** and a bag of ammunition was found"

"Lund now risks prison for at least six months."

You really have to love those nationwide clampdown raids with no previous suspicions, breaking into people's homes to see if the police can uncover evidence of any crimes. These raids targeted the nationalist movement in the country, and people found their computers and such equipment seized as well, along with cash. Naturally the police have to perform the raids before people have woken up too.

Just about all the media in the country covered this man's crime:

"Klas Lund released [from custody]"[1]

"Klas Lund sentenced to prison[2]

Klas Lund, one of the leaders of the right-wing extremist organization The Swedish Resistance Movement was on Thursday sentenced to six months in prison for major weapons crime at Lidköping district court."

"A Nazi admitted weapons crime - was released[3]

Right-wing extremist Klas Lund wasn't taken into custody."

Oh no... He's actually walking the streets as a free man just like almost all suspected criminals in Sweden, although now completely stripped of any guns the state could find in his home.

---

1   dn.se, 03-11-27

2   svd.se, 04-05-13

3   sydsvenskan.se, 03-11-27

"Nazi escaped from prison[4]

The infamous Nazi Klas Lund, 36, escaped from the Mariestad institution."

"As soon as his disappearance was discovered he was declared wanted in all of Sweden."

And that would naturally happen to a non-political person as well...

Getting a gun permit... And maybe avoiding getting eaten by bears

Surely the aforementioned people who were sent to prison simply made the mistake of not attempting to get legal permits for their intended weapons? The following court case will illustrate just how meaningful it is applying for one.

RÅ 2004 ref. 32

"M.O. is since the 1970's in the business of sheep grazing with pasture management. The sheep, some 300 animals, are grazing freely in the forest from 1 May to 15 November. During this period, M.O. is moving around the grounds a lot to watch his animals. He then carries a rifle and has a dog on a leash. Since the end of the 1980's the sheep stock has been attacked by bears on numerous occasions. M.O. applied in May 2001 for a permit to keep a large-bore revolver (handgun). To support his application, he stated that he needed the revolver in case of a bear attack. The police authority in Västernorrland fief rejected M.O.'s application in a decision on 8 June 2001. According to the police authority there were no exceptional reasons to grant the applied for permit. The guns M.O. already had permits for could be used for the purpose."

M.O. (Mats Ohlsson out of Ånge) appeals the verdict, and

---

4   aftonbladet.se, 04-10-12

the district administrative court to process the errand has this to say on 24 October 2001:

(plenty of law citations cut)

"According to the position of the National Police Board, which is also supported by the Swedish Hunter's Association, a revolver is a less suitable weapon than a rifle or in some cases a shotgun loaded with rough shells or massive shots for both pursuit hunting as well as protective hunting. The guns that M.O. since earlier is in possession of can be adequately used for the potential needs he feels exist. In any case no exceptional reasons can be considered to exist to grant the applied for permit. The National Police Board objects to approval of the application."

"The administrative court makes the following assessment. - From the investigation into the case **it's clear that no doubts about M.O.'s personal suitability concerning gun ownership exist.**"

"The administrative court doesn't find that what M.O. has stated can be considered to be such exceptional reasons as to grant the applied for permit. Thus the police authority has had good reason for its decision, why the appeal will be rejected."

M.O. appeals the verdict, and this time he makes a more personal plea for the necessity to own a revolver. As quoted from court documents, released at the time of the verdict on 11 December 2002:

"By law he's required to keep watch over his sheep every day. He must also locate attacked sheep, for among other reasons to be compensated for them. This often means he's forced to move into brushy and dense forest, where the damaged animals are. The damage to the animals must be documented and an inspector must be contacted. He's out in the grounds just about every day and often resides in the vicinity of bears. His fear increases all the time and he's convinced that sooner or later he will be attacked. You can't scare away a bear by firing into the air. When he's watching the sheep he carries two rifles along with a video camera, regular camera and binoculars. If a bear would attack him it can be very hard to defend himself with a rifle. He also works in the forest, among other things by cutting pathways, and then he can't carry a rifle. He needs a short-barrelled gun as a last resort to be able to defend himself at close quarters if a bear would attack. The revolver is intended to be used only when it's gone as far as the bear having come over him and he can't turn a rifle barrel towards the bear."

"The police authority contested approval to the appeal and stated among other things the following. M.O. can adequately use one of the three rifles he's already in possession of for the designated purpose of protection."

"Any exceptional reasons to grant M.O. the applied for permit don't exist. There appears to be more practical and convenient reasons behind the application."

You simply have to love the police telling a man approaching retirement age who's worked his whole life that he doesn't have the right to spare himself discomfort.

This court seems to want to show a bit of mercy, however, actually granting his permit:

"The administrative court of appeal finds during an assessment of this part concluded that M.O. has an absolute need of a gun to protect himself. From the other information M.O. has delivered, it's clear that the purposes of protection according to the court can't be sufficiently met with the rifles he's already in possession of. For this reason the court finds that M.O. has the type of qualified need for a handgun that's required for the applied for permit to be granted. Exceptional reasons to grant M.O. a permit to possess the revolver in question for purposes of protection are therefore deemed to exist in the case. Considering also that M.O.'s personal suitability concerning gun ownership hasn't come into question, the court finds in a total assessment that M.O., among other things taking into consideration the, as far as can be told, special situation that he in the practise of his profession finds himself in, should be granted a permit to own a handgun in accordance with his application. Changing the decision of the police authority and the district administrative court, the administrative court of appeal grants M.O. permit to possess a revolver, Smith & Wesson, calibre 44, for purposes of protection."

The police aren't very happy at this point and appeal the verdict to the supreme administrative court. From the verdict on 31 March 2004:

"The police authority appealed and insisted that M.O. shouldn't be granted a permit to possess a handgun and stated among other things the following. M.O. can adequately use one of the three rifles he's got a permit for. There exists neither a qualified need for the applied for weapon or an absolute need of this for purposes of protection. If M.O. is granted the applied for permit, everyone who spends time out in the wild and risks coming into contact with a she-bear with kids could be granted a permit for a large-bore handgun. This can't have been the intent of the legislators."

This time around, the police side focuses on legal history to justify their rejection of his application. They are still disputing whether a revolver is a proper weapon for defence against bears, however.

"A revolver is particularly bad for shooting an attacking bear, among other things for the very real risk of missing the target or wounding the bear. When M.O. because of his dog's behaviour or other signs, notices that there's a bear in the area, he should choose to either retreat and avoid confronting the bear or arming his rifle and carrying it in his hands when he approaches the assumed location of the bear. Such a solution offers better protection for M.O. than a revolver and can't in any decisive way be considered an obstacle in advancing towards the bear. That it generally would be more comfortable for M.O. to carry a revolver than a rifle can't be considered an exceptional reason to approve of his application."

For the idea that a revolver is bad for killing bears, I'll refer to the man who shot dead a grizzly bear in self-defence in Denali National Park in May of 2010, using a .45 calibre handgun, as well as the claim on the gun webpage sixguns.com that that the very revolver M.O. was applying for has been successfully used to kill bull elephants. This is also the gun that was made famous by Clint Eastwood's Dirty Harry character.

(A couple of pages of court deliberations cut.)

"Considering what has become evident in the case about M.O.'s options to meet his need for protection with other weapons than handguns and about the suitability of a handgun for the stated purpose, the Supreme Administrative Court finds that the exceptional reasons required for a permit to possess a handgun to be granted do not exist.

The decision of the Supreme Administrative Court. Approving of the appeal of the police authority of Västernorrland fief, the court nullifies the decision of the administrative court of appeal and establishes the verdict of the district administrative court and the decision of the police authority."

So in the end, after three years of litigation, he still wasn't able to get a permit for a revolver. As a good a time as any for practising civil disobedience.

Soft on the tough (ones), tough on the soft (ones)

... to paraphrase the Swedish expression *mjuk mot de hårda, hård mot de mjuka.*

Perhaps one of the most ruthless confiscations of guns in modern day Western history took place during the autumn of 2008 in *Torsby* near the Norwegian border. During the month of October, two biathlon clubs would be hit with police raids, ending in the authorities seizing all the weapons and handing suspicions of weapon crimes to a large number of people. Biathlon is a sport which Sweden has been quite successful at, but this hasn't stopped the police from interfering in the practise of the sport through their raids.

On 13 October, well-established biathlon club SK Bore Biathlon in *Torsby* is hit with a raid, where the police seize 15 rifles; due to an earlier investigation concerning how one of the members of the club had stored his rifle, which three weeks earlier had led to this man's permits being revoked, now they raided the club itself since it was possible that it wasn't up to date with new regulation concerning the storage of the rifles. They also charge the club with suspicions of weapons crime. A month later, the police notifies the club that it doesn't have the right to store weapons any more, making it impossible for its members to practise the sport, though the weapons crime charge is dropped. One of the complaints by the police on the management of the rifles is that the required alarm isn't of the correct security class.

SK Bore Biathlon wasn't just any club, either - it staged the junior world championships 27 January to 2 February 2010, and is in a bid for the European championships of 2013. Let's just hope no local despot decides to interfere again if the club gets the event.

On 22 October, a high school in the same town - Stjerneskolan - is raided as well. Stjerneskolan has a so called *idrottsgymnasium*, a sports high school, and here they practise biathlon in connection to the school. Without any advance warning, the police storm the school, seizing all 31 rifles they can find and notifying the students that they're suspected of weapon crimes. The rifles are stored in locked safes, with the ammunition in another locked safe, arrangements that were perfectly adequate when the facilities were installed during the 1970's. This year they've introduced new regulation, however, and the conclusion after an examination on 23 September was that the arrangements didn't meet present-day standards. The police remark about both the locks and the alarms being inadequate for the new regulation.

An unnamed source within the police critically describes the proceedings as a crusade when talking to *Värmlands Folkblad*.

Now these students as well find themselves unable to practise their sport, and are suspected of crimes that can render them prison sentences, a highly confusing situation. Instigator of both raids is Jessica Ölvestad, head of the legal unit at the Värmland police authority, and she defends charging teenagers with weapon crimes by saying that the lack of criminal intent doesn't matter, negligence is enough.

> "- When I got to hear about the state of things I made the decision that all the weapons should be confiscated, Jessica Ölvestad says. Considering the state of things I had no other choice.
>
> But Jessica Ölvestad neither wants to, or can, tell us what's actually flawed."[1]

Though most of the people whose rifles were confiscated in these raids would eventually get them back, for quite a few of them it would take several months. A small number of people lost their permits and couldn't keep their weapons.

These children wouldn't be the only victims of Ölvestad's peculiar use of authority; in early 2008, an 82-year-old man by the name of Lennart Olsson, who had been a gun owner for 70 years and had gone his whole life without committing any crimes, suddenly came across police searching his home and taking his guns. The authorities had declared the man deceased and for this reason the police was tasked with taking the guns that he was registered as owning. Only thing is, when they entered his home, they found him alive and well. Still, this doesn't stop them from

---

1   nwt.se 08-10-23

taking his guns as ordered. A few weeks later, Olsson gets a letter in the mail saying the reason his guns were taken was because the owner, he himself, had passed away.

After he's learned the details of the matter, he sends a letter to Ölvestad notifying her that he's pursuing all legal routes available to him to get his guns back, including turning to the European Court of Human Rights. This author unfortunately doesn't have the resources to investigate what later became of the matter.

When you think about it, it's really bizarre sending people to prison for possession of a weapon that they haven't used in a criminal manner and only intend to use for self-defence. A crime in the traditional sense is an action whereby someone or something is hurt or infringed upon. A responsible person could have a room full of mini-guns at home without anyone ever coming to harm. When you leave natural law behind, there's no limit to what you can criminalize, and ironically you can outlaw something that many people consider to be an actual natural right, the one to keep guns for self-defence. Gun ownership is truly a victimless 'crime.'

Abortions on demand - We'll let you pick gender too

If I told you that there was a country in the world where if given special permission, a woman can abort a foetus at any state of pregnancy until the child would be able to survive on his own; where you can abort your baby if you don't approve of his or her gender; and where physicians can be sentenced to prison if they refuse to perform the procedure - then I guess you'd assume I was joking? As sad as it may be, there is such a country, where it's completely taboo to question a woman's right to kill her offspring. Portions of the Swedish abortion law read as follows:

> 1 § If a woman requests her pregnancy to be terminated, abortion may be performed if the measure is taken before the end of the eighteenth week of pregnancy and it can't because of an illness in the woman be assumed to bring about serious jeopardy to her life or health.

> 3 § After the passing of the eighteenth week of pregnancy, abortion may only be performed if The National Board of Health and Welfare grants the woman a permit for the procedure. Such a permit may only be granted if exceptional reasons exist for the abortion.

> 4 § If abortion in the case designated by 1 § is refused, the matter shall be immediately put in front of The National Board of Health and Welfare for examination.

> 10 § If a doctor intentionally disregards ordinance in 4 § or, if nothing else follows by 6 § second paragraph, in 3 § or 5 §, he's sentenced to a fine or prison for at most six months.

The 1974 abortion law is the result of government bill 1974:70 under the management of Lennart Geijer, and though the criminalization of the refusal to perform abortions wasn't discussed at any great length, this is what was stated on page 74:

"Likewise doctors who neglect to observe their duties in matters of abortion ought to be subject to penalization."

A pair of very controversial abortions took place in Eskiltuna during 2008 and 2009; a mother of two daughters got pregnant with the intention of having a boy. After she was pregnant for the first time, she asks for an amniocentesis to see the gender of the child and found it was a girl. Six days after receiving this information, she requests to have the foetus aborted, and the pregnancy is terminated.

After disposing of the first foetus, she gets pregnant again, hoping for better luck this time around. This time too, she asks for an amniocentesis, but now it's denied. Struck with this setback, she realizes in a couple of weeks she'll still be able to see the gender through ultrasound, and when she finds out it's a girl this time as well, she requests a second abortion the same day she receives the screening. Though it sickens the staff having to assist this woman in her doings, they're legally required to do so, facing possible imprisonment otherwise, and certain loss of employment.

Afterwards, Kaj Wedenberg, head of the clinic where the woman has had the two abortions, writes a letter to the health authorities asking for clarification on the issue of whether they can't opt out of having to perform gender abortions. In May of 2009, the health authorities respond to the inquiry and reaffirm that doctors have no right to refuse a woman an abortion she wants because of the child's gender.

Since 2008, foreign women as well are able to have abortions in Sweden, at a cost of about 4500 crowns, or roughly $600. The largest portion of the women performing this procedure come from Asia, and there is no requirement to inform their families of the terminated pregnancy. Though most of the developed world has legalized abortion, very few countries explicitly permit gender abortions the way Sweden does.

Circumcisions and the Swedish state

> "And God said unto Abraham, Thou shalt keep my covenant
> therefore, thou, and thy seed after thee in their generations.
> This is my covenant, which ye shall keep, between me and you,
> and thy seed after thee; Every man child among you shall be
> circumcised.
> And ye shall circumcise the flesh of your foreskin; and it shall be
> a token of the covenant betwixt me and you."

Genesis 17:9-11

"Thou shalt have no other gods before me."

Exodus 20:3

Formally, Swedes enjoys freedom of religion, though it's often said that people shouldn't bring their religion into politics or into public life. As long as people keep their religion to their private lives, no one will bother them, or so the story goes...

Sometimes, however, the state appears to not even respect the integrity of people's own family life, or their religion. This is the case with male circumcision. As few people are unaware of, this is an ancient tradition that in Semitic religion goes back to Abraham's covenant with God in Genesis chapter 17. This tradition has been respected universally without much controversy, but in the late 1990's in Sweden, public debate started turning against the procedure. Though little in the way of actual evidence was cited, the debate expressed a general fear that male circumcision might have serious complications, and legislators became involved.

In 2001 a new law was enacted, *Lag om omskärelse av pojkar*, "Law on circumcision of boys," which made circumcision punishable with prison unless it was performed by a licensed physician or an individual with a special permit. Anesthetics also became a requirement. To quote the law:

> 4 § The procedure shall be performed with anesthetics catered for by a licensed physician or licensed nurse, under satisfactory hygienic conditions and with concern for what's best for the boy.

> 5 § Circumcision may be performed only by a licensed physician or by one who has a special permit to perform circumcision on boys. Other person than a licensed physician may not perform the procedure on boys older than two months."

Hence, the state introduced legislation that prevented people from keeping their religious traditions by themselves, and without a special permit, it had to be entirely on the terms of the state. This struck the two religious minorities performing the procedure, Jews and Muslims, differently; Jews typically circumcise on the eight day of the boy's life, while Muslims do it later in life, some time before puberty. Hence Jews could still have one of their own perform the actual procedure, though they certainly didn't welcome the presence of the physician or nurse required for anesthetics. For Muslims, the ceremony was taken completely out of their hands, if they were to follow the law.

Physicians in Sweden are generally not very keen on performing the procedure since it has no medical indication, and quite often refuse to perform it. They're often not keen on performing abortions either, but unlike circumcisions, they can't opt out of abortions. This leaves Muslims in a difficult situation when they attempt to have their boys circumcised legally - waiting lines for the procedure in the public healthcare system often become extremely long. If they afford it, they can pay up to $1,000 to have a private physician perform it, but that option isn't open to very many. To be able to do it under these conditions, for many families the only solution becomes fellow Muslims without medical training.

In 2004, the circumcisions performed in Sweden were surveyed. Out of the 3,000 or so that are performed every year, only 850 had been performed in the healthcare system. Hence some 2,000 a year are performed the traditional way, by untrained individuals.

The year after that, in 2005, the effects of the law were also evaluated in a report by The National Board of Health and Welfare. (2001:499)

> "The National Board of Health and Welfare is, due to the complications that have been registered in the public hygiene and health care along with information in connection with other oversight of operations, of the opinion that circumcisions are being performed on older boys (in preschool age) outside the hygiene and health care."

> "According to the registration of complications, five boys have been registered with complications in connection with circumcision since 2001."

Oh my, we have a national crisis on our hands, five registered complications. It would be interesting to see a compilation of the complications suffered through legal abortions in the healthcare system, but it's an understatement to say that that would be politically unfeasible. Judging by discussions online, plenty of pregnant women who consider having abortions fear the potential complications, however.

It is indeed quite peculiar that the state cites complications as reason to attempt to blot out circumcision while abortions are a highly prioritized procedure within the public healthcare. If medical complications are a concern, shouldn't the state warn women about the potential ones in connection with abortions, if this is the real reason for attempting to prevent circumcisions?

In this author's opinion, the complications are only used as an excuse. The real reason is that the circumcision gives the boys a religious identity of their own - they're brought into the world to be God's children, with the circumcision signifying their covenant with him. With the requirement to be present when this procedure is performed, the state signals to these religious minorities that the Swedish state doesn't respect any other gods but itself, that the state owns a human being from the cradle to the grave.

Thou shalt have no other gods before the Swedish state.

CRIME AND NO PUNISHMENT

"And if a man cause a blemish in his neighbour; as he hath done, so shall it be done to him;
Breach for breach, eye for eye, tooth for tooth: as he hath caused a blemish in a man, so shall it be done to him again.
And he that killeth a beast, he shall restore it: and he that killeth a man, he shall be put to death." *Leviticus 24:19-21*

Chapter 1, section 6

"No sanction shall be imposed upon a person for a crime committed before attaining the age of fifteen."

Chapter 26, section 6

"A person serving imprisonment for a fixed term shall, unless it follows otherwise from the second or third paragraph or by Section 7, be conditionally released when two-thirds of the sentence, but at least one month, has been served. *Swedish Penal Code*

§ 9

"An inmate shall be treated with respect for his human dignity. He shall be met with understanding for the special difficulties that accompany residence in a correctional facility."

§ 14

"An inmate shall be provided with opportunity for suitable leisure activity. He should be encouraged to spend time with hobbies of his own that can contribute to his development. To the extent it is suitable, he should have opportunity to through newspapers, radio and TV follow what happens in the outside world. His need for recreation should be provided for to a reasonable extent."

Lag om kriminalvård i anstalt - "Law on the treatment of offenders in correctional facilities" (not an official translation)

Imposed sentences

A century ago, Sweden still decapitated convicted criminals, but alas in 1921, the death penalty was repealed after having been used very sparsely the decades before; since then, the evolution has been a gradual process towards more and more leniency shown towards criminals, with the most serious transformation taking place in the 1970's. Until 1962, convicts could still be sentenced to forced hard labour, but the political activists that came to dominate the debate during the sixties saw the criminal as a victim of society, and that it was cruel of society to actually punish the criminals - by the logic of these activists, that would constitute punishing the rapists, murderers and such two times over. So, it was instead argued that society had a duty to treat these "victims of society" instead of asking them to pay back any debt to the community.

The application of the sixties ideas took place during the seventies, culminating in the 1974 law *Lag om kriminalvård i anstalt*, "Law on the treatment of offenders in correctional facilities," usually abbreviated *KvaL*. In here, a large number of rights are enumerated that will be expanded upon in a later section. During this era, regular prison sentences were also cut in half with something called *halvtidsfrigivning*, half-time release, which meant you only had to serve half your sentence if you didn't attempt to escape. However, after massive protests, this provision was transformed into the 2/3 rule in 1998, which meant the convicts had to serve 2/3 of the sentence instead. Left-wing politicians aren't too pleased with this, unfortunately, and there have been calls to revert back to half-time release once again, something that could have become a reality if the Social Democrats had won the 2010 election.

In *Brottsbalken*, the penal code, sentences for crimes are listed, sentences that to an international observer must appear extremely light. Murder is listed as having a sentence of between ten and eighteen years or life. The paragraph beneath defines manslaughter as a murder with extenuating circumstances or a less severe case, punishable with between 6 and 10 years in prison.

Lifetime imprisonment in Sweden is a sentence without any definite length, though after 10 years of served time, the prisoner has the option to apply for a determinate sentence, with a minimum of 18 years. The lifetime sentences usually officially become between 18 and 25 years, before the 2/3 rule is applied. Hence, the minimum sentence for murder becomes 4 years, and so called life only has a minimum of 12 years, with the typical lifetime term being around 15 years.

Rape is listed as having a punishment of between two and six years, though underneath, less severe cases are given a maximum of four years with only an implicit one month minimum.

Something else of concern in Swedish crime prevention is that in 1989, the earlier regulation in *Brottsbalken* 1 § 7 supporting the need for general deterrence was removed. Hence society ceased believing in the notion that imposed sentences had any effect on the likelihood of a potential criminal committing a crime. The delivered sentences were no longer thought to send a message to the criminal population. This meant more lenient sentences, and unfortunately sowed the seed of coming crime waves as well.

Let's look at the sentences handed out by the courts under these regulations:[1]

The figures in these compilations of statistics list the number of sentences within a given bracket, not every individual sentence.

In 2005, this is a breakdown of the 78 murder sentences:

1-2 years	1 offender
2-4 years	4 offenders
4-10 years	52 offenders
'Lifetime'	21 offenders

The average sentence length was 102 months, hence the offenders would have to serve five years and eight months on average.

In 2008, the most recent available statistics, only combined murder and manslaughter sentences are listed. These are the brackets for the 122 prison sentences for homicide that year:

1-2 months(!)	3 offenders
1-2 years	1 offender
2-4 years	22 offenders
4-10 years	86 offenders
'Lifetime'	10 offenders

Average sentence length 83 months, hence about four years and seven months of served time. The same year, two rape sentences were in the 1-2 month bracket, though average sentence length for rape and gross rape combined was 29.8 months, hence about one year and eight months in prison.

---

1   Source: Kriminalstatistik, Brottsförebyggande rådet

Youth offenders ages 15-20 get even more lenient sentences; these are the four homicide sentences to secure youth care (LSU) from 2005:

1 year	1 offender
1-2 years	2 offenders
2-4 years	1 offender

The seven rape sentences for youth offenders to secure youth care the same year:

2-3 months	1 offender
3-4 months	1 offender
4-6 months	1 offender
6 months	1 offender
6-12 months	1 offender
1 year	1 offender
1-2 years	1 offender

From the looks of it, criminals in Sweden have learned that holding a job and paying 2/3 of your income to the government just doesn't pay - a life of organized crime is a better career option. There are no "three strikes and you're out" rules in the country - no matter how many convictions you have behind you, you still get the same lenient sentences. The last couple of years, there's been a joint EU TV show called *City folk*, portraying individuals from various European cities. One of the representatives from my town of Sundsvall was a 48-year-old man who had served no less than 43 prison sentences. Funny as it may sound, the other week at the grocery store, I spotted this very man. This time he didn't appear to be stealing anything though, he was simply standing in line at the checkout. Then again, who knows what he had in his pockets?

The stereotypical behaviour of going in and out of prison, or to be more specific, the individual cycle of this lifestyle, is called a *volta* in Swedish. Directly translated, *volta* means 'overturn' in English, the phrase was possibly coined because sentences are so short that you're out in no-time.

It can be interesting to look at the recidivism rates with these sentence lengths. Proponents of humanitarian crime prevention often claim that short sentences provide the best readjustment to society. Surely then the recidivism rate will be low? Here are the actual statistics (keep in note that these are all sorts of crimes – violent criminals tend to relapse more than say the typical drunk driver.):[1]

In 1994, 20% of offenders had relapsed into crime within one year and 32% within three years;

In 2004, the figures were 24% within one year and 38% within three years.

Some statistics are quite dramatic. The recidivism rates of the 5400 offenders with at least ten previous convictions were these:

74% within one year; 89% within three years.

Out of this group, the 55 18- to 20-year-olds with 10+ convictions had these recidivism rates:

78% within one year; 95% within three years.

You can clearly tell how well it works attempting to avoid sentencing the youngsters to prison, with these relapse rates. The 5% that didn't relapse also include offenders who have sustained injuries during the course of their crimes and hence aren't very able to commit new crimes.

---

1   Source: "Återfall i brott" / Brottsförebyggande rådet

The world's most luxurious prison system

Long gone are the days when criminals in Sweden could be sentenced to hard time and forced labour. These days, rehabilitation and recreation are the watchwords. The basic idea is that criminals are victims of society and that it is society's duty to readjust them to everyday life, by providing them with everything they need to do that. In 1974, a law was passed, "Law on the treatment of offenders in correctional facilities," which granted inmates generous rights and entitlements, a product of a very liberal era. It also introduced something called *öppen anstalt*, open prison, which as far as the building complex goes isn't an actual prison - it's rather like a motel, where inmates are provided ordinary rooms to live in, and where they're allowed to freely roam the premises when they're not on work duty.

Some of the most generous entitlements provided by this 1974 law are 37 §, guaranteeing an inmate healthcare, at an ordinary hospital if necessary; 33 § imposing upon government the duty to secure the inmate's need for housing, employment, education, financial support and "support and treatment measures" if necessary after release; 30 § giving the right to keep in touch with the outside world through the phone; 14 § providing leisure activities and recreation, such as game consoles in one's room as well as barbecue nights with family and other inmates.

7 § of said law reads as follows:

> "An inmate should be placed at an open prison, if placement at a closed prison isn't necessary for security reasons or to let the inmate be granted the opportunity of such work or such teaching, education or special treatment that can't reasonably be arranged at an open prison."

My, they sure are being accommodated if their needs are taken into account when deciding placement. And on the topic of placement - amazing as it may sound, convicted criminals actually get to choose which institution they're going to be placed at, if they qualify for placement at an open prison. *Lag om beräkning av strafftid m.m.*, "Law on the calculation of sentence length etc," from 1974 deals with the execution of sentences, and provides additional rights to inmates. Convicted criminals are generally free to roam society for a brief period after their guilty sentences have been received, perhaps given a deadline to show up for the sentence in a month's time. Up until that time, this law grants them the right to show up at whatever open prison they prefer and produce a *nöjdförklaring*, "declaration of satisfaction with a judgement," and the institution is then forced to take them in and let them start serving their sentences the moment they check in. 3 § grants the general right to produce a *nöjdförklaring*, while 10 § deals with the duty of prison employees to take the convict in if he produces this declaration.

On top of these privileges, 12 § grants the right for the convict to apply for a postponement of up to six months of the sentence if he can cite "state of health, work or education situation or other circumstances." An additional six months are possible if "exceptional reasons" exist. Sometimes the law text almost seems to be instructions for the convict on how to dodge serving his sentence; to quote the last paragraph of 12 §:

> "If the convict shows that he's filed an application for postponement at the latest on the day he according to first paragraph 10 § was meant to report to a correctional facility and if a postponement hasn't been applied for earlier in the case, the execution shall be deferred awaiting the decision of the Prison Service."

So if you feel like postponing the sentence another one or two weeks, just file such an application the day you're supposed to check in. 13 § provides the same option for an application for clemency. And let's not forget 29 §, which entitles the convict to appeal rejected applications for postponement or clemency to an administrative court.

Life in "prison"

Ljustadalen institution, a summer evening in 2010.

About three kilometres from my house, the closest prison is located, one housing women. Up until 1996, it housed both men and women, but then became an exclusively female institution. Ljustadalen is an open prison whose amenities include a football (soccer) field as well as a special ordinary house for family visits; a children's room inside the building and a playground outside. It's beautifully situated some ten kilometres north of Sundsvall up on a hill with a great view of the surrounding area.

I have a confession to make. My half-sister has served time

in this institution, though she was free in July when I took this picture. Knowing her, she might very well be back there by the time you read this. I think incarceration is good for her, she mostly just messes up her life even more when she's on the outside.

But to stay on topic. Sweden's prisons have a classification of their security levels from A to F, with open prisons such as Ljustadalen being F. On the website for the Prison Service at www.kvv.se, they've got listings of all the prisons in Sweden with the programs they offer, what comforts are available and such, contact information and other data that might be of interest. All prison pages also include pictures of the facilities, and the general appearance is very much as that of a tourist guide for people undecided on just where to go.

Though I have no personal experience of prison life myself, some of these prisons do indeed look very comfortable, almost appealing to live in. *Asptuna*[1] is also well-situated on a wooden peninsula right next to a lake, and the amenities listed on the webpage for this institution are these: "Swimming, fishing, football [soccer], volleyball, jogging track, table tennis, pool and a gym."

Another attractive placement is *Gruvberget*[2], where inmates live in separate regular wooden houses in a cleared area in the middle of a huge forest, seemingly with two inmates per 2-floor house. Leisure activities here include miniature golf, skiing, swimming, fishing or simply picking berries. Regarding housekeeping, this is what the webpage says: "The institution provides three meals a day, but in the bungalows there is the opportunity for the inmates to do their own housekeeping." This "prison" is so attractive that only in the last two years, there have

---

1   http://www.kvv.se/sv/Fangelse/Vara-anstalter/Asptuna/

2   http://www.kvv.se/sv/Fangelse/Vara-anstalter/Gruvberget/

been at least three JO complaints from inmates who found their requests to transfer there unsuccessful. (Registration numbers 5482-2009, 497-2008 and 496-2008. JO Cecilia Nordenfelt criticized the prison management in all the cases.)

Family visits are encouraged in general at prisons, and even field trips are possible if you successfully apply for a permission. The requirements for visiting a prison sure are harsh. To quote the Prison Service webpage: "As a condition for a visit, you and the things you carry **may** be subject to examination." You'd think frisking visitors would be standard procedure, but maybe I'm just too much of a traditionalist to ask for that.

These two mentioned prisons are of course open ones. So, how do "closed" prisons look? This is the inside of a "cell" in such a facility. Well, to be honest, they don't call it a cell, but a "room:"

Naturally, personal TV sets and bathrooms belong in a prison cell. It sure has to suck being locked up at 20:00 every night and be confined to no other activity than watching primetime TV and maybe playing your own Xbox or Playstation game console. I kind of wonder what's the difference between life on the inside and on the outside - I mean, many young people today in general tend to lock themselves up in their own rooms and doing these very things. Oh, I just forgot... If your parents don't serve you breakfast, the most you can do is bitch to them personally, but if you're incarcerated and you suffer the same fate, you can file a complaint with the JO. Don't worry about having to procure an envelope and paper to write on, though - simply go to whatever PC they've got in your prison that's hooked up to the Internet and use that one.

It has to be said that rooms at closed prisons don't appear quite as comfortable as ones at open prisons; the following picture is from inside such a one, also from the kvv.se webpage:

Sometimes I ponder committing some crime for the sole purpose of being placed at such an institution, to gain a more relaxing environment in which to pursue a writing career. Of course, with the way the Swedish penal system is designed, I'd have to go through at least five convictions to even get into an open prison.

Prison inmates discuss correctional facilities

If the information on life in the various prisons available on that webpage isn't enough, there's also the option to exchange information on what prison to apply to online on Internet forums. One of the biggest such forum, and probably also the home of the largest portion of society's rejects, is *Flashback*. What follows here are excerpts from discussions between mostly current or former inmates on life in correctional facilities. To get into the spirit of comprehending the depictions of these institutions, I would suggest listening to Cliff Richard's song "Summer Holiday" while reading the quotes.

Tips på bra öppna anstalter

Jag behöver tips på några bra öppna anstalter , helst med bra studiemöjligheter.

Vafan har Bahamas med det här att göra?

"I need advice on a couple of good open prisons, preferably with good studying options."

Harry_
Medlem

Citat:

Ursprungligen postat av **frio**
Jag behöver tips på några bra öppna anstalter , helst med bra studiemöjligheter.

Asptuna
där har dom Jacuzi o pool

--::::Håll käften när du pratar med mig::::--

"Asptuna - they've got jacuzzi and swimming pool there."

Sök till Skenäs en öppen anstalt som ligger i östergötland. Enligt dom som satt där så var det den bästa anstalten i landet. Dom har verkstad och snikeri. En skola. Enda anstalten i sverige som har ett motionspår på 3.5 km, en fottbollsplan...en badbrygga. I kiosken kan man köpa det mesta och det som inte finns där kan dom beställa hem. Sök till skenäs....en blandning melian ett sommarkollo och plugga på folkhögskola. Det enda negativa med stället är att man måste ge tvättkillarna 20 kr i veckan för att få tillbaka sina egna kvv-kläder.

"Apply to Skenäs, an open prison in Östergötland. According the people who sat there it was the best institution in the country. They've got workshop and woodwork. A school. Only institution in sweden that has a 3.5 km jogging track, a soccer field... a bathing bridge. You can buy most things at the kiosk and what they don't have you can order home. Apply to Skenäs... A mix between summer camp and studying at a community college."

sätilla e soft bra mat hyffsat gym grillkvällar llite knepigt folk o inte så mycket grupperingar där

försök få kökstjänst då har du det helt ok

Lätt att få in biltele o massa gömställen o ha den o andra grejor om du nu använder sådant

"Sätilla is soft good food decent gym barbecue nights. [...] Easy to get cell phone inside and lots of hiding places to keep it and other stuff in case you're using."

hmm

Jag har suttit på skenäs ett halvår eller nått...

Det är en helt OK anstalt.. Som någon sa finns de lite olika sysselsättningar som du måste vara på under dagtid. Det finns bland annat snickeri där du kan få utbildning i cnc svarvning eller svetsning. Kan även ta truckkort o lite annat sånt. Sen finns de komvux där du kan läsa alla grund ämnen (matte, svenska, engelska, samhäll, spanska, naturkunskap o franska).. Sen kan du läsa vad du känner för på distans. Ett plus är att de finns internet i skolan om man gillar sånt. Visserligen bara modem men va fan de är ju ändå på kåken 😊
Gillar du inte något av ovanstående kan du jobba i tvätten, köket, skogen eller som städare. Personligen var jag städare då man har egna tider o i princip kan softa på avdelningen framför digitaltv boxen..
Just de, alla avdelningar har en digitalbox..

Motionsspåret är guld, dels kan man gå ner o sitta vid en badbrygga o ångra sina synder eller så kan man bara gå en runda. Även ett populärt ställe att ta in i sprit o andra olagligheter 😈

Andra sysselsättningar som finns är styrketräning, pingis, tennis (en hel sporthall med allt vad den innehåller), solarium o ett rum med instrument där du kan spela instrument...

Kiosken är skitbra, man kan köpa i princip vad som helst. Bland annat hade dom långa silvriga rizla & OCB där hahaahha 😊

"I've been to Skenäs for half a year or so... It's a perfectly ok institution. [...] Can also get a truck driving licence and some other stuff. Then there's adult school where you can learn all school subjects(math, Swedish, English, civics, Spanish, science and French)... Then you can read whatever distance courses you feel like. What's nice is that they've got Internet at the school.[...] All sections have digital boxes. The jogging track rules, you can either go down and sit at a bathing bridge and repent your sins or just go for a walk. Also a popular place to bring liquor and other illegalities."

"No computers are harder... worked for a while but then they removed it. On the other hand it's no problem bringing a cell phone... just be a bit careful as you enter..."

"How do you mean... Don't they have any searches?"

"Exactly... They search your bags and then you get to post an arrival U.P... I always kept my cell phone in my pocket... Even smaller objects are even easier...

I can recommend prison drug rehab as an occupation by the way...
sit down, gossip and have some coffee."

"Bring your own TV if you've got one... They were short on those
last time I was there."

"What the hell don't you get a TV?????"

"You're going to get a TV first, at the reception quarters, but you'll
have to share the room there.

In your own room you can either rent one from the trustee council
for $2 a week or something. The downside is they're short on
them. I should have brought TV... a pain not having one.

109

They've got a channel where they show DVD movies too, by the way... a couple of movies they change once a week..."

"So how do you go about bringing a TV? You're supposed to take it along when you enter? "

Kmaan
Medlem

Reg.datum: Sep 2005
Inlägg: 67

exakt!

eller så kan ju besök ta med sig...

"Exactly. Or you can have visitors bring it."

Svinpäls
Medlem

Reg.datum: Dec 2004
Inlägg: 602

Citat:

Ursprungligen postat av **lipton**
När jag satt så fanns det en speciell paviljong med äckel (sexdömda) men dom fick man inte ha nån som helst kontakt med.
Som Boddie sa så finns det m,öjlighet att röja i skogen eller vara på ett snickeri o hamra lite, finns även möjlighet till att lära sej svetsa och liknade saker. Finns speciella raklöddersflaskor med riktigt raklödder i toppen och ett lönnfack i botten som är grymt lämpliga att dölja mobiltelefonen i har jag hört 😊 och när jag var där så fanns det till och med en ingående telefonlinje på varje paviljong men var snack om att det skulle försvinna redan då så lär nog inte vara så längre, då fick man även använda sina egna kläder.

Helt seriöst! Jag vill fan dit! Ett par månader skulle fan sitta fint! Vila sig från det vanliga kneget samtidigt som man lär sig svetsa och får betalt!!

Topic: Anyone that's been to the Skenäs institution?

"Seriously! I f***ing want to go there! Hell, a couple of months would do me good. Rest from the ordinary grind at the same time as learning to weld and get paid for it. "

"I agree with Mr Svinpäls [Swine fur] above. Since I live fairly close to Skenäs institution as well and love to fish, it would rule being able to slack for a few months there. Anyone have any advice on how to get in there? That is, as far as crime goes?[...] How long time do you have to serve to get free dental care, by the way? That's something a white man doesn't afford any longer without going to Hungary. I could bring beer there in advance if the fence consists of marking sticks."

"Hello, a while ago I was arrested for aggravated assault and they found a bit of cocaine on me as well, which I was only bringing to a friend, but they didn't buy that. Now it's like this that I'm going to court very soon, and I'm most likely going to be incarcerated, it's the first time I've been arrested, never been put in custody or stuff, so how's life in prison? What are the chances I'll spend my time in an open prison or a 'closed' one? What should I think about in there? Appreciate answers. "

"It's cool, fun to spend time, you'll get far less than you think, it's always that way. I got 40 days now for 5 different things, 2

111

assaults on patrolmen on 2 different occasions, that's 2 of the 5 things, so don't worry, and you can apply to an open prison, you'll exercise, eat well, play table tennis, all that good life, tv in your room, sooo it's cool."

The taxpayers' bill

Since the Swedish prison service doesn't worry much about security at facilities, surely that will mean that costs are low? Think again. Sweden most likely has the highest cost in the world per inmate for incarceration. The kvv.se webpage states that the costs in 2009 were these:

2280 crowns / day in custody, or $310.

1599 crowns / day at open prisons, or $220.

2455 crowns / day at closed prisons, or $335.

There are some Western countries that unlike Sweden prioritize taxpayer money on other things than the good life of prison inmates. Keeping an inmate for a year in a closed prison in Sweden costs roughly 900,000 crowns, or $120,000, pretty exactly three times the average salary in the country before taxes. In the USA on the other hand, the national average cost per inmate in 2009 was $28,689[1], less than a quarter of Sweden's. Some American states are even better than that - in Montana, the cost was $11,268, or less than one tenth. Obviously the swimming pools, 1-man rooms and other luxuries cost a bit of money. The notoriously tough and secure American Supermax prisons which cost roughly $50,000 per year per inmate and have critics lamenting the high costs are not even close to Swedish expenses.

In Swedish prisons, the food the inmates eat costs 45 crowns per day, or $6.15. For comparison, in most of Alabama, the maximum allowed cost of food per inmate per day is $1.75, with

---

1   Source: National Institute of Corrections

the prison administration netting the difference if the expenses are less than that. One Florida prison was quoted as able to keep the cost at less than a dollar, quite a feat that Sweden should learn from. Maybe then inmates would stop putting on so much weight? Just about everyone released from prison in this country bitches about how much weight you put on while incarcerated. I guess those cell room TV dinners are to blame.

Prisoner rights, a rapist and porn magazines

A man in his 40's with the initials K.G. had been sentenced to eight years in prison for *gross rape*, a crime classification that usually involves multiple cases of rape. K.G. was spending this time in Härnösand institution, a prison with security class D - class A being the two top ones Kumla and Hall; F being open prisons. In spite of his rape sentence, he's initially making use of the right convicts have of enjoying recreation in their prison cells. In his case, this consists of 20 porn magazines. In 2004, the staff at the prison decide that the magazines interfere with the treatment of his criminality and might encourage him to rape women again in the future, so they seize them. Consequently, he files an application with the prison authority in Härnösand for the permission to keep these magazines in his cell, but this is denied on 3 May 2004.

K.G. then appeals the verdict, and on 15 June, he's denied the privilege as well. Then he appeals to the national Prison Service, which repeats the same verdict as the previous instance on 24 February 2005. After K.G. has exhausted the prison chain of appeal, he turns to the administrative courts and files a complaint with the one in Härnösand. On 31 August 2005, the district administrative court sentences in K.G.'s favour, and the prison is ordered to provide him with the magazines. The prison service appeals the verdict, but this is rejected on 17 March 2006.

The following week, K.G. requests to be handed the magazines which the courts had given him the right to. On 10 April 2006, the prison service rejects the request. They instead appeal again, to the supreme administrative court - *Regeringsrätten* - and request inhibition; that is, that the magazines will stay with the prison until the case has been tried. *Regeringsrätten* starts its examination of the case on 17 May 2006, but rejects the inhibition request, hence legally the magazines must be returned at once. Learning of this, on 20 June,

K.G. yet again files a request to get his magazines, but the prison rejects this the following day. The coming winter, new porn magazines are seized in K.G.'s cell at two separate occasions, which he must have bought during furloughs.

After Härnösand institution had neglected to comply with the court sentences to hand K.G. his magazines, he files criminal charges against the employee of the prison service who had denied his requests, alleging that this man had violated his duties. The investigation is dropped on 31 August 2006, however, with the prosecutor's office stating that the conduct by the employee doesn't fall under criminal law. True to his style, K.G. appeals the matter twice, both times failing to get a court case started.

On 21 June 2007, *Regeringsrätten* rejects the appeal of the prison service, hence the magazines are to be returned to K.G., which they indeed are now after some three years. This verdict sets a legal precedent. Following this, plenty of convicted sex offenders take the opportunity to have their seized magazines returned as well, and receive subscriptions of new magazines to their cells. The head of the Prison Service, Lars Nylén, wants to have the law changed so that convicts can be denied access to pornography, but know-it-all criminologist Jerzy Sarnecki counters by telling media that he's not certain that pornography will really contribute to recidivism, protesting the calls for a general ban. Sarnecki has been one of the most influential people in Swedish crime 'prevention,' a regular guest on the state TV when crime is discussed.

By now, you'd think K.G. would have displayed enough audacity for a whole lifetime, but next he files a complaint with the Chancellor of Justice, which at this time is Göran Lambertz. K.G.'s complaint is about the handling of the return of the magazines, the ones he was denied, and in his complaint he also asks for 200,000 crowns in damages, about $25,000.

On 7 August 2008, Lambertz produces his 6-page decision on the matter.

(Registration number 7545-07-40)

"DAMAGE CLAIMS CONCERNING A DECISION ON THE PART OF THE PRISON SERVICE TO NOT DELIVER CERTAIN MAGAZINES WITH PORNOGRAPHIC CONTENT

The decision of the Chancellor of Justice

The Chancellor of Justice denies K.G.'s request for damages from the state.

The Chancellor of Justice criticizes the Prison Service for not having delivered so called men's and porn magazines to a convict after the administrative courts had established that the refusal on the part of the Prison Service violated the law."

So a case of a serial rapist wanting to keep his 20 porn magazines led to this legal circus:

* **Three applications within the Prison Service to be able to keep the magazines.**

* **Three administrative courts trying the matter.**

* **Two applications within the Prison Service to have the magazines delivered after a favourable verdict.**

* **Three applications to file criminal charges against the employee who denied him the magazines.**

* **One complaint to the Chancellor of Justice for damages.**

Aren't prisoner rights great? Isn't Sweden great too?

Jonas Fernqvist - child molester working for the public day care

In 1977, a man was born who would later in life show an extraordinary interest in children. When he reaches high school age in the mid 1990's, he enrolls in a school program called *Barn & Fritid*, "Children & Recreation," aimed at teaching the profession of caring for children. As part of this program, he has a brief internship at a day care centre in his home town of Örebro in southern Sweden. After graduation, he starts work at the municipality's day care facilities, and because of the good hand he appears to have with minors, he's also entrusted with babysitting children in his spare time.

On the surface, he seems to live a well-ordered life, forming a romantic relationship with a woman by the name of Marie Friberg, whom he meets at the day care centre. Marie is almost ten years older than Jonas and has two children of her own from a former marriage, over which she's managed to gain sole custody. Due to a custody dispute, the social services is present in her family life, monitoring how the children are doing, though apparently not being very observant as we will see. It doesn't take long for Jonas and Marie to move in with each other, with Jonas settling in Marie's apartment in October that year, but soon Marie would learn of a terrible secret of her new boyfriend...

For about a year, since September of 1996, Jonas has sexually molested children at the day care centre where he works, as well as the children he's personally acted babysitter for, videotaping these excesses for his own enjoyment. At first it's a case of not too intrusive but of course still depraved experimentation, involving Jonas playing with the genitalia of these boys; as time goes on, he craves a more intimate experience, outright raping them in ways that are extremely painful for them.

When Jonas has moved into Marie's home, he assumes parental authority over her children, which includes locking them into their rooms on an almost daily basis for breaking some arbitrary rule he has set up for them. Jonas also installs a camera indoors to monitor what the children might do at night time, such as taking candy without permission. Just about every day when Jonas comes home from work, he tells Marie to leave the house and go see a friend, which she does willingly. Though struck with the peculiar realization that her boyfriend keeps her children locked up most of the time, she rarely has much to say about it, except when they bang the doors to be let out to be able to go to the bathroom. The rooms of the children have windows of their own, but Jonas has turned these rooms into prison cells by removing the handles on the windows so they can't be opened. On a couple of occasions, Marie locks her children into their rooms on her own as well.

Gradually, Jonas becomes ever more cruel towards the children and torments them, though the emotional plight this caused them appeared to go unnoticed by their guardians. During the later investigations, Marie told the police she was very tired at this time, both from her children being hard to manage and her former husband fighting her for custody over them. Hence locking the children up was the easiest way to deal with the situation. When Jonas is home alone with Marie's children during the afternoons, he molests and rapes them, videotaping this activity as well.

As early as May of 1997, Jonas had been spreading these videotapes over the Internet to a large community of paedophiles, and the movie clips he uploaded would include many taped sessions of him molesting Marie's children. All in all, between September of 1996 and February of 1999, the total duration of the taped clips would amount to over 20 hours, across 355 clips. In court, Marie would claim she had no knowledge of Jonas videotaping sexual molestations or collecting child pornography.

Though Jonas sexually violates at least thirteen different children during this period until the couple are arrested on 25 February 1999, no one becomes aware of what's taking place. In fact, the reason the affair came to the attention of the police was a crackdown on Internet paedophiles, a community to which Jonas was a major contributor. At first, he's assumed to be merely a distributor of child pornography, but when the police watch the tapes, they would come to a shocking realization - that Jonas has spent the last 2.5 years molesting children entrusted to his care and spreading the video clips all over the world. Now a major investigation into his activities would be underway, and Marie's children are taken into state custody.

In mass media, even though he's clearly guilty due to the video evidence, his personal identity isn't revealed and neither is his face shown; he's given the nickname *Örebropedofilen*, "The Örebro paedophile." As mentioned above, on the other hand, "Nazi leader Klas Lund" being sentenced to prison because of a pistol that was in his possession when the police raided his home wasn't spared the publicity, being named and shamed before he was even declared guilty.

In police custody, Jonas and Marie are both declared suspects of a large number of crimes, though in two weeks time, Marie is released until the court proceedings, while Jonas remains in custody. The subsequent investigation would result in no less than 57 counts of criminal charges against Jonas for such crimes as *gross rape, gross sexual exploitation, unlawful deprivation of liberty*, aggravated assault (*grov misshandel* in Swedish, *gross assault* official translation) and *gross child pornography crime* against thirteen children ages three to eleven.

On 23 July 1999, the district court of Örebro delivers sentences against the couple. What follows here might be quite shocking in its graphic description of the excesses committed, and sensitive readers might want to skip reading this part. To quote the 36-page sentence and its enumeration of the crimes:

"Färnqvist has during several occasions on 2 January 1997, at a day care centre in Örebro, had sexual intercourse with plaintiff 1 in attachment C in the plaint. Färnqvist has thereby been employed by the child care system."

"The sexual intercourse has consisted of among other things Färnqvist sucking, licking and fingering the penis of the plaintiff."

"During playback of the video tape concerning count 5, it has, according to the court, due to the pictures compared to the pain the plaintiff has expressed, become clear that Färnqvist has inserted his penis into the rectum of the plaintiff."

"From the film it's evident that Färnqvist by sitting on the plaintiff completely deprived him of his mobility, which is particularly expressed when the plaintiff had attempted to get loose but wasn't successful. Evident is therefore that Färnqvist has forced him into intercourse. For the reasons the prosecutor has stated the deed shall be deemed gross rape."

"Concerning count 11 it's evident that Färnqvist with sexual intentions has made the plaintiff attempt to empty his bowel at the same time that he's touched the plaintiff in the way stated, whereby Färnqvist also has taped the procedure in its entirety."

"... evident that Färnqvist through intimidation attempted to make the plaintiff urinate in his underpants."

"Färnqvist has taken an active role in the event by carefully instructing the children in their conduct. He has also on an actual physical level participated in the execution of the act by grabbing the hand of one of the plaintiffs and inserted one of his [the boy's] fingers into the rectum of the other plaintiff."

"Concerning count 45 it's primarily verified through what the court has been able to observe during playback of the video tape that Färnqvist sitting over the plaintiff has emptied his bowel on the plaintiff. It has become evident through Färnqvist's statements that this has taken place primarily to satisfy his sexual urge."

"On the topic of count 51 it's among other things through what the video tape has verified evident that Färnqvist has proceeded in such a manner with the water hose as has been stated. Among other things by taking into account the force with which the water jet has been sprayed into his rectum and the violation of integrity this proceeding has constituted, the deed shall be considered equivalent to forced intercourse."

"Through his conduct he's caused the plaintiff intense pain and the way he's proceeded testifies to exceptional ruthlessness."

The court's verdict:

"Färnqvist's criminality has a very high sentencing guideline. The court has found him convinced [sic] of excesses against eleven children. The excesses have taken place over a long period. Some of these, relatively speaking, have been of a less serious kind while most have been of a very serious nature with deep violations of integrity. He has in a manipulative way created a relation to the children, a relation he's been able to use to - through promises of rewards or in some cases violent threats - make the children participate in his exploitation of them."

"One of the plaintiffs has also in connection to being put through a deeply degrading excess asked the question "am I human," which, according to the court, is a testament to the level of violation that has taken place."

"According to 30 chap 6 § of the penal code, a person who commits a crime under the influence of a serious mental disorder may not be sentenced to imprisonment."

"A unanimous investigative team has found that Färnqvist during the crimes and during the investigation has **suffered** from a serious mental disorder."

Yeah... Way to go, using the word 'suffered' about the perpetrator.

"The diagnosis has been determined to be paedophilia as well as a personality disorder with[...]"

Blah, blah, blah... Am I the only one finding it a bit strange that paedophilia can be considered a 'serious mental disorder' that makes a person unaccountable for the molestation he puts children through? Note to the court - paedophilia is what we call the **behaviour** of molesting children. It's only a matter of time before all criminal behaviour is explained away with some 'disorder' invented ad hoc, with the criminals sentenced to care instead of incarceration.

"With this background it shall be considered having been made clear that Färnqvist committed the acts under the influence of a serious mental disorder, causing the sanction to be determined as delivery to care under forensic psychiatry with a decision on special release inquiry."

... the sentence that in the USA is usually called "Not guilty by reason of insanity."

"In the statement by forensic psychiatry, it's been noted that the risk for Färnqvist to relapse into crime is very great. The excesses have accelerated and they've become more and more bizarre and repulsive. Färnqvist has been determined to be dangerous with risk for additional escalation of his perversion. He himself has during court negotiations stated that he, if the opportunity were given, would yet again molest children. On these circumstances there's reason to remember that Färnqvist, when other adults have been present, has acted in a soft way towards the children, to, when he's alone with them, molest them."

Apparently he wanted to make sure he was sentenced to care instead of prison. Perhaps he realized just how the other inmates would treat him if he were to be sentenced to prison? I'm astonished that someone who's apparently manipulative can be considered to be 'suffering' from a 'mental disorder;' the only 'disorder' is his perversion. The execution of his own behaviour is something he's completely in control of. A civilized society would sentence him to death.

Marie Friberg is sentenced to 1.5 years in prison, being spared all the charges but unlawful deprivation of liberty, for locking up her children.

Fernqvist's time in psychiatric care

The very day Jonas is sentenced to care, he's placed at *St Sigfrid hospital*, an enclosed complex of psychiatric facilities - what used to be called a mental hospital, before that term was deemed politically incorrect. This hospital houses both convicts considered to have committed crimes under the influence of a mental disorder, as well as law-abiding citizens who have been involuntarily committed because their mental health was brought into question. One could say he was put in the right place, being surrounded by Sweden's most deranged and depraved individuals; but alas, unlike what's the case for many of the other inmates, the 'disorder' this man is 'suffering' from doesn't leave him very disabled, and the strongest drug they put him on is the 'anti-depressant' Paxil, not even any anti-psychotics to really sedate him; neither is he physically restrained.

Not much is publicly known about his activities during the first couple of years in psychiatric care, perhaps due to the great secrecy he's afforded as protection, apart from in 2004 when the head psychiatrist at the facility declares having been successful with the therapeutic care of Jonas. However, in early 2005, police investigating child pornography on the Internet trace distribution activities to a Swedish mental hospital. Jonas appears to have been pretty much left alone in his room at the hospital, with little in the way of actual searches of his quarters. He seems to have been able to make quite a comfortable residence out of his room, with a wide-screen TV, a home audio system and a cell phone which is his personal property, something the staff isn't legally allowed to take away from him.

Quite a few inmates at this facility have their own cell phones, and there have been public complaints about them using these phones to call people to harass and intimidate them; yet when the staff has attempted to seize the phones, administrative courts haven't approved of the actions and they've had to return them. The staff are told they're there to provide care, not take on a police role.

Shocking as it may seem, like just about all convicted inmates at Swedish prisons and psychiatric facilities, Jonas has been granted regular unsupervised furloughs, able to freely roam town like any regular citizen. Even as a free man, his activities in his hospital room are what preoccupies Jonas, however. During furloughs, he purchases computer hardware, one piece at a time, and smuggles into the hospital, gradually assembling a PC that he hides inside his home audio system. For a display, he uses his wide-screen TV. Then to top it all off, he uses his cell phone to connect to the Internet and hooks it up to his PC. Now he's back in business, downloading child pornography and helping to spread it as well, using his TV to watch the movie clips inside his hospital room.

When the police after having learned of the source of the child pornography distribution enter his room on 17 February 2005, they seize his cell phones and computer equipment; after searching his hard drive, they find he's got 7682 pictures and 14 video clips of children being sexually molested. During the autumn of 2006, he's on trial again over child pornography charges, but this conviction doesn't change his sentence. Jonas has also been given a new identity by the authorities and his appearance today isn't known. What's known, however, is that this man still freely walks around Swedish society during his furloughs.

Undoubtedly, this story isn't over just yet. So what's the moral of the story? That it just might not be a very good idea entrusting government day care with your children. And of course that the insanity defence is an abomination that shouldn't be permitted.

Protecting the public?

A madman running amok around children

On 19 May 2003, a 32-year-old man with twelve previous convictions, six for violent crimes and one for sexual crimes, is walking Stockholm town armed with an iron stick he's stolen from a construction site. His sanity is questionable - he's convinced people are trolls and that they're after him. Then he suddenly goes berserk near an elementary school and attacks everyone around him with this stick, killing a 71-year-old man and injuring six others, among them a 12-year-old girl coming home from school on her bike. The man strikes panic into the area, with people fleeing inside the school building. As the police catch up with him at the nearby subway and wrestle him down, he yells at them to shoot him, to no avail. Sometimes you'd wish the police were more flexible in the execution of their duty.

On 25 August, he's sentenced to psychiatric care for the murder and assaults he committed that day. In spite of the great danger he had constituted to the public, the justice system doesn't take many precautions to protect society from him - in four years time, he's practically a free man. In 2007, he's on furlough 321 out of 365 days, only having to keep in touch with outpatient psychiatric care during this time. The doctor in charge of him states that he's no danger to society as long as he doesn't use drugs, yet during his furloughs, he's been caught doing just that.

It's believed the 12-year-old girl would have died too if she hadn't used a bike helmet. Apparently in Stockholm today, you need a bike helmet to protect yourself not only in traffic, but from lunatics as well.

Most likely to be continued...

Psychiatric care for convicts

Ever since the 1970's, there's been a great belief in society's ability to treat criminals - they're seen as victims of society, and society apparently has an obligation to remedy them. For this reason, a large portion of violent criminals in the country are sentenced to psychiatric care rather than actual imprisonment. Out of 97 people convicted of murder in 2005, 18 were sentenced to psychiatric care under the LRV law, *Lag om rättspsykiatrisk vård*, or about 20%.[1] In 2006, 23 out of 106 convictions led to psychiatric care, about 20% as well.[2] Initially there's no defined duration for this form of incarceration, though an administrative court has to approve of the continuation of this care at least every six months for it to go on. When the doctor in charge of the patient decides the patient isn't in need of care any more, he's to be immediately released back into society. This can theoretically happen as well in the unlikely event the court doesn't approve of further care too.

Gradually, the care is meant to be reverted to open forms, with the convict residing in society and only receiving outpatient treatment while generally being a free man. To quote LRV 3 b §:

"The one who is provided with care under forensic psychiatry according to 31 chap. 3 § the penal code (*Brottsbalken*) with a decision on special release inquiry may be provided with open care under forensic psychiatry if

1. he or she still suffers from a mental disorder,

2. it is no longer called for to keep him or her in a healthcare facility for qualified psychiatric inpatient care that's accompanied by deprivation of liberty and other coercion, and

---

1   Source: Kriminalstatistik 2005, BRÅ

2   Source: Kriminalstatistik 2006, BRÅ

3. he or she because of his or her mental state, personal circumstances in general or the risk for recidivism into crime of a serious nature needs to observe special conditions to be able to be provided with necessary psychiatric care."

Hence, as soon as condition 2 is met, the convicted criminal gains his freedom, only having to keep in touch with his doctor as an otherwise free citizen. If the sentence includes a special release inquiry, an administrative court has to approve of the convict's release, but this is mostly a mere formality.

So, how long time all in all do the criminals sentenced to care spend in this care? In 1995, the National Board of Health and Welfare started an investigation into this matter, monitoring people sentenced to care, and followed them as they were released. The findings were reported in the document *Rättspsykiatrisk vård - utvärdering – omvärdering* in 2002. On page 30, average time in care is listed for a number of different crimes. The 38 people convicted of murder had an average time of 4.6 years, and the 24 convicted of manslaughter had an average of 4.3 years. This time included time out in society with care in open forms. The shortest care time for murder was 1.4 years, while 0.8 years was the shortest one for manslaughter.

Seems the psychiatric care must do wonders with its clients when it's releasing them this fast, doesn't it? Well, recidivism rates tell another picture. Within the time the clients were monitored after release, an average of two years, 21% had relapsed back into crime again. Page 34 has a breakdown of different types of treatment the inmates had received and its impact on recidivism rates - it turns out not a single one of them had made a statistically significant difference. There were two factors that did have a clear impact, however - social networks and drug abuse. Out of the ones that had relapsed into crime, 59% had adequate social lives while only 41.7% of the ones that didn't relapse had that. 35.9% of the recidivists abused drugs, while only 9% of the non-recidivists did. Hence the mentally ill people that both have social networks and abuse drugs are the most dangerous to society.

The furloughs granted the inmates proved hazardous to society; during the time in care, 185 out of 665 had been convicted of new crimes, or nearly 30%. Out of these, 19 were cases of sex crimes, eight cases of manslaughter, seven cases of murder and nine cases of aggravated assault.

If this lenient and ineffective psychiatric care wasn't bad enough, occasionally courts decide on a dropping of charges called *åtalsunderlåtelse*, which is similar to 'Nolle prosequi,' except that the Swedish version requires proof of the suspect's guilt. The Swedish *åtalsunderlåtelse* is usually given as a show of good faith to minors for misdemeanours; sometimes it's called the "young and dumb" rule. Well, in 2005, one person guilty of homicide was granted *åtalsunderlåtelse* too.[1] Essentially, he had killed another person yet the court simply decided not to prosecute the crime. I guess guilty criminals should focus on attesting to their own personal development rather than finding an alibi - "That guy I killed was only a case of youthful foolishness... I've learned to be a better person now, surely you wouldn't force poor little me to be prosecuted when you can just give me *åtalsunderlåtelse?*"

---

1   Kriminalstatistik 2005, page 169

Mattias Flink - homicidal misogynist on a state payroll

Sometimes in a modern society, especially in such a one as Sweden with very restrictive gun laws, you ask yourself whether you should look for safety in the government, or instead from the government. On 11 June 1994, a second lieutenant in the army named Mattias Flink, stationed at I 13 in Falun, had had a fight with his new girlfriend at a club, after they had hit town to spend the night out. Among other things, he shouts "I'm immortal, this is my town," out in the street with his arms raised above his head. After being thrown out of the club, he returns home to get his service uniform, and then heads for his regiment. Here he picks up his service rifle, a Swedish type of assault rifle named AK 5. Then he leaves the regiment armed to go woman-hunting.

The first victims of his wrath would be six female volunteers previously stationed at the same regiment, who were returning to their post after their discharge party as he came across them. Four of them die right away, and one would die shortly afterwards at the hospital. Then he continues his rampage and shoots dead two young men he comes across. Later during the night, the police catch up with him and disable him with a shot to his leg, when he a moment earlier had fired on them. Seven young people died this night:

Karin Alkstål, 22
Maths Bragstedt, 35
Therese Danielsson, 20
Helle Jürgensen, 21
Lena Mårdner-Nilsson, 29
Johan Tollsten, 26
Jenny Österman, 22

It was later learned that during May of that year, he had physically attacked his girlfriend and his other friends, though this didn't have any consequences. The forensic examination finds that all of the 48 located shell casings from his rifle had hit their targets, hence it appears not a single shot missed, and this with a blood alcohol content of 1.69 permille taken a couple of hours after the shooting. Flink however denies the murder charges, pleading for manslaughter instead, though he doesn't remember the events that have taken place.

During the subsequent trial, the court is charged with determining if Flink suffered from a mental disorder at the time of the shooting and proceeds with a lengthy psychiatric examination, but in spite of the insistence of psychiatrists that his actions are a case of alcohol psychosis, this examination ultimately finds that he's prosecutable and he's sentenced to a whopping 14 years by the district court, for seven counts of murder and three counts of attempted murder. Both defendant and prosecutor appeal the verdict, and in Svea Court of Appeal, Flink pleads for a sentence to psychiatric care instead, though the court sentences him to 'life' in prison. The same psychiatrists are called in this time as well, but now they have another explanation for his behaviour. one claimed to be deeply rooted in his personality, requiring a long treatment time. Finally in the supreme court, Flink pleads for psychiatric care or the district court's 14 years, but on 13 February 1995, the supreme court establishes the verdict of the previous court - 'life' in prison.

All is not so bad for Flink now, however - after spending only a couple of years in prison, he's soon moved to the low security institution Beatesberg due to good behaviour, a 'prison' with only fences keeping the inmates inside.

During his regular unwatched furloughs once a month, he often goes kayaking in Sankt Anna archipelago, a seaside resort outside Söderköping town, sometimes with old friends of his who don't mind his company.

(The people in the picture have nothing to do with Flink.)

Though there's plenty of resentment among the public towards these furloughs, Flink has nothing to worry about since he's acquired himself a new identity and the last close-up photos of him are from before the 1994 shooting.

As he's reaching the spent time behind bars that's required to apply for a definite term for his imprisonment, he does so, though initially without success. In 2008, he requests a 24 year sentence which would make him a free man by 2010, but all the three courts he appeals to deny him this.

Due to these setbacks, he lets himself be interviewed in TV for the first time since becoming incarcerated. On 28 March 2009, he's on the TV 4 show *Nyhetsmorgon* for 30 minutes, though he demands that they will not show his face. This is because of his monthly furloughs, he says, he fears people might become uneasy if they see him on a train or something and he doesn't want people to spot him.

The interview is mostly about his 'life' sentence, which he feels he doesn't deserve, arguing that he should instead have been given a definite sentence by the court. Quoting the legal precedent set by the Supreme Court in a case from 2009 where they stated that no one who's believed to be unlikely to relapse should get more than a 24 (16 in practice) year sentence no matter the crime, Flink feels this should apply to his case as well. When asked the question of how he sees himself today, he describes himself as "a pretty ordinary Swedish man." Flink says he'd like longer furloughs than 24 hours at a time, but the Prison Service doesn't give him that. He laments that since he's not believed to be likely to relapse, he shouldn't have to be incarcerated.

When asked to explain how he ended up murdering seven people, he states in true remorse that a number of ingredients contributed to it, which included both his friends and his girlfriend. He explains that since he's learned not to go into "such relationships" any more, these ingredients aren't present any more, hence he won't relapse.

Asked how the interaction with his fellow inmates works, he responds "You'll have to scratch that question;" the interviewer doesn't press him on the matter. Flink laments that he's forced to pay damages to the families of his victims for the rest of his life, never realistically being able to pay it all. "It's like a punishment within the punishment," he says. Funny when the damages were actually part of the original punishment. "It's not enough doing your time, but you also might have to spend the rest of your life on subsistence level." Oh, poor you, forced to live in poverty after killing seven people. He also laments that though initially his good behaviour in prison gained him more furloughs and benefits, the last couple of years there haven't been any improvements.

On 7 July 2010, Örebro district court finally converted his lifetime imprisonment to a definite one of 32 (21) years, and he's scheduled for release in August of 2015. Hence his sentence will total three years for every person he murdered. His lawyer said in TV that Flink was ecstatically happy about this. If his homicidal and psychopathic tendencies don't make some private army recruit him, I propose he should form a new association called "Released mass murderers with most of their lives still left in them." Or perhaps a Facebook group with the name "Misogynist killers looking for company." In today's western world, I think that one would attract quite a few female members.

The crime rate

After being exposed to tons of propaganda over the years about how criminals are just victims of society, how prisons only contribute to crime and so on, Sweden's laissez-faire policies must have resulted in a low crime rate, right? Especially with all the expenditure towards treatment, with all the fancy psychological theories they've come up with over the years? Unfortunately, over three decades of this approach towards crime prevention has taken its toll in much death and human suffering. In the mid 20th century, Sweden was one of the most peaceful and safe countries on the planet; now it's in the top internationally in several types of violent crime.

In 1950, there were 7382 reported cases of assault, 350 rapes, 2829 sex crimes, 20714 burglaries and 66 homicides.[1]

In 2009, there were 86281 reported cases of assault, 5937 rapes, 16069 sex crimes, 95516 burglaries and 231 homicides (in 2007, 261 homicides).[2]

Hence 11.7 times as many assaults, 17 times as many rapes, 5.7 times as many sex crimes, 4.6 times as many burglaries in 2009 compared to 1950, and about 4 times as many homicides in 2007.

---

1   Source: Kriminalstatistik, Rättsstatistisk årsbok and Statistisk årsbok

2   Source: Brottsförebyggande Rådet

Chart of rapes 1975 to 2009 (in 2003, the USA invaded Iraq and Sweden granted asylum to a large number of refugees.):[1]

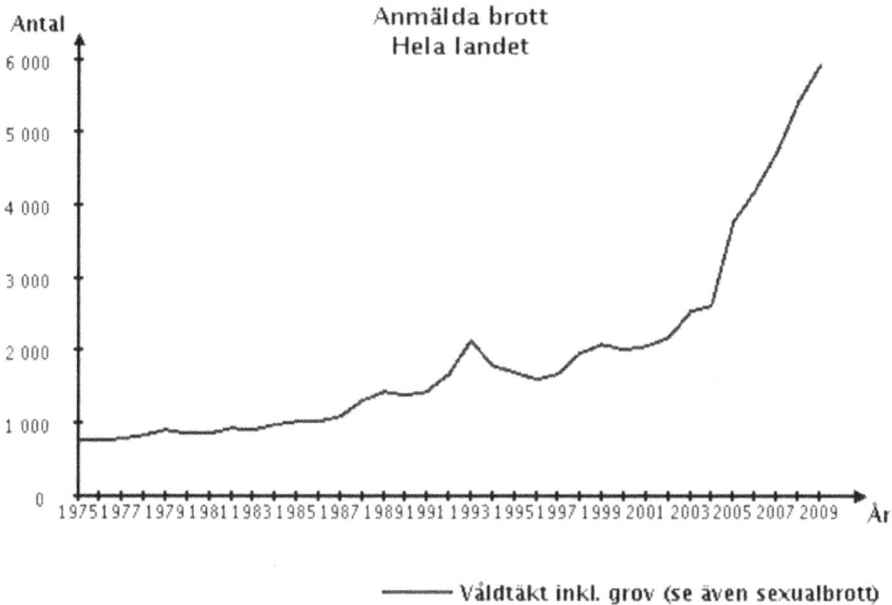

Already before the spike in the incidence rate during the 2000's, an EU report concluded that Sweden had the highest number of reported rape cases per capita in Europe; "Rape - The Forgotten Issue" from 2001 quoted Sweden as having 50% more reported cases per capita than the #2 country - France. And since then, the Swedish statistic has tripled.

---

1   All three charts generated on the website of *Brottsförebyggande rådet.*

Chart of assaults 1975 to 2009:

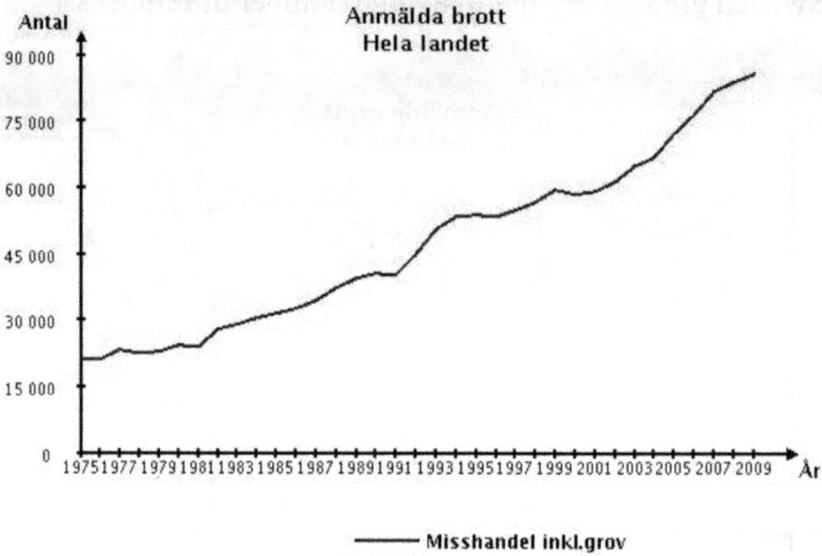

Chart of homicides 1975 to 2009:

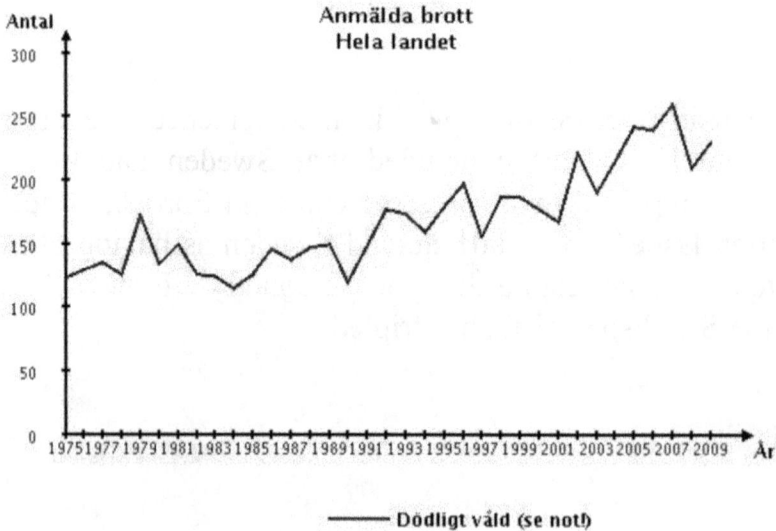

Most of Europe has gone through a similar development, but

137

perhaps not quite as dramatic as the one that has taken place in Sweden. France for example had an explosion of crime in the 1990's following the reception of large numbers of third world refugees. There are countries that have managed to break this destructive trend, however; notably the USA. The 1960's and 70's had seen the crime rate rise in the USA, with violent crime increasing by 270% between 1960 and 1980, quite possibly as a consequence of liberal crime policies, but during the 1980's when it was realized that society's only possible response to the crime wave was incarceration, that rehabilitation wasn't possible, crime was brought under control.

In 1980, the USA had 10.17 reported cases of homicide per 100,000 people, 36.63 rapes and 593.5 counts of violent crime.

In 2008, the USA had 5.4 reported cases of homicide per 100,000 people, 29.3 rapes and 454.5 counts of violent crime, a dramatic decrease.[1]

There are some differences in definition between countries concerning what constitutes a specific type of crime, and naturally the tendencies to report crime may vary as well, making comparisons between countries and possibly parts of countries as well far from perfect, but the number of reported crimes is still the best method we have of telling how many crimes take place. Hence, we'll have to go with this statistic and let it speak for itself. The United Nations Office on Drugs and Crime has for some time now made compilations of the reported offences in countries that make these figures available. The following is a comparison from 2003 to 2008 between Sweden and the USA. Sweden has 9.2 million people and the USA about 310 million, about 33.7 times more; but the figure to the right, the number of offences per 100,000 people, lets one compare the crime rates per person.

---

1   Source: Bureau of Justice Statistics, sourced from FBI:s Uniform Crime Reports

UNODC
United Nations Office on Drugs and Crime   **Motor Vehicle Theft at the national level, number of police-recorded offences**

Definition: *'Motor Vehicle Theft' means the removal of a motor vehicle without the consent of the owner of the vehicle. 'Motor Vehicles' includes all land vehicles with an engine that run on the road, including cars, motorcycles, buses, lorries, construction and agricultural vehicles.* (UN-CTS M4.4)

Country/territory	Count						Rate per 100,000 population					
	2003	2004	2005	2006	2007	2008	2003	2004	2005	2006	2007	2008
United States of America	1 261 230	1 237 850	1 235 860	1 192 810	1 095 770	956 846	424,8	412,9	408,2	390,2	355,0	307,0
Sweden	67 199	60 980	56 719	51 639	49 249	44 717	749,2	676,2	625,6	566,7	537,7	485,8

UNODC
United Nations Office on Drugs and Crime   **Assault at the national level, number of police-recorded offences**

Definition: *'Assault' means physical attack against the body of another person resulting in serious bodily injury; excluding indecent/sexual assault; threats and slapping/punching. 'Assault' leading to death should also be excluded.* (UN-CTS M3.2)

Country/territory	Count						Rate per 100,000 population					
	2003	2004	2005	2006	2007	2008	2003	2004	2005	2006	2007	2008
United States of America	859 030	847 381	862 220	860 853	855 856	834 885	289,3	282,6	284,8	281,6	277,3	267,9
Sweden	65 177	67 089	72 645	77 019	82 262	84 566	726,6	743,9	801,3	845,2	898,1	918,7

UNODC
United Nations Office on Drugs and Crime   **Total sexual violence at the national level, number of police-recorded offences**

Definition: *Total 'Sexual violence' means rape and sexual assault; including sexual offences against children.* (UN-CTS M3.3)

Country/territory	Count						Rate per 100,000 population					
	2003	2004	2005	2006	2007	2008	2003	2004	2005	2006	2007	2008
Sweden	10 142	10 419	11 711	12 147	12 563	14 342	113,1	115,5	129,2	133,3	137,2	155,8

(American data not present in UN report)

UNODC
United Nations Office on Drugs and Crime   **Rape at the national level, number of police-recorded offences**

Definition: *"Rape" means sexual intercourse without valid consent*

Country/territory	Counts						Rate per 100,000 population					
	2003	2004	2005	2006	2007	2008	2003	2004	2005	2006	2007	2008
United States of America	93 883	95 089	94 347	92 757	90 427	89 000	31,6	31,7	31,2	30,3	29,3	28,6
Sweden	2 235	2 261	3 333	3 703	4 269	4 901	24,9	25,1	36,8	40,6	46,6	53,2

UNODC
United Nations Office on Drugs and Crime   **Total Drug-Related Crimes at the national level, number of police-recorded offences**

Definition: *"Total Drug-Related Crimes" means all intentional acts that involve the cultivation; production; manufacture; extraction; preparation; offering for sale; distribution; purchase; sale; delivery on any terms whatsoever; brokerage; dispatch; dispatch in transit; transport; importation; exportation; possession or trafficking of internationally controlled drugs.* (UN-CTS M5.2)

Country/territory	Count						Rate per 100,000 population					
	2003	2004	2005	2006	2007	2008	2003	2004	2005	2006	2007	2008
Sweden	42 308	46 060	51 807	66 857	71 546	78 188	471,7	510,7	571,4	733,6	781,1	849,4

(American data not present in UN report)

139

As we can see from these figures, the USA has managed to uphold the law while Sweden appears to collapse under a never before encountered surge in crime. Sweden has a vastly higher rate of assaults (more than three times as high), motor vehicle thefts and rapes (more than twice as high). Though the Swedish government often attempts to explain away the drastic increase in the crime rate as a result of increased reporting and distort reality in doing so, it can never manage to make reports such as these from the FBI in 2009:

> "Preliminary figures indicate that, as a whole, law enforcement agencies throughout the Nation reported a decrease of 5.5 percent in the number of violent crimes brought to their attention for 2009 when compared with figures reported for 2008."

In Sweden, the crime rate instead increases by about as many percent every year.

While as stated, the rate of violent crimes per 100,000 people in the US has gone from 593.5 to 454.5 between 1980 and 2008, the Swedish rate has experienced an enormous increase. Between 1975 and 2009, it has gone from 331 to 1200 per 100,000 people. The rate of sex crimes has gone from 33 in 1975 to .173 in 2009. And the rate of homicides from 1.51 in 1975 to 2.85 in 2007.[1]

In Sweden, only 5.8% of violent crime is resolved and only 4% of sexual assaults, perhaps a result of an underfunded police force given the wrong priorities. Who can argue with the need to have the police monitor religious sermons that might contain 'hate speech' when all that's happening elsewhere is that a woman is being raped? And the EU International Crime Survey of 2005 found that 10.8% of Swedish women had been victims of sex crimes the last five years, an increase from 4% in 1994.

---

1   Source: Brottsförebyggande Rådet

The USA can on the other hand report great successes in crime prevention; the National Crime Victimization Survey from 2005 reports that the number of victimizations per 1,000 population age 12 and over has gone from 47.7 for all violent crime in 1973 to 21.0 in 2005. Rape victimization from 2.5 per 1,000 to 0.5. Aggravated assault from 12.5 to 4.3. The total assault victimization rate was 17.8. This is to be compared with the Swedish one quoted in SCB Statistical Yearbook 2010 of 2.9% or 29 per 1,000. The Swedish victimization rate lists people ages 16-79.

To further quote the American survey: "From 1993 to 2005, the violent crime rate was down 58%, from 50 to 21 victimizations per 1,000 persons age 12 or older."

Sweden has made great effort to attempt to rehabilitate criminals; provide them with work; listened to their complaints about being mistreated in prison. The USA has on the other hand stood tall in the face of bleeding-heart liberals and simply locked the criminals up. It should be quite evident which strategy has proven to work. Alas, if only Sweden's elitist political establishment would take heed and stop denouncing as uninformed brutes people who want a tougher stance on crime.

Something that was removed a long time ago in Sweden and something that will have you dismissed as a lunatic if you simply bring it up, is the death penalty. The establishment maintains a dogmatic line that the death penalty in no way helps with crime prevention. Little evidence to support this is provided, however. But to give an idea about the potential effectiveness in having access to it, I will here present statistics from Saudi Arabia, ranked third in the world in the number of executions performed. If the opponents of the death penalty are correct, that it simply encourages suicidal people to commit crimes for which they are executed, the country's crime rate should be high, right? The available statistics paint a very different picture.

Saudi Arabia has a population of 28.7 million, a little more than three times that of Sweden. Yet about the same number of homicides per year, hence only one third as many per person. 18,717 car thefts to be compared with Sweden's 19,401 in 2008, hence same deal here. The assault rate is very low; 13,864 assaults, or 48.3 per 100,000 people. Sweden has 19 times as many as stated above. It appears as if the death penalty has contributed to making Saudi Arabia a safe country.[1]

If any country in the world is to be crowned the biggest loser in the war on crime, it has to be Sweden. I guess pampering criminals just doesn't work.

---

1   Source: nationmaster.com

THE GOVERNMENT AS PARENT

"Myndigheterna tror de är ofelbara förmyndare men då säger jag bara det... ta er i häcken!"

"The authorities see themselves as infallible guardians but I've only got one thing to say... up yours!"

"Jag ger fan i allt" by Eddie Meduza

As the industrial society had brought on urbanization and poverty, and with that potentially dysfunctional family environments, in the early 20th century Swedish Socialists wanted to remedy the situation through a caring government that would make sure that the people's need for a decent life situation was met; this vision was called *Folkhemmet*, "the people's home." As part of this vision, the upbringing of children became a concern of the social engineers. In other parts of the world at this time, eugenics was a large movement - scientists in this field feared that portions of society had a tendency towards degeneration, and this problem would become worse with every generation. It was argued that society should attempt to prevent the designated people's genes from being spread through means such as sterilization.

In Sweden, the eugenics movement never became too

influential, but instead the Socialists felt that one could come to terms with the problem of degeneration by providing the children of these families with other environments to grow up in - what would later be called foster care. In the 1920's and 30's, there was a great belief in the government being able to engineer solutions for society's problems. These social engineers felt society could take children at birth from families where they were expected to grow up to become degenerates; even put them in state-run orphanages with no real family structure, but instead a hierarchical replacement with staff providing for them. This was particularly necessitated by the shortage of foster families for the intended scope of the new plans.

In 1924, the first major step was taken with *Barnavårdslagen*, the Children and Young Persons Act, which defined what society's responsibilities were. Among them was the introduction of the option for society to seize children against the will of the parents. The children taken into custody were divided into three classes: Degenerate (*vanartade*), neglected (*försummade*) and abused (*vanvårdade*). The authorities would be quite judgemental in determining which families would produce degenerate offspring, and the country's gypsy minority would be heavily targeted for this; they often lost touch with their biological parents at birth and were instead raised as part of the majority culture.

Sterilizations

Shortly after this law was introduced, society also started forcibly sterilizing people deemed not fit to raise children. Leading in this matter was Gunnar Myrdal and his wife Alva, Gunnar being a prominent Social Democratic economist and politician. These social planners were mostly concerned about the low nativity rate among the Swedish population in general and advocated remedying it through political means, though they also

144

wanted to eradicate physical and mental defects. In 1934, forced sterilization became an option through a new law that, though it was inspired by the Myrdal advocacy, nevertheless was restrictive in its initial application, its proponents failing to fully establish this radical measure. The government is dissatisfied with the limitations put on the law and attempts to educate local authorities on how to get more 'voluntary' sterilizations to compensate for the limited number of forced sterilizations taking place. As society introduces a general economic safety net during the 1940's, the law is extended, however, and forced sterilization often becomes a condition for receiving financial assistance. Though Nazi Germany is condemned after the war for its forced sterilizations, Sweden is unaffected by this criticism, with the late 1940's being the peak of the number of people sterilized.

Targets for forced sterilization were of three classes - people with 'medical,' 'eugenic' and 'social' indications. Eugenic indication being genetic heritage deemed damaging to society, social indication being preventive measures against members of society whose parenting abilities were in question, and medical indication being protective interventions against women whose potential pregnancies might jeopardize their health or lives.[1]

The social indication was the one that allowed for the most liberal application - even if not the one used the most on its own, it still commonly accompanied the other indications. In 1941, the definition was extended to the following:

> "where someone because of mental illness, mental deficiency or other disruption of mental state or because of antisocial manner of living is found to be for the future apparently unfit to manage the care of children."

Poor people on government support often found themselves becoming victims of the social indication clause, when society

---

1   SOU 2000:20

wanted to prevent the added cost of another child to the family. Children having grown up in orphanages sometimes found themselves forced to go through with it to be released from institution life. People living on the fringes of society, outcasts and such, often became victims too.

In the 1950's, *raggare*, perhaps equivalent to the American Greasers, were an unwanted subculture in Swedish society, whose members rode hotrods, listened to music and drank beer, though who still worked for a living and adhered to an alternative to society's norms - *Raggarlagen*, or the "Greaser law." In the early 60's, a 17-year-old woman from these circles became yet another case of a social indication. The application to request a forced sterilization had this to say about her:

> "During conversation she demonstrates her lack of judgement in many ways. Tells with pride that she's a Greaser chick and also tells openly and uninhibitedly about her life among the greasers. Completely lacking in ethical-moral terms. Doesn't say she likes the Greasers, since they have to obey the "*Greaser law.*" She probably has intercourse to the extent *Greaser law* permits and is required by her."

Though you'd expect people that advocate eugenics such as the Myrdal couple would raise prime stock offspring, their son proved quite an embarrassment to them - Jan Myrdal, born in 1927. Jan was a dyslectic boy who had displayed both learning and behavioural problems at school, and already in his early teens he became a Communist, in the middle of World War II. Since he was the son of what was generally considered to be the father of the people, his controversial activism didn't go unnoticed. Sweden had during the war formed a coalition Government comprising all the political parties but the Communists, whose loyalty to the nation was in doubt, in order to present national unity during this time of crisis. Jan rebelled against both his father and the national consensus through Communist agitation at this time, even speaking his mind on the Government's position in the war. This saw prime minister Per-Albin Hansson tell Gunnar Myrdal to silence his son, and he became estranged from his father.

In 1982, Jan published a memoir about his childhood entitled *Barndom*, "Childhood," where he laments the lack of parental attention in his family with his parents busy elsewhere. In this book, he also tells peculiar stories about soiling furniture with his excrement and forming a ring with ten other boys to sexually 'entertain' the boy next to you, as well as other not-too-refined tales, using the most crude language imaginable. Following the publication, his father rejected the claims in the book and attempted to sue his son for defamation. This Jan did however eventually leave a legacy as one of the most important icons of the Swedish far-left.

Forced sterilizations became illegal in 1976. All in all some 63,000 people were sterilized, about half through various degrees of force – if they were not outright forced, many were coerced into agreeing with it, or simply tricked into believing it was a reversible procedure. No other country in the world forcibly sterilized as large a portion of its population as Sweden did, about 1% of the women.[1]

For most of the later half of the 20th century, the forced sterilizations of the past was a topic you weren't supposed to touch upon in society's debate. This changed in 1997, when sociologist Maciej Zaremba published a series of articles in *Dagens Nyheter*, which even resulted in international attention being brought to the matter. Though not much effort had been made previously to atone for past atrocities, now the political establishment and mass media almost universally condemned what had taken place. This disappointed Social Democrat Carl Lidbom who in a DN article 2001 countered by justifying the sterilizations and pointed out that

---

1   SOU 2000:20

very few people at the time had anything negative to say about them. Maybe he's got a real point - how many of the people condemning it in this day and age would have done it back then?

Following the attention brought to the matter, the incumbent Government delivered a bill (proposition 1998/99:71) to the parliament on 18 March 1999, offering limited compensation to the affected parties. Forcibly sterilized people would during a two year period until June of 2001 be able to apply for a sum of 175,000 crowns or about $25,000. Complaints were raised by the victims that they had to file an application when the government had them all on file anyway, which was humiliating. About 2,300 people applied for compensation, and 1,600 were granted the specified sum. The bill decreed that after June of 2001, any further applications would be denied. This would settle the matter for good and get it out of the nation's memory.

Foster children speak up as well

As the victims of forced sterilizations had their albeit small share of compensation for what had been done to them, the people who suffered abuse in state-run orphanages also started looking for redress. Following this, in 2006, the newly elected centrist Government launches an investigation called *Vanvårdsutredningen*, "The abuse investigation," into what had taken place in these orphanages and how many people had suffered abuse. The National Board of Health and Welfare had the same year compiled a report on possible abuse in orphanages between 1950 and 1980 entitled "*Förekom övergrepp och kränkningar vid institutioner inom den sociala barnavården 1950–1980?*" which was the product of about a hundred interviews with people who had been placed in orphanages.

In this report it was found that at least 100,000 children had gone through institution care during this time, when the country's population went from seven to eight million. At least 2.5% of society's children had spent parts of their childhood institutionalized, if not all of it.

In 2007, *Vanvårdsutredningen* publishes an interim report called "*Delrapport 1 från Utredningen om vanvård i den sociala barnavården,*" summarizing the experiences of 60 interviewed former residents of foster care between 1925 and 1980. The interviewed people recall both physical and emotional abuse. The following is an excerpt from afore-mentioned report:

"Battery and outrages

Several interviewees recall how they've been hit, in their faces, on their bodies, with or without clothes on. They've been hit with broomsticks, carpet beaters, chains, gallows, whips, planks or with bare hands. Many people say that this has taken place, not once but systematically and repeatedly, without any other explanation than that they're "evil," "possessed by the devil," "bastards," "vagrant kids," "hopeless cases," "just stupid."

Many have recalled how they've been forced to adapt to pointless rules, have been pinched, have had their body parts twisted about, have had their hair pulled, have been mocked and kicked, thrown into the air to free-fall to the floor, kicked down stairs, have had their possessions and toys destroyed as punishment for some misdemeanour.

There are examples of how children have been spit on, locked into closets, toilets, boiler rooms, locked out in the snow, with urine-drenched clothes, have been beaten and mocked for wetting their beds, forced to eat vomited food, forced to watch as younger siblings have been tormented. Children have also been threatened with firearms, with knives and kept outside windows at high altitudes.

Several also recall that they've been molested as children, forced to perform sexual acts on foster mum, foster dad, institution

149

manager, other staff, have been raped since they were toddlers, not once but systematically and repeatedly.

Foster children have been forced up at dawn to have time to milk cows and feed pigs before it was time to sleep their way through a school day, to then get to work peeling potatoes, doing laundry and cleaning, before it was time to sleep in something that to and fro might not be their own beds or a nook of one's own.

Mentally ill foster parents and institution staff have subjected children to systematic outrages to satisfy sadistic and perverted inclinations. One man tells us how his foster mother now and then forced him to cut himself with a razor while she stood next to him, making sure it bled properly.

Many say they've not understood why they've been torn from their environments, how they've been separated from siblings, friends and relatives. There hasn't been anyone there to explain to them. They've not been told why, for how long or what is going to happen. These are children that the representatives of the child care and supervision hasn't seen, hasn't spoken to. Interviewees recall how they as children have been moved from one foster home to another, from one institution to another, without understanding why."

Stolen Childhood / Stepchildren of Society

With attention brought to the matter, people who for their whole lives have been forced to take a back seat now step up and get organized, forming two non-government organizations to speak for them. In 2004, *Samhällets Styvbarn*, the Stepchildren of Society, is founded at a former orphanage. Its stated intentions are:

* mutual support between all the [members of] Stepchildren of Society.
* redress for people subjected to acts of cruelty or abuse in society's child care.
* monitoring of today's child welfare policy concerning society's

150

custody measures.

They've got a website up at www.styvbarn.se with brief information in English.

Stulen Barndom, Stolen Childhood, is another organization founded in 2006 by Peter Lindberg, who had spent 17 years in foster care, starting at age three, with the specific aim of pursuing damages for people abused in foster care during the mid 20th century. Traditionally it's been quite hard seeking compensation for damage you've suffered at the hands of the state, with individual lawsuits simply unrealistic; the complainant has to pay his legal representation himself, and law firms aren't awarded any part of the damages in case of a successful suit, unlike what's the case in countries with contingent fees such as the USA. If the case is lost, the complainant is required to pay all legal fees for both parties.

In 2003, something that made it a bit more feasible seeking compensation was introduced, however - class action lawsuits, called *grupptalan* in Swedish. Still, even with this new option, few cases have had much luck getting through the courts, which are notorious for stalling these cases. So far, less than a handful of cases have even been approved for examination.

Stulen Barndom decided to pursue this route in 2006. In April of that year, 32 former foster children file a joint lawsuit against the city of Stockholm, with Ruby Harrold-Claesson as their legal representative, announcing too that as people are able to retrieve the journals from their foster homes and orphanages, another hundred names will be added. Lindberg demands one million crowns per year in care per person in the lawsuit, or about $125,000, which initially means roughly 100 million crowns. Hundreds of people start flocking to the organization hoping that they can get compensation for what they went through as children.

In June the same year, the district court of Stockholm

decides it will not try this lawsuit and instructs the complainants to have their cases tried individually instead. Lindberg doesn't give up this easily, however, and continues to pursue the matter. In February of 2007, the Supreme Court rejects the lawsuit as well, saying cases have to be tried individually since everyone has different experiences from different locations.

With all Swedish legal venues exhausted, *Stulen Barndom* sets its sights on the European Court of Human Rights. Legal analysts commenting on the initiative point out it's futile attempting to try a class action lawsuit at the ECHR, but Lindberg isn't deterred - "I will fight until I die," he says. In June of 2007, Lindberg personally travels to Strasbourg, France, to deliver the complaint. Initially he had estimated that 4-500 people would join the lawsuit, but when it's filed there are 137 complainants, with their foster care acts in tow, asking for the same compensation as in the district court - one million crowns per person and year.

In May of 2008, the ECHR notifies that it will not try the lawsuit either, it's considered inadmissible, hence the last possible option fails as well. Lindberg tells mass media that *Stulen Barndom* will still not give up, though with the setbacks the complainants have suffered, the steam has run out and they disperse from the organization.

Today the Government still foments the notion that at some point the former foster care children will get compensation, though with all the procrastination, you get the impression it's waiting on them to pass away instead, one by one. And maybe, just maybe, the political system is attempting to avoid the loss of prestige it would mean having to concede yet again that Swedes suffered abuse at the hands of their own government.

Society learned from its dark past... or did it? Enter LVU

In 1982, a new law called LVU, *Lag med särskilda bestämmelser om vård av unga*, was introduced to replace the old child care law that had its roots back in 1902. The official English name of the new law, *Care of Young Persons Special Provisions Act*, is like its Swedish name somewhat Orwellian - critics are more prone to call it *Lag om tvångsvård av unga*, "Law on forced care of minors," since the purpose of this law is to be able to "provide care" whether the recipients and their families agree to it or not. As part of the transformation of the former child care law, voluntary care ended up being covered in the more general social services law, *Socialtjänstlagen*. In this law, usually abbreviated SoL, the natural role of the government as a complementary parent in all families residing in Sweden is detailed. The previous two decades had seen societal debate diminish the role the nuclear family was expected to have in raising children, and these two laws provided the regulations for the state to take on this role instead.

Chapter 5 of SoL, the section on minors, includes the following provisions: (My bold emphasis.)

"1 § The social council shall

- work for children and youth to grow up under safe and good terms,

- in **close cooperation with the homes** encourage a versatile **development of personality** and a favourable physical and **social development** of children and youth,

- with special attention follow the development of children and youth that have displayed signs of an unfavourable development,

- in close cooperation with the homes see to it that children and youth **who risk** developing unfavourably receive the protection

153

and support they need and, if the concern for the best interests of the minor justifies it, care and fosterage outside one's own home."

Hence with this law, at least on paper, no homes are exempt from being under the watchful eye of the state, and the provisions are wide-reaching and vague. Just what is an "unfavourable development?" That's up to the social workers to decide. And what does the state consider a proper personality to develop? Why, naturally one that looks up to the state as its father - not an independent individualist.

A certain Third Reich had a law enacted in 1936 with a similar wording, the Law on the Hitler Youth. Paragraph two of this law read:

> "The German Youth besides being reared within the family and school, shall be educated physically, intellectually, and morally in the spirit of National Socialism to serve the people and community, through the Hitler Youth."[1]

The experience from previous decades had convinced legislators that you couldn't always predict every situation in which society might want to intervene in family life. The 1960 revision of *Barnavårdslagen* had for example had a clause concerning when to take children from their homes, paragraph 25a, that wasn't quite the catch-all clause that they now wanted:

> "25a § if someone less than eighteen years old is being battered in the home or is otherwise treated in such a way that his physical or mental health is exposed to danger, or if his development is jeopardized due to the unsuitability as fosterers of the parents or other fosterers or their lacking ability to foster him."

Though this paragraph was quite wide-reaching, the 1982 law introduced general clauses - paragraphs that have no

---

1   Source: http://germanhistorydocs.ghi-dc.org/sub_document.cfm?document_id=1564

limitation in scope, being able to provide for situations the legislators aren't able to predict. The use of the word 'any' makes this clear:

"1 § The one that is less than 18 years old shall be provided care supported by this law, if it can be assumed that necessary care can't be provided the minor with consent from the one or the ones who have custody of him and, when the minor is 15 or older, from himself.

Care shall be provided the minor if

1. lack in his care or **any other condition in the home** constitutes a danger to his health or development or

2. the minor exposes his health or development to serious danger through abuse of addictive drugs, criminal activity or **any other to that comparable behaviour.**"

In 1990, the law was revised again and we arrived at the unlimited general clauses we have today. The two clauses from 1 § formed paragraphs 2 and 3 of the new law:

"2 § Care shall be decided on if because of physical or mental abuse, improper exploitation, lack in care or **any other condition in the home**, there is an obvious risk that the health or development of the minor is harmed.

3 § Care shall also be decided on if the minor exposes his health or development to an obvious risk for damage through abuse of addictive drugs, criminal activity or **any other socially destructive behaviour.**"

Now the social workers were provided with a concept that would later become infamous - the term "socially destructive behaviour." Society could take minors into custody under this paragraph until they were 20 years old, if they engaged in what the social workers considered such behaviour. To date, children have been taken into custody for spending too much time on the

Internet; hanging out with the wrong crowd; joined skinhead groups; joined religious 'cults' (other countries might just consider these 'cults' religious minorities); used steroids; truancy etc; more on this later.

Children's need of protection

The most widely supported reason to take a minor into foster care has traditionally been, apart from the outright demise of his or her parents, to protect the minor from potentially abusive guardians; now and then we read about the occasional horror story concerning sexual abuse and violence to the point of killing the child in his or her very home. Child protection agencies make sure that everyone gets to hear these stories over and over, to justify the calls on the part of these agencies to have access to monitor family life.

Urban myth has it that abuses against children is largely a problem of the poor sections of society - since most violent crime is committed by the lower classes in society, the belief has been that these same people also commit violence against their children. If the origin of the children ending up in foster care is a proper indication of the need for protection, this is indeed so - poor families are most definitely over-represented in this area. But few people are probably aware of just how large the difference is. Indeed, I myself was taken by surprise when I read a report by the social authorities entitled *Social rapport 2006 ("Social report")*, a compilation of statistics over life in Sweden along with analysis.

On page 273 of this report, the frequency of children born 1992-1996 ending up in foster care before age seven is compared between two different socio-economic groups. In the group where the mother is in a couple relationship, is college-educated, was employed on 1 November 1997 and was not on welfare at any point 1996-98, less than 1 in 2,000 children were taken into foster

156

care. In the group where the mother is single, has at most an elementary education, was not working in 1997 and received welfare every year 1996-98, 1 in 7 children were taken into foster care, hence about 300 times as likely. The same report found that children born outside the country are three times as likely to reside in foster care.

Now is this a true indication of there being a greater need to protect children in poor families from their mother/parents? Or might they simply be easier targets for the child "protection" agencies? A report from 1966 cited in aforementioned document *Förekom övergrepp...* from 2006 had interesting information on this matter:

> "The National Board of Health and Welfare conducted an investigation in 1966 of children treated in hospitals during 1957-1966 after being victims of child abuse. What emerged in the investigation was that child abuse wasn't related to the children living in squalor or in criminal environments but that there was also a group of healthy and apparently well-functioning parents who severely abused their children."

The 2006 statistics then highlight two wrongs - not only is 1 in 7 welfare mothers having their children taken into custody an unreasonably high figure; 1 in 2,000 children from well-established families is an unreasonably low one. Sweden has during the last half a century taken great pride in its child welfare policies, claiming children in this society are taken well care of and having their needs met. Looking at these figures, it would rather appear as if society "protects" children from poor families from their biological parents, while one doesn't concern oneself with what goes on in well-established households.

It's quite well-acknowledged that foster care is often harmful to the development of a child. Though occasionally a child can end up in a foster family where he or she is well taken care of, about half the foster placements end prematurely.[1] The same *Förekom övergrepp...* report also cited a government investigation on foster care from 1974:

> "Performed investigations and long-term experience shows that institution care as such can increase the risks for a negative development of the person cared for. The sharply marked disruption in the normal social contacts in the local environment can for the smaller children cause both temporary and long-term damage as a result, especially following extended care."

Social rapport 2006 also contained an analysis of the outcome as adults of teenagers ending up in social care:

> "Almost all foster care of teenagers consists of unevaluated treatment. That is, society through coercion, threat of force or persuasion makes these intrusive interventions without knowing if the measures have a beneficial, neutral or even harmful effect on the development and life chances of the children on a longer perspective. Generally the outcome for minors placed in foster care because of behaviour problems appear so dismal[...]"

The suicide rate for former foster children is quite elevated as well. Depending on the duration of time spent in foster care, the suicide rate as adults is between four and five times higher for this group compared to the normal population.[2]

When coupling the great potential for damage from being placed into foster care with the uneven class selection for entering this care, one spots the real danger that class roles might very well be cemented due to the government stepping in as a parent, even though these interventions are said to be for the sake of the child's protection, and are supposed to have the effect of enabling class mobility instead.

---

1   Sammanbrott i familjehem / Socialstyrelsen
2   Social rapport 2006, page 294

But enough statistics, law texts and analysis for now. Here follow five dramatic stories of children taking their lives during or shortly after time spent in orphanages.

Suicides as a consequence of institution placement

In most of the Western world, the idea of placing children into orphanages takes people back to the time of Charles Dickens' early 19th century London. Not so in Sweden, where in 2010, orphanages are seen as an essential part of the arsenal the government has at its disposal for coming to the rescue of "vulnerable children." Yet the question is - are these children vulnerable because of their environment, or due to living under a government that wants to care for them? I'm personally more inclined to suggest the latter.

Troubling statistics concerning the mental well-being among the growing generation in Sweden today do indeed exist. During the summer of 2009, Gothenburg newspaper *Göteborgs-Posten* had conducted a survey sent to all ninth-graders in this metropolis, where they found that one in five girls had already at that age inflicted harm on themselves - what's commonly described as self-cutting. As can be expected, Swedish society has extensive public facilities available for helping these troubled children, but can the government really offer anything of value to them? Can these vulnerable children find proper support from taxpayer-financed counsellors and staff? These coming vignettes will have you thinking otherwise; the common theme among all of them is that the children ended up at modern Swedish orphanages, what's called *HVB-hem* or HVB homes, from its acronym. *Hem för vård och boende*, "homes for care and living."

Felicia Pettersson, dead at 14

Felicia was a somewhat troubled girl, born in 1990, who after having been bullied at school for a while suffered from depression as she was entering her teen years. After attempts by her mother Anneli to find help in open forms had been denied, in 2005 the social services instead decided Felicia was in need of placement at an orphanage; Anneli and Felicia are coerced into agreeing with "voluntary" care, threatened with involuntary placement under the LVU law if they refuse. At this orphanage, Felicia would spend the last 55 days of her life until she was found hanging from a tree with a noose around her neck.

23 March	Committed to Kastellet HVB institution for her problems, against the wishes of both herself and her mother.
26 March	Her cell phone is seized by the staff and they set restrictive limits on when she can see her mother and her boyfriend. The coming weeks she would still sneak out at night to be able to see her boyfriend, even though she is rarely able to do that during daytime.
19 April	Felicia buys a pack of cigarettes; the staff confiscates them as she returns to the institution.
24 April	The staff finds a lighter in her room, confiscates it.
12 May	Her boyfriend, seemingly frustrated with the complications placed on their relationship by the staff, suggests they should put their relationship on hold.

16 May   Felicia is nervous, sad and anxious. Yet another fight over cigarettes and cell phone. She cuts her arms.

17 May   Felicia locks herself into her room. The staff break in and find her lying in bed in a state of apathy. She doesn't respond when spoken to. They pour water on her and carry her outside her room. Staff tell her she can't see her boyfriend at all the coming week, which infuriates her; she has a fit of rage and throws things around her. During the afternoon, Felicia requests to be transferred to a hospital instead of the orphanage, which is denied. She walks out out of the orphanage and doesn't return. The following morning, she's found dead from an apparent suicide, hanging from a tree.

On the 19th of May, after her family has been notified of the death and they've paid their last respects to Felicia's dead body at the hospital, her mother demands to see Felicia's belongings. Of particular interest is her diary, which has been a nuisance to the staff, who have frequently confiscated it to see what she's written about them. Anneli is presented with the torched remains of this diary, which makes her suspicious of how it ended up in this state. She's also upset with the staff all the time having told her everything was fine, with no real friction between them and Felicia.

Anneli spends the next couple of years attempting to get the police and other authorities to investigate what's happened, without any luck. She's told by one government official to see if she can get Amnesty International involved, but realizes this organisation doesn't involve itself in cases such as these. Neither does any other of society's institutions, though Anneli is able to find some support on Internet communities. She's got a website up in Swedish at *www.feliciasliv.se* , with plenty of pictures of her daughter up under the heading *Bilder,* along with heaps of documentation. Anneli is accusing several institution workers and government officials of mismanaging their duties, for which criminal charges have been filed against her by the named persons, who are alleging that she's violating their personal integrity. No one involved has suffered any consequences for the suicide that has taken place under government care. Anneli has doubts whether it was actually a suicide, pointing to forensic details that might be from involvement by other people - she argues that it's possible Felicia was strangled to death before being hung from the noose, though this belief probably has more to do with her not accepting that her daughter just couldn't cope any longer and bailed on her, than that there is really something to it.

For tribute clips, search for "Till minne av Felicia" and "Sov gott, Felicia" on Youtube.

Elin, dead at 13

In her youth, a woman named Susanne had suffered a traffic accident and was left disabled - moving around on a walking frame, with a disability pension already at age 20 from not being able to work. The next couple of years, she has three children - two daughters and a son. The first years of the lives of these children would be very happy, though soon the father disappears from the picture and the mother is overtaken by the burden of raising her family with her disability. When her middle child Elin, born in 1994, is six years old, the social services becomes involved in family life and Elin is relocated to a foster family, something Susanne agrees to since she admits she's not capable of being a mother at this point in time. Elin isn't treated very well by this new family, however, becoming the target of frequent insults thrown at her by her foster parents. She attempts to get the social services to listen to her when she tells them that everything isn't all right here, but they don't give her the time of day, in spite of Elin showing up for school malnourished and with discarded clothes. According to her records with the social services, everything is just fine with the placement.

After a couple of years, Susanne starts feeling she's fit to take over parenting again, and Elin also has a great desire to return to her mother, but the social services isn't very interested in interrupting the placement - it's gone from entirely voluntary to thinly veiled coercion. Eventually, when Elin is twelve years old, the authorities launch a new investigation, and both Elin and Susanne want to be reunited. The social services has other plans, however, deciding to place Elin with a new foster family. Susanne is told that if she doesn't agree to this placement, they will go through with a forced placement under the LVU law. Elin isn't happy here and spends as much time as she can on the phone with

164

her mother and sister. On the other hand, she's not very interested in socializing with her foster family, and when the social services learns of this, her phone is taken away from her. As she writes in her diary:

"If you hate life, you have to be able to talk to someone... And then I don't mean psychologists, but someone you can trust."

"The only thing that gets me up when I'm sad, is mom and Linda. But now the social services has decided I'm only allowed to call them once a week."

"The only thing that could make me feel good was if I was allowed to return home to mom."

Elin tells the social services she's being battered in this family but pleads with her handler there that they don't tell her foster parents, which they still do. At this time, Elin starts cutting her arms.

Before too long, this foster family decides they don't want Elin with them any more, and once again Elin hopes she can be reunited with her family. This time around, the social services actually pulls out the LVU law, forcibly placing Elin at an HVB institution some 200 km away from her mother. Now it's 2008 and her short life would soon come to an end.

26 March   Placed at *Carl Bobergsgården* as a single girl at age 13 with up to 10 boys, ages 11 to 20, most of them placed there for conduct problems.

30 March   Elin is physically assaulted by one of the boys.

3 April   She's assaulted again.

7 April   Elin is once again badly assaulted and has to X-ray her

wrist due to a possible fracture.

10 April   She runs away from the orphanage and spends the night in the nearby forest.

13 April   Elin is assaulted by six older boys at the orphanage. At around 15:00, she tells the boys at the orphanage that she's going to go hang herself. Then she walks out and spends the night in the forest again, never to return.

14 April   Elin is found dead hanging from a tree - an obvious suicide - 18 days after having been placed at the orphanage.

Elin had told friends at school that she was both assaulted and sexually harassed at the orphanage, but refused to tell the authorities since she knew from experience she couldn't trust them. Among other things, she was forced to 'entertain' one of the boys sexually with her hands. Her family was not briefed on any of the fights she had been in. During the autopsy, evidence of 19 punches and kicks is found on her body, with 43 bruises. Initially, criminal charges would be filed against two of the boys, but these didn't lead to any prosecutions, since Elin was dead and couldn't testify. During police investigations, at least one of the boys pleads guilty to assault, but this didn't make any difference. The staff remained sceptical of there having been fights at all at the orphanage. "Neither I or the staff ever saw them punching each other or anything like that," one of them said.

In her room, a farewell letter is found along with her diary. As she writes during her short stay here:

"Let me go, let me run away from Boberg. Let me run off and get out, I can't take this any more."

"Please, I can't deal with this. I'll let go of my knives and fly off to

166

heaven."

"My life is ruined, thanks to the Linköping social services."

"The only thing they do is destroy other people's lives, so stay away from them. If your parents need help, just tell them to ignore getting help, because that's the safest."

Elin had apparently intended to become a writer and was in the process of composing a memoir entitled *My sad life*, but this life became simply too much for her to bear to finish it.

About a year later, during the summer of 2009, Elin's little brother Simon is allowed to return to Susanne from his foster home - now the social services feels she can take care of her children again. Alas, if only they had made that decision a little more than a year earlier...

(All of the names in this story have been replaced and are the ones used in mass media.)

Sophie Lohede, dead at 15

A girl named Sophie, born in 1993, had been struggling with a learning disability at school, and her self-esteem was suffering from poor academic achievement. This sparked her mother to ask the authorities for assistance in open forms. The municipality however denied her this, and during the summer of 2008, Sophie instead found herself involuntarily committed to the HVB institution *Lövingstorp* under the LVU law. During her stay here, she made at least one friend, but overall the environment here was deplorable, with rampant drug abuse and even child molesters frequenting the orphanage. An older man named Torbjörn Hasse Puke, born in 1966, had shown quite an interest in the children taken into care here and provided them with amphetamine; during Sophie's stay at Lövingstorp, he would also rape her and her friend repeatedly, starting when she was only 14 years old. Both of the girls disintegrate in this environment, becoming addicted to drugs and losing their balance in life. Sophie has an older sister who was spared institutionalization, who talks in her Internet blog about how much she misses her little sister during this period.

In November of 2008, Sophie contacts the police about the rapes she had been subjected to and files charges, spawning a criminal investigation. She testifies to the police on numerous occasions about the crimes committed, often falling into tears while relating her experiences; yet when the time comes for the trial on April 7, 2009, the prosecutor still demands that she appears in court to testify, with Puke present. A couple of hours before she's due in court, Sophie commits suicide, not able to muster the courage to go through with the proceedings. Puke is then acquitted of the charges due to no testimony. Tribute video clips in her memory are up on Youtube as well, this being her real name.

Jonas Skoglund, dead at 17

A troubled boy born in 1988 had spent much of his teen years hanging out with outsiders and using alcohol and other drugs. Even though he hadn't committed any actual crimes, this behaviour of his had made the social services decide on forced institution care for him at age 15, supported by the LVU law. He had spent this time in several different orphanages, among them one in *Sundby*, where many of the residents had multiple felonies to their names already in their teens; there was even a murderer there at the time, who in 2004 along with his older friend had called on two 18-year-old girls to pick them up one night. When they arrived in a car belonging to one of the girls, the two boys had changed their plans. They told the driver to stop the car out in the backwoods, after which they proceeded to assault the girls and bludgeon them to death in Ted Bundy style. After a short ride in the stolen car, they crashed it and soon found themselves picked up by the police. The younger of the boys had then been sentenced to care under the social services.

Jonas had detested his time in the orphanages with these people and for a brief period in January of 2006 had found himself a free man again, after two years of institution life. On the Thursday of 12 January, he had been summoned to a meeting at the social services, where he was told they had decided he was going to have to spend the coming two years as well institutionalized. He and his father protested the decision and attempted to reason with the social workers, to no avail. Jonas was given one day to present himself at the orphanage, with 15:00 on Friday set as deadline - if he didn't show up, a warrant for his arrest would be filed.

Jonas has no intention of letting himself be locked up again, however. He ignores the deadline and spends Friday with his girlfriend, hitting Kumla town for a party. He tells his girlfriend he'd rather kill himself than go to that orphanage. At first he's in a merry mood, but at 2:20, the police catch up with him and pick him up. Crying, he tells his girlfriend they won't be able to see each other for two years. The police place him in custody at the station, to be transported to the orphanage the coming day. At 3:57, Jonas has hung himself in his cell, using his clothes as a noose.

Mass media only brings limited coverage to the case, though Siv Westerberg from the NCHR files a 1600 word complaint with the parliamentary ombudsman, JO, to see if this government agency would launch an investigation into how the case has been managed, calling for responsible parties to be reprimanded. Among other things, she quotes a boy whose case she had worked with as a lawyer, who just like Jonas had stated that he'd rather die than go back to the orphanage he had been placed at.

A week later, she receives a 60 word response back where the JO states:

> "Your complaint doesn't give any reason for an assumption that action on my part is called for. The case is closed."

(Registration number 322-2006)

Anonymous girl, dead at 14

A girl born in 1995, living in Piteå in the northern end of Sweden, had at the age of 11 had her first encounter with the foster care system. She had become a troubled child with anxiety problems, and at first she receives help in open forms, which includes a personal assistant who follows her to school and attends classes with her. Eventually, however, Piteå municipality would decide on institution placement for her. The last six months of her life are spent at the *Egehem* HVB institution, from which she runs away no less than four times. The last time she runs away is on 3 November 2009, when the children placed at the institution are out on a field trip. At 19:30, she seizes the opportunity to make a run for it and leaves the staff behind.

Police patrols with dogs are immediately dispatched to find her, though it wouldn't be until the next day they would come across her; at 13:30, her dead body is found in a creek.

Local newspaper *VästerviksTidningen* writes, "For three years, society did everything it could to save the 14-year-old." This apparently didn't include interpreting her running away as a sign that the orphanage wasn't a good placement.

As of 19 May 2010, on the webpage of the HVB institution, *www.egehem.com*, there is no mention of this suicide, but instead the institution is presented in a highly favourable light. A personal account from 2010 by a girl staying for four years gives a positive portrayal of her time there.

Personal LVU accounts

In 2008, the newspaper *Smålandsposten* interviewed 68 people who had been seized in accordance with LVU recently.[1] These are translated excerpts of what they had to say, with gender of the youngster underneath:

"I got to read what they had written about me and my case. I didn't feel it was in line with what had been said, but they didn't want to change it."

"But I don't think LVU helped me. It was only when they removed it from me that I could start focusing on feeling better."

(girl)

"The whole s*** about LVU was insulting. I ran away several times and tried to explain that it wasn't that great at the orphanage where I was placed."

(girl)

"It felt like you were watching a movie about yourself. Everyone else decided everything, how I felt, what I wanted to do and so on. I didn't get anything through. I was with a family at first, but then the ones in charge decided I was going to be at an orphanage instead. I ran away from there back to the family. I wanted to stay there, the family wanted me to stay there, but the ones who were in charge didn't feel it was any good."

(guy)

Wonder if that had anything to do with the 4000 crowns or $550 per child and day the orphanages get in taxpayer money? I

---

1   *Smålandsposten*, "Omhändertagna ungdomar berättar" 2008-12-19, http://smp.se/ung/omhandertagna-ungdomar-berattar(1044439).gm

wonder how many social workers have been offered bribes under the table due to this potential income, placing children for profit.

"I didn't know anything about why I had to live in this orphanage. When I asked, they said stuff like that I was so messy and didn't go to school. But surely you had to do something more than that?"

(guy)

"But when I had been at the orphanage for a while I realized that hell I would become more depressed there than at home. There were also two other girls there who had attempted to commit suicide and we talked about how to successfully do it. The staff overheard us talking and in an almost cocky tone said something like: If you do it this or that way maybe you'll succeed."

(girl)

I wonder how much the staff at the orphanages where the five afore-mentioned children who took their own lives were placed had encouraged them.

"I think the worst thing about LVU is that no one listens to what you say. Even if I'm messy and get angry, my own opinion must still count? It's about my life after all. I also don't like that they lock the doors. I get panic attacks."

(girl)

Sweden - the country that provides mass murderers and paedophiles with furloughs, and locks up children taken into foster care.

"I lost my faith in adults when I was seized according to LVU. It was so much about prestige on their part.

Who had done what and so on so they forgot about me in the whole thing."

(girl)

"I didn't feel the staff that made the investigation were that good. They were stressed out and didn't really listen to my view. I really didn't want to be placed at an institution but I still was. It was a disaster. I became even worse and suicidal."

(girl)

"What p***ed me off was that they just appeared one day and said I was going. We had had a meeting at the social services, but I never understood why they wanted to put me in an orphanage. I wanted an explanation why, but I never got one."

(guy)

"It was f***ed up at that orphanage. The staff mocked us and one guy got beaten up once. We didn't feel there was any point reporting it, no one listens anyway and you only get a worse hell afterwards."

(guy)

"Violated. That's what I think about when I remember that period. You felt so f***ing violated."

"Yet one's self esteem has taken a bit of a beating from the LVU period. So that's my advice for the ones who work with LVU youth, think about how you treat them. You affect them for the rest of their lives."

(girl)

"What I remember from my time at an LVU institution was that the staff didn't show any f***ing respect at all. You could be sad and they didn't give a s***."

(girl)

"To this day I still don't understand why I was seized."

"But still I think it's bad that I couldn't get an answer to why I was seized."

(girl)

Sweden - the country where children are arbitrarily put into orphanages and not even told why.

"When there was a decision made that I was going to move, I didn't understand anything. I hadn't been allowed to have a say in anything at all. Once we were at a meeting. Then I think mom was at the social services some other time. Simply sick."

(guy)

"I remember one time when I sat at the social services crying. I couldn't stop crying. Then my officer told me that if I was just going to cry all the time, she might as well go drink some coffee. That felt f***ing insulting."

(girl)

Ok, that last one sounded a bit silly to be honest. I personally don't think government workers should have to sit around and wait for teenagers to stop crying. I guess that's something socialists expect them to do though, a service you can't expect in practice. You just can't expect government workers to be anything but cold and distant.

"Children's gulag" in the Swedish welfare state

The atrocities within Swedish foster care haven't gone unnoticed in the international community. After plenty of child seizure cases had ended up with the European Court of Human Rights (ECHR) in Strasbourg, the German magazine Der Spiegel on 8 January 1983 published a 4,000 word article on the state of foster care in Sweden, called *"Kinder-Gulag" im Sozialstaat Schweden*[1], "Children's gulag" in the Swedish welfare state. From the introduction:

> "All-powerful social welfare workers take children from parents by force to deliver them into state care. Every day five children are moved into state custody this way. In spite of all the protests of parents and lawyers, the Swedish welfare state clings to this practice. Help is now expected from Strasbourg."

At the time, Sweden had about ten times as many children per person in foster care as Germany did, and the scale of the enterprise shocked the magazine, when due to similar demographics, one could expect the child welfare of the two countries to be quite identical. Der Spiegel interviewed a couple of Swedish lawyers who had worked with parents whose children had been taken, cases that were now in the ECHR due to the failure of the Swedish justice system to protect the families from the state.

One of the cases was that of Alexander Aminoff, who had been taken the first time from his mother Eva living in the affluent Stockholm suburb of Lidingö at six years of age. Eva had earlier married Alexander's father, but now the two had divorced, and Eva had sole custody. In her early 50's, she gets a new man some 30 years her junior. Everything seems fine for the moment, the two

---

1   http://www.spiegel.de/spiegel/print/d-14019042.html

being very enthusiastic about their new relationship and their future together, but this was about to change. The couple runs into more and more friction with the authorities and the surrounding community as they're both pronounced individualists with little interest in what their peers think about them, and then one day someone reports them to the child welfare authorities. The civil servants deem both the home and Alexander's own behaviour at school problematic, and when they approach Eva with their findings, she fires back and publicly in the media she's got access to names and shames the two female social workers. Her words are harsh, depicting having the two employed as a complete waste of taxpayer money.

On 2 September 1974, a team of civil servants shows up at the Aminoff residence: Four social workers, one doctor and two police officers. The social workers demand that Eva hands over Alexander to state custody, but she doesn't do this willingly, so they break up the door and drag him away screaming from his guardians. Now Alex is put through psychiatric examination for a couple of weeks, with his whereabouts being held a secret to Eva and step-father Martin. The authorities decide that Alex is going into foster care, but they let the three meet up one last time before the actual placement. Martin decides they're going to use that opportunity to make a run for it; as they sit with him and the civil servants in a building, Martin tosses Alex out the window and then follows him along with Eva, entering their car and speeding down the road. They eventually make their way to the closest airport and start a 2.5 year escapade globe-trotting their way through many different countries.

In 1977, they decide to return to Sweden, assuming that the authorities have lost interest by now. The couple have gotten the story of their conflict with the Swedish child welfare published in several different countries, which these authorities have learned. Instead of dropping the investigation, the child welfare has added quite a lot of material to it, possibly angered by the disrespect the journalist Eva has shown in international media.

Swedish authorities are generally extremely displeased when they find a citizen has criticized the country abroad. As a later prime minister, Göran Persson, would put it during a speech before parliament on 14 June 1995:

> "I will, along with the Government I'm a part of, at all times with force brand the ones who speak ill of Sweden abroad."

Facing personal consequences for what you say about Sweden isn't exactly unheard of, something many Swedes have learned the hard way. Nevertheless, the authorities don't act upon the investigation for now, but still document all the suspicions they can find against the home. In August of 1979, the family had planned to live in Bolivia for a period, and Eva had explained her plans to the authorities, that she was going to let Alexander attend a Swedish school over there. Now the child welfare authorities strike again and take Alex at school, quickly hiding him from his guardians as they place him into foster care. Martin goes to great lengths to learn the location of Alex, and Eva hires a private eye, but his whereabouts remains out of their reach.

Now Eva reaches out to international mass media again, and is able to attract seemingly enormous attention to the matter, with world-renowned figures such as R.D. Laing and Birgitta Wolf visiting their home and becoming involved. Articles are written in newspapers in many different countries. Said Birgitta had intervened on the behalf of many prison inmates whom she felt weren't treated in a humane manner, and often got the opportunity to meet up with them in her travels. Now she requests to get to see Alexander, but the authorities don't disclose his location even to her, which has her contact newly re-elected Prime Minister Olof Palme.

When asked about the matter, Palme says he's not familiar

with the Aminoff case, but that he will look into it. He holds a press conference, which mostly becomes an attempt on his part to avert foreign criticism of Swedish child welfare policies, rather than actually scrutinizing these very policies.

Alexander is at this time placed with a foster family on a remote island in the lake of Mälaren, and objective accounts on the state of things are hard to find. The Aminoffs would later claim that the foster father was a career criminal, that he liked beating up the children in his care, that he was a sadistic alcoholic and that his wife was both a whore and a fraudster. On the other hand, the child welfare alleges that Alexander has taken emotional damage from his relationship with his mother, a relationship they describe as symbiotic. Eva has apparently taught her son that the world consists of only a few people capable of rational thought, and then nothing but idiots; she elevates herself and Alexander up on a pedestal above the rest of the world.

As for Swedish society, Eva describes it as 'racist' towards her as a Finnish immigrant, and that the surrounding community in her home town of Lidingö had ostracised the family, even having their children set fire to one of the family cars. The police never uncover anything with which to start an investigation, however.

In May of 1984, after almost five years in uninterrupted foster care, Alexander escapes the island on a raft and reconnects with Eva, at a time when the Swedish authorities are in negotiations about permanently transferring custody of him away from her. They now head off to Finland and file a suit against the government over the Alexander case. In October of that year, the social services decides that the public care is to be discontinued. Two years later, in the autumn of 1986, the Swedish state settles with the Aminoffs for 200,000 crowns, or $27,000, for the wrongdoings that have taken place, the case having been taken to

179

Strasbourg after the Swedish courts had consistently decided in favour of the social services. (*Aminoff v. Sweden*) The deliberations in Swedish courts are still classified.

But to return to the *Der Spiegel* article; here are some quotes:

> "And as is almost always the case with these procedures, an administrative court confirmed the decision of the social services this time as well."

> "Coercive measures by the social services as the ones against the families Lilja and Magrell, by which children are separated from their parents through brutal force, are in Sweden neither single, nor extreme cases."

The Liljas were Karl and his wife Bozena, who left a middle-class life in Sweden behind when the child welfare wanted to take their newly born son, taking refuge in an uncertain future in New York as illegal aliens working odd jobs instead.

> "All too often however, the lawyer Brita Sundberg-Weitman finds, the social services uses completely normal family conflicts and developmental crises of the children and adolescents, sometimes even their own prejudices, as justification for the decision to take children from their childhood homes."

> "The house was unbelievably filthy and untidy, the hygienic condition in the kitchen, bathtub and toilet beneath contempt. Beer boxes, beer cans, wine and liquor bottles were all over the house when we visited.

> The social services had placed the 30 children in state custody into this neglected home, among them epileptic and disabled children."

> "For the lawyer Lennart Hane, who has learned a lot in his long fight against the "nationalization of our children", there is a simple reason for the placement into institution care: The

admission of children into care is often outright business."

They also interview a representative of the government - Hans Danelius, Under-Secretary for Legal and Consular Affairs at the Swedish Ministry for Foreign Affairs, who would later become a Supreme Court Justice and a member of the ECHR and other international courts. He's asked about the many child seizure cases that have ended up in Strasbourg:

> "Danelius explained openly that human rights conventions such as those of the Council of Europe from 1950 and those of the UN from 1966 are not binding in Swedish courts. They are not to be used by Swedish courts. That is our perspective on all international agreements."

It seems Swedish officials are very happy to criticize other countries and attempt to get them to follow Swedish directions, but certainly not the other way around.

The Swedish people did however learn something from the Aminoff and similar affairs; it's generally not worth it putting up a fight with the authorities - if you thwart their plans, they simply give you a harder time and you lose in the end no matter what. Alas, the option to get restoration through the ECHR when Swedish justice fails is long since gone, and Swedish families are today in a significantly weaker position than back then, in spite of the government's position being that the type of problems described in this article are history. And these days, escaping to another Nordic country won't be enough to get away from the social services. To quote official policy on child seizure:

> "Extradition for care between Nordic countries
>
> The Nordic countries have identical legislation regulating extradition to another Nordic country of persons subject to care. The principle is that in Scandinavia, you respect each other's laws on care in the areas at hand.

See the general counsel by The National Board of Health and Welfare [Socialstyrelsen] (1989:5) "Cooperation concerning children and youth Sweden-Finland."[1]

1   SOSFS 1997:15, "On the application of the LVU law," page 101

Taken at birth

A poor woman named Christina Ekman became pregnant in 1998, and during this pregnancy, she found herself evicted from the camping cottage where she had lived. Along with the father of her baby, she applies for help from the social services in getting housing, but this is denied. Being homeless and pregnant, she contacts a documentary film-maker who records her calamity and the events that take place for posterity.

The social services demands she complies with their request to receive the assorted services they want to provide her with, but she's only interested in the housing support this societal institution is legally required to provide; Christina and the authorities don't get along.

As the time comes for the expected birth and Christina fears the social authorities might involve themselves in the matter, she asks the doctor at the maternity hospital to keep the birth confidential; the doctor assures her they won't inform the social services. Yet in the journal, the doctor writes, "welfare officer, social services, psychiatry and proposed foster parents have been contacted."

During the autumn, Christina gives birth to a boy she names *Månstråle* - Moonbeam in English. Shortly after the birth, with Christina still in the hospital bed, the staff ask to separate the infant temporarily, even though his mother wants to keep him with her. They tell her they'll return with him and that she can have some sleep meanwhile.

When she wakes up from her sleep, she finds the child isn't with her, and she's instead dragged off to a psych ward by the police, involuntarily committed. The film-maker meets up with her at this institution and asks the doctors why she has been committed - they cite a suicide risk from having had her baby taken. The same question is posed to the social services, who cites her involuntarily commitment as reason for seizing the infant.

During the coming period, the social services vehemently refuses to allow the mother access to her baby, though the father is promised he can retain fatherhood if he accepts moving into assisted living facilities and keeps Christina from seeing the child. Reluctantly he sees no option but to go along with this.

On 27 January 1999, a documentary called *Att ta ett barn*, "To take a child," is shown on Swedish TV. This sparks furious protests, and no less than ten complaints are filed with the parliamentary ombudsman, JO, among others one by the NCHR, which specifically mentions two social workers, one psychiatrist and one gynaecologist. There would be no consequences from what had taken place, however, and the JO ends the response to the NCHR complaint with these words:

> "I also therefore find no reason to launch an investigation when it comes to the complaints against hygiene- and healthcare.

> What has otherwise come up doesn't motivate any action on my part.

> Decision

> I will not investigate the complaints any further."

A discussion of ethics... or tactics?

The National Board of Health and Welfare (*Socialstyrelsen*) has a webpage for ethical questions to guide government employees on how to deal with certain situations. Some of the questions asked here display a blatant disregard for the personal integrity of the clients of these employees, and sometimes it appears to be more a discussion about tactics on how to deal with a problem, rather than ethics.

When to inform, not whether to proceed

The following question is from the autumn of 2009:

http://www.socialstyrelsen.se/etiskafragor/etiskafragestallnin gar/narinformerautvecklingsstordbl

(My bold emphasis.)

"When to inform a mentally retarded expecting mother that her child will be seized?

The social secretaries feel it's unethical to wait until after the child is born to tell Sofie that it will be taken at the maternity hospital. At the same time, she can run away to give birth somewhere else than at the hospital if she's told in advance, which presents a danger to the child.

Sofie is a 20-year-old mildly mentally retarded woman who's pregnant with her second child. The father is a young man who's also mentally retarded. The first child, a girl, was taken and placed at a foster home pretty soon after birth because it became apparent that Sofie didn't realize the needs of her daughter and couldn't look after her.

The social secretaries have concluded that Sofie isn't capable of caring for a child, because she doesn't have the ability to see the needs of the child or protect it from danger. This child as well will be removed after birth. The social secretaries want to tell Sofie what is going to happen as soon as possible, but are anxious about what will happen if they tell her before the child is born. Sofie is very industrious and has far-reaching plans to move to another town, where she's got friends she's hooked up with over the net. Her friends are people with problems of their own. Many of them have some form of diagnostic label and most of them have or have had substance abuse problems."

You know you're in a great society that respects personal integrity when government workers keep track of what friends someone keeps.

"Discussion by the board of ethics

Social work often-times is founded on prognoses on what will happen in the future, and decisions are made based on what will probably happen. This applies as well to as intrusive decisions as seizures and forced measures. The social secretaries make a prognostic assessment about what Sofie will manage when the child is born and about how she will manage to protect the child, and they then conclude that Sofie won't be able to care for and protect the child."

Hence no actual proof that she so far has proven herself unfit to be a mother, and the authorities won't even let her try being one.

"To tell Sofie

The social secretaries are required by law to tell Sofie what they intend to do. A public authority may never withhold what it intends to do respective to an individual. If the social secretaries don't tell Sofie that they will seize the child at birth they withhold important information.

The investigation may be initiated before the child is born and Sofie may be made aware that the child will be seized. The social secretaries are concerned that Sofie might disappear if they tell her that the expected child will be taken. If Sofie disappears, it's the responsibility of the social secretaries to find Sofie, when they've launched an investigation.

Several of the members [of the board of ethics] felt that Sofie should be informed about the proceedings during a possible seizure. Withholding information is an injustice that's not insignificant and can't offset the possible gains one would achieve by not mentioning the plans to seize the child. Sofie ought to be told that it's only when the child is born that the decision to seize it can be made. **At birth a decision to immediately seize in accordance with LVU can be made**. Then the decision is put before the administrative court for examination; it establishes the decision or cancels it. She should also be informed about the possibility to appeal a decision on a seizure.

When Sofie is informed about what will happen when the child is born she might consider heading to her friends to give birth. **She should be informed that she thereby probably worsens her chances of getting to keep the child**; this will be interpreted as a sign of want of caring ability."

So if you take the matter in your own hands and claim the natural right of a biological parent to raise your child without going through the legal routes the government presents you with, you will be punished by most likely not getting to see your child at all. It's shocking how a public authority in a "Western democracy" in 2009 can be so explicit regarding fascist measures in its instructions.

In an earlier case that reached the office of the *HSAN*, the disciplinary board for hygiene and health care, in a different errand, a chief physician had declared a couple as mentally retarded without any closer examination. The written statement by this chief physician was introduced as testimony to support the social services in seizing the couple's three children; in *HSAN*

461/82, this disciplinary board doesn't hold the physician accountable for failing to review the requested information. When the social services seizes children in accordance with LVU, they often employ professionals as expert witnesses on the state of family affairs, with no consequences for the professionals if they simply forge the statements required to warrant an approval by the administrative court that tries the placement. Hence there might not be any truth whatsoever to allegations of the mother or both parents being "mentally retarded," "mentally ill" or "drug abusers," the claims most commonly used to form an LVU case.

Sofie is described as mentally retarded even though she's got an active social life maintained through the Internet and has plans for the future. You get the impression that the social services subjectively decides early on that a person can't handle being a parent, and then more or less purchases professional statements that support their perspective. Just how "mentally retarded" would this Sofie appear to a layman? And if the social authorities see fit to hide plans of this nature to their clients, what else do they keep them uninformed about?

Sometimes the parents that the social authorities have described as mentally retarded, mentally ill or abusing drugs contact doctors in order to prove their mental abilities and lack of a substance abuse problem. According to the NCHR, the doctors that comply with such requests generally see themselves reported to the National Board of Health and Welfare by the social services, intimidating them from coming to the defence of the accused parents.

And this takes place in 2009 in a country that's signed the UN declaration of human rights - probably also the country that has lectured other countries the most on the implementation of these rights.

Only in Sweden

"How to act when a person doesn't want to receive granted assistance?"

http://www.socialstyrelsen.se/etiskafragor/etiskafragestallnin gar/hurhanteranarpersonintevilltam

From the spring of 2010:

"Helen has a case of mild mental retardation and lives in a service apartment in accordance with the LSS law. She's granted assistance measures from the municipality but doesn't want to let the staff in when they come visit. How can and should the staff act?

Helen is 35 years old and has a case of mild mental retardation. She's physically disabled (in a wheelchair) and lives in a service apartment in accordance with the LSS law. The apartment (2-room) is in a housing block that's rented by the municipality, and the users have second hand contracts. Helen has a cohabitant her own age who has a trustee, and according to him the cohabitant has a diagnosis within the autism spectrum but he has no LSS decision for any measures.

How can and should the staff act to make Helen receive her services in accordance with the LSS law? The services are voluntary, but at the same time Helen is taking a spot in a municipality-owned LSS residence."

How about this for an answer - come to terms with the fact that she doesn't need your services! You might want to have a look in the mirror concerning that 'retarded' part. This is what you get when society adheres to the principle that "everything is politics;" society decides what a person needs, not the person himself, viewing him or her as an object. Many people have complained on online forums about the government deciding that they supposedly need care that they have to be provided with, while they themselves don't see any need for it - this is a complement to the

189

stories of people with real special needs that apply for the services they're legally entitled to but for which no resources are available. Isn't Sweden great?

A similar question, also from the spring of 2010:

http://www.socialstyrelsen.se/etiskafragor/etiskafragestallnin gar/hurhanteranarpersonkraverhjalp

"Question: How to deal with a person requiring assistance but refusing to accept it?"

"Märta is a woman around 65 who's got her own home and who's enrolled in the municipal home nursing. She's alert and at her senses but has since a number of years had back problems with certain physical ailments and illnesses, which have now become worse."

"She's got a borderline-kind of personality, which presents itself as mental instability and a manipulative manner. This is not "on paper," and she doesn't want anything to do with psychiatry."

Perhaps you social workers ought to ask yourselves whether you have the ethical right to diagnose people with mental illnesses? To add my own two cents on ethics - it's highly questionable that social workers disseminate claims about certain people supposedly having mental disorders, entering these claims into their journals without any proof.

"Five nurses are tied to Märta and there's a plan on who will visit [her] what day (for the sake of work environment, the same person shouldn't have to go every day). There's a nurse in charge of the patient and a doctor, but Märta doesn't want to see them."

"Märta barricades herself in her apartment except for some days when she throws out the key to the nurse, who can then enter. Märta is aware that there's a risk for sepsis, falling damage etc. The staff don't consider Märta suicidal and LPT isn't in question **at present**. She refuses all forms of commitment to a hospital and she's received several offers for different residental options, but she always backs out at the last minute, for what appears to be banal reasons such as the wrong people being in the transport car."

LPT = *Lag om Psykiatrisk Tvångsvård*, the law on involuntary psychiatric commitment. So in other words, locking her up in a psych ward was on the table when she didn't act in the way the government employees expected her to.

Your life belongs to the state

Another story on the same topic from the spring of 2009:

http://www.socialstyrelsen.se/etikisocialtjansten/hurskaparm anettdragligtliv

"How to create a tolerable life?

Ulla has a case of mild mental retardation and lives in a residence with special services in accordance with LSS. There are suspicions of drug abuse but Ulla doesn't meet the criteria for involuntary psychiatric commitment or addiction treatment. How can the staff help her to a tolerable life?

Ulla is 32 years old and has a mild case of mental retardation with autistic traits. She's got difficulties with contact and interplay and distances herself socially. She's also very sensitive to sounds and self-centered. She's provided assistance by a trustee.

Since eight years back, she lives in a residence with special services in accordance with LSS. She's very hard to motivate to do anything. Earlier she's taken part in daily activities, but since five years back she's not had any form of occupation."

"Ulla's residence is very messy and dirty. It's decaying. Ulla doesn't open the door, and she doesn't answer the phone when staff at the residence attempt to get in touch with her. Neither does she allow anyone to help her, and she refuses all contact with care- and nursing staff. The staff basically only go to her to make sure she's still alive.

The staff at the residence suspect that Ulla abuses alcohol and pills since empty bottles and dispersed pills have been spotted by the ones who at some point have managed to get inside to her. Ulla doesn't meet the criteria for LPT or LVM. The staff have filed a report in accordance with Lex Sarah that Ulla isn't doing well.

The ethical dilemma of the staff

What can the staff do to get Ulla a more tolerable life?"

I'd respond by telling them to just let her manage her own life, but I guess that would be too simple and obvious a solution for the Swedish system. LVM is the law on forced treatment of drug addicts, and *Lex Sarah* is the popular name for a paragraph in the social services law (SoL) that was introduced after an assistant nurse by the name of Sarah Wägnert had brought it to the public's attention that residents at an elder nursing home were being mistreated. How ironic that government employees now use this paragraph to attempt to protect an adult human being from herself. I'm a bit suspicious of the claims that they've spotted drugs in her apartment – my experience of government workers tells me that they will happily make up such allegations for the purpose of reaching the criteria required to have someone committed.

The government will always treat you as nothing more than a mere object - government services are nothing like services you buy from a private caregiver. I wonder just when the government employees will understand that they through their condescending attitudes contribute to the misery of their clients, as well as to their potential substance abuse? How can you have a decent life if the government doesn't entrust you to make your own decisions about it? It's all profit to the government workers, though - by providing a person with services he doesn't need which deprives him of his dignity, you can get a coworker at the social services work dealing with the person's inflicted substance abuse problem.

All in all it's just another brick in the wall.
All in all you're just another brick in the wall.

The administrative courts

So, in the hands of what esteemed institutions of law are LVU cases settled? Who has the power to decide on whether the social council will be allowed to take a child into state custody? These cases are handled by something called administrative courts, presided over by a judge and three lay assessors, who in closed legal proceedings make the decisions. The social council has one legal representative making its case for forced care, and both the legal guardian(s) and the child itself have one representative each. It's no understatement to claim that the game is rigged against the biological parent(s) and in favour of the state; in practice, the "best interests of the child" on which the child's representative act, are almost always synonymous with the view of the social council, and the one representative of the other party rarely make too strident a case against forced care, for several reasons:

* He/she generally doesn't get to partake of the case the social council has compiled in favour of care until mere minutes before the trial, even though this material is sometimes the result of months of work, including statements by doctors, teachers and other public employees, whose written testimonies are presented before the court. There's no requirement on being physically present to have one's testimony delivered, and oaths aren't required to make statements in front of administrative courts.

* The court both picks the legal representative and pays him or her, which introduces a problem with challenge. Since the judge can determine if a lawyer should receive his full due or a reduced one, there's a very present risk that ones who defiantly oppose the state's case and challenge its claims might have their pay cut.

In lawyer magazine *Advokaten*, issue 8 2009, a researcher

194

and a lawyer are interviewed on this matter, after researcher Anna Hollander had published a study highlighting the shortcomings of these courts. To quote the article:

"Compulsory institutional care: Consensus in the courtroom threatens legal security

Cases concerning administrative forced seizures are characterized by a spirit of consensus, where legal security gets the short stick. This is the opinion of researchers who have studied cases involving forced care in a number of county administrative courts. But judges at a county administrative court doesn't recognize this picture."

"An aura of consensus is established, where the purpose of the decisions is defined by therapeutic motives that are hard to question. In many cases, this means that the legal review disappears and that the court trusts that the social services does this for the good of the individual," Anna Hollander says.

"We saw clearly in our study that the court wants to tone down divergence of opinion between the individual and the public authority. The investigation isn't reviewed and during the verbal negation, questions are asked that rather have the intent of convincing the client that the proposed decision on forced care is for his or her own good."

"The courts are at the mercy of other professions here, and may not be able to judge the social assessments that are made in the investigation. They must be able to review the arguments and that they are correlated with the facts and circumstances that are accounted for, Anna Hollander says, who feels that the administrative courts don't live up to the demands of the *officialprincip* that the case is satisfactorily investigated."

"The researchers' study also shows that the negotiations in cases of forced care are short and that the public attorneys that represent the ones who will be taken into care and in LVU cases the parents as well, as a rule request compensation for between an hour and a whole work day. Anna Hollander feels that the public lawyers have an almost impossible task, who in this short time have to find time to both speak to the client and to review the written basis that dominates the administrative process."

Attorney UllaBella af Klercker relates her experiences as well:

"Investigations by the social services concerning LVU and LVM have great shortcomings too.

- There's a lot of personal opinion and emotion and conclusions of one's own that are mixed in a mishmash with objective facts, she says, and establishes that the ones that write the investigations, the social secretaries, often are so involved in the case that they have a hard time separating facts and conclusions."

"- I can feel an immense frustration at times. That the public authority steps over the line without taking all of the facts into consideration, one abuses one's power against an individual. That's frustrating, she says."

On the futility of appealing a verdict:

"- Since these are relatively short cases, it's hard to get a case to a superior instance. Many don't even feel there's any point in appealing, since it's somewhat of a fresh product, she says.

In for example LVM cases, the decision is on care for six months. Unlike in criminal cases, the verdict is carried out immediately. If it then takes four months before the case reaches the administrative court of appeal, many feel there's no point in appealing."

Decisions on care under the LVU law are also for six months at a time. And unlike what's the case in the American legal system - in the Swedish one, verdicts from administrative courts can't be appealed to judicial courts. In an article in *Dagens Nyheter* from 27 October 2006, Hollander and two other researchers address the

196

same topic:

> "Many individuals therefore leave the negotiations not only disappointed in that the forced care goes on, but also frustrated that the legal motives in the verdict haven't been clarified. Fact is that it's not uncommon that no questions at all are put to the representative of the public authority. Instead the negotiations are dominated by questions to the individual. These questions are however rarely put in such a way that it becomes comprehensible to the individual what legal relevance they have. Hence the court negotiations are transformed into a renewed examination of the individual, whose legal interests they're meant to protect."

> "Our impression is that in these negotiations on forced care, a special therapeautic culture develops among involved judges, psychiatrists, social workers and legal counsel. The starting perspective is the well-meaning "we're all here to achieve what's best for the individual.""

To quote another authority on the topic - Brita Sundberg-Weitman, former *lawspeaker* (president) of Solna district court, in her 1985 book *Rättsstaten åter*:

> "Power without responsibility: Through the use of general clauses without content, the legislators in Sweden of the 1970's and 1980's have made it possible that authority decisions in certain areas *can't* be wrong, since anything the public authorities find suitable automatically *becomes* right."

Apart from this stated book, Brita also wrote *Sverige och rättsstaten på 2000-talet* in 2008, returning to the same topic of the rule of law having gone AWOL in Swedish society.

Hence, to summarize: It's safe to say that children at the risk of being taken into foster care are rarely given a fair trial, and the social council has little reason to fear their cases being denied.

The social services and the rule of law

LVU, paragraph 43:

"Police assistance

43 § The police authority shall provide assistance to on the request of"

"2. the social council or any member or employee that the council has ordained to carry out decisions on care or taking into custody supported by this law"

Hence the social services has the legal right to call on the police for taking children into custody, potentially placing them in locked rooms at youth institutions. This clause was obviously necessary to avoid the problem that the children who are meant to be provided with "the care they need," might disagree with receiving this very care. When social secretaries seize children, they usually have a squad of police officers accompanying them, quite often in uniform. This differs from the way actual criminals are dealt with - they're generally *picked up* as it's called, by officers in civilian clothing.

The role of the traditional police authority has been shaped over centuries, its procedures having been made ever more humane, while this new-found power of the social services hasn't been very scrutinized. Now why would anyone have a problem with giving the social services strong legal authority in providing its intended clients with the "care they need?" After all, the very wording suggests that it would be a disservice to the child "denying" him or her the care he or she "needs," and any attempt on the part of the client to dodge the care is only the manifestation of the problem to treat - the individual can't be entrusted to look after himself. While traditionally in Western law, the rule has been that the law is clearly defined so that it can't be misunderstood, and everyone is equal before it. With the concept of "the care people need," it's bestowed on the profession of the social workers to make such decisions on the other hand - the grounds for someone "needing care" in the therapeutic state are described in loose "I know it when I see it" terms.

If you've not grown convinced by the material in this chapter so far, here is yet more discussion of the inherent problem in granting the social services this power.

The documents the social services has produced to instruct its employees in the exercising of its craft give very free reigns. To quote *SOSFS 1997:15*, on the application of the LVU law:

> "It's in the nature of the matter that a complete basis for a decision is often missing in situations where an immediate taking into custody comes in question. In acute situations, sometimes a fairly high degree of uncertain must be accepted."[1]

> "A decision on a request for police assistance ought to be delivered in writing to the police authority. The JO has while reviewing an errand concerning immediate taking into custody found that in acute situations, decisions can be made verbally and thereafter as soon as possible be documented and signed."[2]

> "Additional decision power

> Decision on an immediate taking into custody may at times have to be made on a very short notice. Therefore the chairman of the social welfare council or other member that the council has appointed in accordance with § 6 paragraph 2 LVU has the right to make those decisions. This decision power assumes that the council's, or in anticipated cases the committee's, decision can't be waited upon. Primarily, decisions on seizures should hence be

---

1   *SOSFS 1997:15, page 43*

2   *SOSFS 1997:15, page 99*

made by council or committee."[1]

Hence a single social worker can simply call the police and have them pick up children, to take them into custody, though an administrative court has to approve of the placement within a week for it to be legally binding. Even if the children are held against their will without a court order for a longer time than this, the social council doesn't face any consequences - about the only thing the child's parents can do then is complain to the JO, who will at most offer mild criticism of the measure.

Some actual cases provide interesting studies of the intersection between the role of the social services and the police authority in governing society. A juvenile delinquent born in 1992 had from 2006 and onwards committed a number of burglaries against schools, and in 2008 even started robbing banks as part of a gang. The justice system in Sweden offers pretty non-existent legal sanctions for juvenile offenders, even for crimes such as these, and to a large extent the work rather falls under the jurisdiction of the social services, which in this case in Helsingborg municipality has an intimate collaboration with the police. By late 2008, this boy T.H. has had eight indictments brought against him, and when the social services learns that he's suspected of robbing a bank, they take the matter into their own hands.

Due to the suspicions, T.H. is legally detained by the police on 17 December 2008 and interrogated that day as well the next. The evidence is weak, and the police release him on the 18th, while an investigation is underway. He doesn't get to stay for very long at home, though - that evening, he's detained by the police again - but this time, it's the social services that has decided that he's going to be put in the Råby youth home, supported by LVU § 6. T.H.'s mother is upset and contacts the social workers to see

---

1   *SOSFS 1997:15, page 48*

what's the matter, and she gets her son back the next day. T.H. is detained by the police again on 15 January 2009 after the social services had neglected to inform the police that the LVU decision had been retracted, hence they assumed it was still outstanding.

T.H.'s mother G.L. now files a complaint with the JO about the way her juvenile delinquent son had been treated, and from the investigation it becomes evident that it had started on 18 December when a social worker had been at the police station as T.H. was being interrogated, and that this social worker had forwarded the information to the social council after he had learned that T.H. was a suspect in a bank robbery.

> "One of the members of the social welfare council, Anna Jähnke, made the formal decision. Thereafter a request for police assistance was made to get help in carrying out the decision."[1]

Though obviously this T.H. should be incarcerated, and his earlier crimes should have resulted in him not being a free man at this time, it's highly peculiar that the government can operate in this manner - who needs legal courts, evidence, trials and such obsolete innovations when you can just decide that someone needs care and should be institutionalized because of it? Have the police perform surveillance and let the social services incarcerate youth who have been found engaging in "socially destructive behaviour;" that is the Soviet Union resurrected.

Ironically, though Råby youth home is the home of some of Sweden's worst juvenile offenders, the "secure youth care" they're sentenced to isn't very secure. As a rule, the residents here are generally not locked up even though being convicted, and at several times the criminals sent here have run away repeatedly. As the police described a juvenile repeat offender escaping from Råby: "He simply walked out."

---

1   JO Registration number 311-2009

This very institution has been the site of other outrageous government actions as well. In 2004, a family from Croatia had arrived in Sweden, seeking asylum. In 2006, they move to Karlshamn municipality and become a case for the social services there, a family of some five children. Late that year, one of the daughters in the family - a girl named Lollo - showed up in school with bruises on her face, and when asked about it, she says it's her dad that has hit her. In early 2007, he gets a short prison sentence for assaulting her and her siblings, but after serving his time, he returns home and has custody of his children again. The social services is involved in family life, and initially doesn't believe Lollo when she tells them about the abuse.

While the family has lived in Karlshamn, Lollo has been through various foster placements as the social services has attempted to rectify the family situation, and this public authority has taken a disliking to her somewhat insubordinate attitude. In April 2007, Karlshamn municipality files an LVU application with Karlskrona county administrative court, citing the need to place her in a locked facility in spite of the actual problem being that her father abused her. To support the need to deprive her of liberty, they would cite some astounding reasons. You see, under the "Reasons for need of a spot at a special youth home" section of the form, they enter these words:

In the field named "Other, state what," they write "Gypsy, Romani tradition."

In the field named "Substance abuse," they write "Hangs out with guys with drug problems."

So now, 16-year-old gypsy girl Lollo is placed in a locked facility with Sweden's worst juvenile delinquents - Råby youth home. In the application, unsubstantiated accusations of shoplifting are also cited. Eventually she is released from this institution and relocated to a foster family instead, but not before being returned back to her father again. The social workers don't believe that he's abusing her until he tries to run them over with his car after they had picked the girls up. Very sparse media attention is brought to the case at the time, but later in 2008, when the family faces possible deportation from failing to be granted asylum, the story of Lollo becomes national news; or at least the story that doesn't include her being deprived of liberty for being a gypsy. Now Karlshamn municipality makes a grandstand portraying itself as the champion of this young girl's rights, when they fight for her being given asylum.

In 2009, Lollo gets a residence permit, but still at this time, the public knows very little about what Lollo has gone through earlier. During the summer of 2010, after some investigative journalism on the part of a reporter named Glenn Möllergren, this part of the story is uncovered as well, and the LVU application with the peculiar reason for taking her into custody is released to the public. Apart from the media of the journalist in question, the matter is only covered by a single newspaper.

Ah, what a society, where neither public authority nor mass media will neglect to look out for the little guy, the ones in vulnerable positions at the mercy of their surroundings. I mean, why on earth would the social services locking children up for being gypsies be of any public interest? The story also highlights the hypocrisy in politicians getting involved in clearly sympathetic cases that will boost their own images, while caring little about limiting the option the social services has for arbitrarily employing the power of the state – which is what would be required to prevent something such as this from being repeated in the future.

A culture clash - Oriental academic tradition meets the Swedish school system

JO registration number 1978-2005[1], or the story of a teenage girl who finds herself forcibly institutionalized when the government learns that the pressure her father puts her through to excel in school has made her depressed. This Chinese family, judging by the documents consisting of father and daughter living in Sweden, while the mother is back in China, found themselves in a precarious situation when the Swedish government didn't respect the father's way of raising his daughter.

"Background

On 13 April 2005, a report arrived at the social services in Österåker municipality from the Berga school concerning fears about T.Y., born in 1990. She had the same day left a letter to a teacher at the school and then disappeared. In the letter she had expressed suicidal thoughts. The school had also reported her disappearance to the police.

The social council in Österåker municipality the same day initiated an investigation in accordance with 11 chap. 1 § the social services law (2001:453), SoL, concerning T.Y.

T.Y. was found later that day by the police. Representatives of the social services held talks with her first at the police station and then at the premises of the social services. Talks were then held with her father, C.Y. After that the council made a decision in accordance with 4 chap. 1 § SoL on placing T.Y. in an HVB home. [An orphanage]

On 19 May 2005 the chairman of the social council decided on an immediate seizure of T.Y. supported by 6 § the Care of Young Persons Special Provisions Act (1990:52), LVU."

---

1   http://www.jo.se/Page.aspx?
MenuId=106&ObjectClass=DynamX_SFS_Decision&Id=2059

Ok, it's noble if people get themselves involved when they hear someone feels like committing suicide, but surely a teenage girl expressing herself this way shouldn't be considered spectacular enough to ship her off to an institution? Especially not as the first thing on the table? I personally also find it offensive that the social services involved themselves in family life that very day without first getting the approval of the father. It's obvious that the Swedish state considers children its own property, not belonging to their parents.

"Complaint

In a complaint, that arrived at the JO on 2 May 2005, along with a supplemental writ which arrived at the JO on 24 May 2005, C.Y expressed complaints against the social council in Österåker municipality. The complaints focused mainly on the council placing his daughter T.Y. in an HVB home without making a decision he could appeal and without his consent."

Now why would a father be upset that the government arbitrarily took his daughter into custody?

Much of the remainder of the available documents recount the interaction between the father and the government, with him unwilling to discuss how he's raising his daughter and only asking the other party if they've got the law on their side. It's interesting to note that a man from a seemingly totalitarian society such as China takes for granted that he's got more freedom in family matters than the Swedish government wants to give him.

"After the first meeting at the social services, C.Y. was summoned to another two meetings, on 25 April as well as on 4 May 2005. He didn't show up for any of these. The council has stated that several letters were sent to C.Y. but that he didn't respond."

Oh, you poor civil servants... The man doesn't listen to you and wants nothing to do with you.

"Judging by the file of the administration in the matter it however becomes clear that two writs from C.Y. arrived at the administration, on 25 April as well as 3 May 2005. In the writs, C.Y. expressed that he wants his daughter back home. He writes among other things that you have to stop keeping my daughter in 'captivity,' you're going to send my daughter back home and I can most definitely not approve of you sending my daughter to a temporary family or any form of adoptive family."

My, the social services must really be astounded here... How could anyone use the word captivity for being placed into state custody at an orphanage? But it's our service to the families, don't they understand that?! This is how JO Kerstin André concludes the matter:

"With this background, what C.Y. has stated in this part doesn't bring about any statement or any action on my part within the scope of this matter."

I guess if you attend school here in Sweden, you're not allowed to focus on the actual studies, then you'd upset the hegemony. Parents here are expected to encourage their offspring to spend their teen years in search of sexual perversion, drug experimentation, left-wing political extremism and various other virtues of contemporary Sweden, not actually focus on learning anything. I guess I'm a great sinner in this regard, I spent most of my teens at the town library, even on weekends. I'm glad the social services didn't catch me there.

Hiding your child from foster care = "kidnapping"

Since children taken into foster care are generally not locked up, though if they've been placed under LVU § 3, they can be - it might be tempting to attempt to defy the law and simply take your child back from the care. It's quite common that children run away from either foster parents or the orphanage they've been placed at, but the state is vigilant in preventing parents from helping their children escape their forced care. You have to give credit to the legislators for a truly Orwellian spirit in describing taking your child back from an institution placement as a *crime against family*. Section 4 of chapter 7 of the penal code, *On Crimes against the Family*, reads this way:

> "[Most of first paragraph cut] be sentenced for *arbitrary conduct concerning a child* to a fine or imprisonment for at most one year.
>
> A person is also criminally responsible under the first paragraph who without authorisation separates a child under fifteen years of age from the person who has the custody of the child by virtue of the Care of Young Persons Special Provisions Act (LVU), unless the crime is one against personal liberty or of furtherance of flight."

If the child is the one that initiates the break for freedom, another paragraph is applied - 17 § 12, under the chapter *On Crimes against Public Activity*:

> "A person who assists someone who is an inmate of a prison, or who is remanded in custody or arrested, or otherwise **lawfully deprived of his liberty**, to gain his freedom or, after such escape, **aids him by hiding him** or by other like action, shall be sentenced for *aiding escape* to a fine or imprisonment for at most one year."

Hence whether you visit the orphanage and save your child

from the placement, or if you simply hide him or actively prevent the social services from taking your child back after you've been allowed to have him come home briefly, you commit a crime with a possible sentence of up to a year in prison. Attempted escapes are common both at orphanages and the prison service's open prisons, but unlike the run-of-the-mill escape from a 'prison,' attempted escapes from orphanages usually result in an alarm within hours, with police sent out to intercept the runaway. It is also interesting to note that while technically the people deprived of freedom at both places can easily escape, foster children are more prone to do so in spite of their care supposedly being in their best interest. I guess the prison service realized that if you make prisons luxurious enough, the inmates won't escape - I mean, why run away when they take care of everything for you - food, dishes, washing clothes, recreation and provide you with stimulating work to do so your life doesn't lose all meaning.

On the same note, Swedish prisons have also solved the problem of violence in prisons - if you let the violent criminals out into the streets instead, the prisons will be safe havens where the worst downside to life is that you might be without yoghurt in the morning! Not only are the Swedish authorities great at hiding their intentions through misleading nomenclature - they also come up with creative solutions for hard-to-solve problems.

The Berlin wall

"Set-surround sound in a two inch wall
I was waiting for the Communist call
I didn't ask for sunshine and I got World War Three
I'm looking over the wall
And they're looking at me"

Sex Pistols – Holiday in the sun

Paragraph 6 of the LVU law reads as follows:

"The social council may decide that one that is under 20 years of age shall be immediately seized, if

1) it's likely that the minor has to be provided with care supported by this law, and

2) the court's decision on care can't be awaited with regards to the risk to the health or development of the minor or that the continued investigation can be seriously jeopardized or **further measures be prevented**."

This is the provision that lets the authorities seize children as their families are attempting to leave the country - they don't even have to provide any written documentation at first, but merely call the police and have them pick up the children.

To quote a policy document by the social services, SOSFS 1997:15, on the application of this law, page 46:

"Another situation may be that the execution of the administrative court's decision is prevented, for example if the parents might disappear with the child or that there is a risk that the child hides or runs away to stop a decision on care supported by LVU from being executed. Special difficulties may arise if the parents are planning to send the child abroad since a decision supported by

209

LVU can't be executed there. In such situations, the child should be immediately seized so that the decision can be carried out."

You know you're in a true democracy when the authorities feel entitled to enter into their policy documents the recommendation to seize the children of families attempting to leave the country. The following are three stories of families attempting to do just that, but where the authorities had other plans.

Leaving the psych ward... twice

In 2007, a single mother of two daughters, aged 10 and 13, had a nervous breakdown and found herself briefly hospitalized. This saw the social services come into family life. These two girls had lived with their mother their whole lives, but now the government saw fit to remove them and place them into foster care; the social services described the mother as a destructive influence on the development of her daughters and had an administrative court approve the LVU order it had written.

Their first placement by the social services is with a family where they're warmly received. The children are content with the placement and they have good access to their own social network. The social services, however, isn't pleased with the placement - within months, they are removed to another family, which already has children of its own. Now they find themselves far away from what they call home, and they feel like unwanted stepchildren. Their foster parents are displeased with them and threaten them frequently with being sent off to an orphanage.

As their mother is back home, the girls want to return to her, but the social services has other plans. Not knowing where to turn, the older daughter composes a letter to send to a local newspaper, describing their plight. A journalist is interested in the story and visits the mother at her house, but when he proposes his article to his editor-in-chief, he finds that he refuses to cover it, citing how it would "be detrimental to the children."

The girl who has written the letter, fearing she'll be put in an orphanage, runs back to her mother. They decide that the only option they have for staying together as a family is to leave the country. As they're aware of how swiftly the authorities can move if they learn that families want to escape their care, they waste no time and take the first ticket out of Sweden, even though they have no plans for their future abroad - all they can think about is getting away from the social authorities.

The younger daughter still wants to keep in touch with her mother, but the social services has put restrictions on this communication - she's only legally allowed to keep in touch with them listening in on the conversations. Though initially she's tempted to agree with the placement voluntarily by being offered a computer of her own, they take it away when they learn she's been corresponding with her mother through E-mail. The final placement for her appears to be with a 60-year-old single woman.

The mother has written on sourze.se about her story, under the taken name "Lena Olsson." She has decided she's never going back to Sweden.[1]

Not without my daughter?

Back in 1991, there was a movie called "Not without my daughter," about a woman who had gone to Iran with her husband and daughter, and found it wasn't possible to leave the country with her child, since her husband intended to stay there. The movie is somewhat loosely based on a real story that had taken place in 1984. In 2009, a family found themselves unable to leave

---

1
http://www.sourze.se/Jag_flydde_Sverige_när_socialen_ville_ta_mina_barn_10680926.asp

the country they resided in, but in this case, Iran was the destination, and Sweden was the country they had gone to for a brief visit, where the authorities had seized their children. The father of the family, Esmail, is of Iranian descent; the mother Susanne Swedish. This was the father's story, posted on the forum of the Nordic Committee for Human Rights (*forum.nkmr.org*):

> "The 28th of May when we were about to fly to Iran to visit my dad who had cancer we were stopped at the passport control. The police said that all three children had been seized by Linköping municipality. We were shocked and couldn't believe it. We were in Arlanda police custody with Filip age 6, Nicole age 5 and Miranda age 2 for three hours. After three hours, two social workers from Märsta municipality came and dragged the children from us. All three children screamed after us. All of this took place in mere minutes. We received an investigation where it said that an anonymous person had reported us for child neglect. We only stayed a couple of days in Linköping and visited Susanne's brother in Linköping. We're not even residents of Sweden. We've lived in Norway for a year, and before that we lived in Iran. Now it's been 182 days since we saw our children."

Contacted on 26 April 2010, the father reports that they're still fighting to get their children back after over a year in state custody, without much luck, without any media penetration. One wonders just how many cases like these there are, when society keeps a lid on the topic.

On the ninth of that same month, a Swedish woman by the name of Helena Högström put up a petition on behalf of the Muslim families of "at least 30 children in Sigtuna-Märsta municipality," stating that this number of children in a town of some 40,000 people had been taken into state custody because of their parents' religion, in particular due to a named social secretary - Maria N. She also sent an open letter to minister of health Maria Larsson, accusing Sweden of violating the UN declaration of human rights through its family policies, and also insinuates that Sweden is in the practise of "ethnic cleansing" against this minority.[1]

The next couple of months, some 500 people sign the petition and add their stories about their encounters with the social services; lots of Muslims pray to God that Maria will see the errors in her ways in taking the children. A man named Youssef adds this story in broken (hopefully correctly interpreted) Swedish:

> "I've also become like you mukhtar! They've taken my children from the daycare centre without me knowing it! Then they said that the "health or development" of the children was in jeopardy. How? About my children - I've personally been to the nurse at a hospital and have everything in order, dentist too, everything there is. Doctor's examinations find that my children are perfect and they're not shy and they don't have anything. F***ing municipality makes lots of stuff up just because some of them do their job or make money from it? [sic] I hope my God will help me and show them that what they're doing is wrong. ;((("

On a news portal called *e-jihad.se*, the plight of Muslim families under the Swedish social services is covered in a couple of articles, where among others a Palestinian family is interviewed - the Qatananis. The father has this to say about how he felt after the social services had taken their four children:

> "I wanted to move here and live here and let my children go to school here. But now it's exactly the same thing here as in Israel. Our children are taken away from us as if we were cattle! We're powerless as parents, this power they've got in their hands runs us over like tanks. We've cried, we've asked for help but we've not witnessed any help."

Sweden has indeed marketed itself as a utopia to come to for

---

1   http://www.ipetitions.com/petition/barn/

people living under unfavourable conditions in the third world, and some half a million people from Muslim countries have made their way here, expecting a great life under a generous welfare system. The Social Democrats take for granted that this will mean that they'll be faithful supporters of the party, yet when these families get a taste of Social Democratic family policies, they realize that they were misled in coming here - the party has no intentions of letting them remain with their religious traditions, but merely make them pieces in a giant welfare machinery.

Maybe Sweden ought to launch a new motto:

Come for the welfare, stay for the legal fight to get your children back.

The world-famous Domenic case

On 25 June 2009, a uniformed police squad enters a plane leaving for India about to take off from Arlanda airport outside of Stockholm. Is it a drug bust? A terrorist threat? Or maybe the escort of a dignitary stepping on board the airplane? None of it - they're there to take a seven-year-old boy named Dominic into state custody, from a family that's leaving Sweden and moving to another country.

The affair had started the year earlier. During the spring of 2008, Swedish Christer and his wife Annie of Indian descent had planned to move to India with their only child, where they had earlier married back in 2000, after having lived together in Sweden since 2001. The plans are put on hold, however, and during the autumn, Dominic is due to start mandatory schooling at a public school on Gotland. At first, even though the family intends to leave the country as soon as possible, Christer still brings his son to school the first day. Dominic is however startled by this noisy and unfamiliar environment, and the family decides they're going to homeschool him until they've landed in India, to

214

hopefully enjoy a more orderly school environment there.

At this time, Swedish law still formally permitted homeschooling, though in practice the only permits that were granted were for cases where geography or illness make public schooling impossible. Christer gets in touch with the school authorities to get his homeschooling approved, and is told he's supposed to negotiate with the principal at the school where Dominic was enrolled. This principal isn't the least bit interested in giving way, however, and Christer's plans come for naught. When the Johansson family still proceeds with their homeschooling, which has resulted in their son being fluent in both Swedish and English by the time he was supposed to enter school, the school authorities put a fine on them for every day Dominic doesn't show up for school. From November 2008 and onwards, the fine is 500 crowns ($70) per day.

During the coming winter, Christer is in regular contact with the school authorities and the social services. The family wants the legal right to homeschool Dominic; the authorities on the other hand attempt to coerce Christer and Annie into sending him to school instead. The affair escalates, and the social services becomes convinced that Dominic's needs are being neglected in his home. In May of 2009, they're in court over the fine the school board has put on them and it's overturned. Soon after this, the social services launches a new investigation into the living conditions of Dominic in the Johansson home, and in early June Christer receives a call about his plans for the future. He tells them they're finally leaving on a plane on the 25th, moving to India indefinitely, taking their son along with them to live in a sort of commune in the city of Goa. As Christer would later explain on an Internet forum - the three constitute "a somewhat different eco-style family," which he feels might have angered the authorities.

Though under reasonable government, the affair would have

ended here... But now the conflict reaches its climax - the family attempts to emigrate with a child who's a Swedish citizen, who the authorities have already made other plans for. The Gotland social services makes a decision supported by LVU § 6 to seize Dominic as the family attempts to leave, and uniformed police officers are called in to execute it. Though you'd think the police taking a child from the arms of its parents on an airplane would make headlines, there's a complete media blackout for the next six weeks. The mother Annie is in shock after the police action, and she visits the hospital emergency room several times during the coming months. The events have taken their toll on Christer, too, who's got a history of being treated for depression.

Initially both Annie and Christer lack the strength to challenge the decision, but the story makes its way through Internet blogs during the month of July, ultimately reaching Swedish mass media in the beginning of August. By then, it was becoming world-wide news as American organizations such as the American *Home School Legal Defense Association* got wind of the connection to homeschooling.

On 13 August 2009, an administrative court confirmed the LVU decision of Gotland municipality, that Dominic for the time being will remain in state custody until another solution can be worked out. Before this, a complaint had been filed against Gotland municipality with the JO about the seizure on the plane, which was quickly dismissed by Hans Ragnemalm.

As grounds for taking Dominic into state custody, the social services has now added additional risk factors to his development in his home, when initially the only problem had been the refusal to place him in public school. The journals from Christer's history of mental instability are quoted, something that sparked him to volunteer for a mental check-up himself, where a psychiatrist later in October states that his mental health is just fine. The authorities also charge the parents with having "isolated" their son from his peers and that his development had been harmed, in spite of Annie testifying to her son being ahead of his peers in schooling as well as being bilingual.

During the autumn of 2009, the story becomes heavily publicized by Christian media in America, which once again acts as a watchdog against a country that defiantly violates natural rights; an earlier time had of course been the Åke Green affair a couple of years back. In September, it's covered by Christian news site WorldNetDaily and subsequently also by the Christian Broadcasting Network. The HSLDA even writes a letter to the Gotland social services to inquire about their version of the story and remind them of the rights granted families under the European Convention on Human Rights as well as by the United Nations.

As of September of 2010, Dominic is still in state custody in spite of the efforts on the part of organizations such as the HSLDA and the Alliance Defense Fund, as well as lawyer Ruby Harrold-Claesson becoming legal counsel for the Johansson family. Though earlier they spent most of their time together with none of the parents gainfully employed, now they're restricted to seeing each other a couple of hours a month, with the social services always present. For two years in a row, the Johansson family has been denied spending Dominic's birthday, 3 September, with him. Though you now get no less than 22,000 hits for "Dominic Johansson" on Google, the overwhelming majority of them for this case, this attention hasn't made the Swedish state budge one bit - there's no end in sight for Dominic's placement into state custody.

The Communists want to erect the Berlin wall... again

In a parliamentary bill entitled "Abduction of children to other countries," *2008/09:So555*, three members of the Left party, the former Communists, call for the criminalization of hiding children from the state. To quote the bill:

> "Sweden is one of the first countries in the world to have approved and implemented the UN *Convention on the Rights of the Child*. The child perspective of the convention therefore shall always be at the centre and be observed in all decisions that are taken at all levels in society and within the family."

> "The child perspective is implemented in the Swedish Social services law and in the founding values of the school [system] which rests on a foundation of democracy, human rights and everyone's equal value."

Sweden is indeed a great example of how "the rights of the child" really is nothing but a catch phrase to transfer guardianship from biological parents to the state.

> "In accordance with the School law, all children between seven and sixteen years old are required to attend school, and education in elementary school is compulsory. No one has the right to prevent the children from taking part in the compulsory education, not even the parents. But unfortunately it often happens that parents and other adults in immediate and extended family send their children to their old home countries, even though the child has been seized in accordance with LVU and even though the child is required to attend school."

Swedish legislators sure have a way with language... To paraphrase: "No one has the right to free the children from state force."

> "Even if the child has been seized in accordance with LVU, nothing can be done about it in another country."

Thankfully for now, Marxists can't demand that children are handed over to them if their parents have other plans. If they have their way with their vision of a global plantation, I guess these non-conformist families shouldn't be safe anywhere.

> "For afore-mentioned reason, we would like the Government to review the *Care of Young Persons Special Provisions Act* (1990:52) (LVU) in accordance with the following principles:
>
> * It shall be liable for punishment for guardians to **abduct their children** to any other country.
>
> * The police shall be given the authority to in the same way as with wanted fugitives be alerted when children that are seized in accordance with LVU leave the country."

(My bold emphasis.)

It ought to be obvious by now that what they really mean by "the rights of the child" is the "privilege" of being a part of their intended plantation. It's a bit frightening that these politicians apparently feel that using force against families can be considered doing the children a favour. Christians have traditionally felt that they've got their children on loan from God, to care for the best way they can, and afterwards be judged by God. In Sweden today, a similar notion is expressed, but the God part has been dropped - you're considered to have your children on loan, they're not your property, but the one that judges you now is the state. Hence a fallible human political invention is to be considered superior to the natural parent human children have always grown up under.

Fortunately, the bill was rejected, but who knows for how long such efforts will be kept at bay? One day we will wake up and salute our personal social supervisor as the first thing we do in the morning and affirm just how happy we are with the system; the state will then truly have taken on the role of God.

Newspeak

In George Orwell's book 1984, old words are replaced by new ones that make up something called *Newspeak*. The aim of this is to make dissent impossible by providing the words for undesirable things with a good connotation, and vice versa. The Swedish government has turned that into a practice as well, especially when it comes to its role as parent. The following three are official words used by the foster care system, before and after:

Fosterfamilj (foster family) -> *familjehem* (family home)

Barnhem (orphanage) -> HVB-hem, *hem för vård och boende* (home for care and living); sometimes referred to as *behandlingshem* (treatment home) in media.

Fostervård (foster care) -> *samhällsvård* (social care)

They clearly saw a need to get away from the negative connotations of the words foster and orphanage.

The opportunity for parents to raise their own children is circumvented, while the government is given the legal right to punish them instead:

Uppfostran (upbringing) -> *barnaga* (spanking)

Frihetsstraff (imprisonment) -> *vård* (care)

So while before, you would *uppfostra* your children so they didn't end up with a *frihetsstraff*, now the government protects your children from *barnaga* by confining them to *vård*.

For most of the 20th century, youth up to the age of 21 could be sentenced to special youth prisons (*ungdomsfängelse / ungdomsanstalt*), but during the 1970's, these were removed since it was considered inhumane incarcerating minors. The 1982 LVU law reintroduced deprivation of liberty of minors in facilities that were eventually known as *ungdomshem* (youth homes), sometimes referred to as § 12-hem due to the paragraph in the law that specifies their use - not only do the new ones have a dubious name, but now minors only guilty of 'socially destructive behaviour' can be imprisoned as well. Of course, now they both receive *vård* instead of *frihetsstraff*, which for minors who have cut classes in school can mean being locked up in your room at the *ungdomshem*. If a parent confines his children to their rooms on the other hand, it falls under Chapter 4, section 2 of the Penal Code - *unlawful deprivation of liberty*.

Dissident -> extremist ("Their dissidents" - "Our extremists")

When mass media discusses political offenders in countries such as China, they're referred to as *dissidents*. Political offenders in Europe are instead called *extremists*. Both of them have in common that they're imprisoned because of their views. It sure would be interesting to learn how China refers to Christian ministers in Europe being imprisoned for teaching the Bible's message on homosexuality - extremists or dissidents? Something tells me they're correctly referred to as dissidents.

Städare (cleaner) -> *lokalvårdare* (keeper of premises)

Fängelse (prison) -> *anstalt* (institution)

For the above one, I do however suggest the word motel instead to better represent what today's 'prisons' are.

Olaga vapeninnehav (illegal possession of a weapon, the term used in the weapons law before 1996) -> *vapenbrott* (weapons crime, the term used after 1996)

To quote the government bill (1995/96:52) introducing the 1996 weapons law:

"The paragraph corresponds to 37 § in the current weapons law. The terms weapons crime (vapenbrott) along with major weapons

221

crime (grovt vapenbrott) have been introduced as crime classifications for the two most serious crimes. This has been done to simplify the denomination of these crimes during the handling of criminal cases and errands of the authorities and courts as well as in connection with registries. **Otherwise the regulation has only been adjusted linguistically.**"

Linguistically... In a Newspeak way. The term "weapons crime" packs a whole lot more punch than "illegal possession of a weapon." I don't think too many people realize that the majority of "major weapons crimes" in Sweden are nothing more than that an individual or a group of people have been caught with an unregistered pistol. The term rather has you thinking someone has been running around with an automatic rifle in public.

And, of course:

Invandringsmotstånd (immigration opposition) -> *hets mot folkgrupp* (agitation against ethnic group)

Meningsskiljaktighet (dissent) -> *hatbrott* (hate crime)

A NATION OF SINNERS

"For this cause God gave them up unto vile affections: for even their women did change the natural use into that which is against nature:

And likewise also the men, leaving the natural use of the woman, burned in their lust one toward another; men with men working that which is unseemly, and receiving in themselves that recompence of their error which was meet.

And even as they did not like to retain God in their knowledge, God gave them over to a reprobate mind, to do those things which are not convenient; "

Romans 1:26-28

Free love for all... including children

Sweden had a leading role in breaking the old Christian norms regarding sexuality, mainly through its movie industry which produced several feature-length films that included scenes of full nudity and even actual intercourse. Movies such as *I am curious (yellow)* from 1967 and *They call us misfits* from 1968 both featured such scenes, and still today, one is shocked at what they contain. For example, in one scene in *I am curious (yellow)*, the lead actress Lena is on the floor having intercourse with her boyfriend, when they suddenly burst into a fight and scream profanities at each other as they don't hide any parts of their bodies. Lena then hysterically runs out of the room and slams the door behind her; the depravity is all-encompassing.

The sexual revolution is often said to have been the liberation of the female gender, though even as a male observer, it's hard to see in what way they became liberated when what it would mostly result in was men taking advantage of women while they're still young, to then discard them as they've grown too old for their men's taste. Women were reduced to objects instead of the life-long partners in marriage they were before.

Sexual moralism may not strike that much of a chord with today's 'liberated' (depraved is more like it) western audience, but the consequences of this transformation of sexuality should provide food for thought even for advocates of unrestricted non-binding free sexuality between consenting adults - you see, very soon after this movement had established itself, children as well became the targets of the lust of these 'liberated' people.

Loosening of the legal framework

Prior to the 1970's, though pornography was legal to produce, child pornography wasn't, and there was a punishable offence called incest. 15 was the age of consent, and an adult having intercourse with a person under that age would be sentenced to prison. During the 70's, the sexual liberation movement would attempt to change all of this. More than anyone else, Social Democrat Minister of Justice Lennart Geijer, who had assumed the position in 1969, would be the one that spearheaded this struggle. In 1971, production and distribution of child pornography became fully legal, though for now, the actual act of molesting a child was still illegal. Little was done to attempt to punish the perpetrators, however. On top of this, the sale of pornographic magazines also became legal in any store, and many a parent had to cover the eyes of their children as they walked past the magazine stands. Christian groups attempted to fight this new development, but theirs was a waning existence with ever less say in public affairs as time went by.

In the view of Geijer and the people of this movement, sexual intercourse between adults and children shouldn't be a crime at all. In 1971, Geijer had launched something called *Sexualbrottsutredningen*, "the Sex crimes inquiry," to propose changes to existing legislation. As he writes in the directive to this inquiry:

> "Prejudices and taboos have long restrained a natural and open view of sexuality and its manifestations. A radical change in perspective has however appeared lately."

The work on this inquiry and the public debate around it would take years, but in 1976, a Government bill was finally produced called "Sexual abuse: Proposal for a new wording of the regulations in the penal code on sexual offences" (SOU 1976:9).

The 233 page inquiry had among other things this to say on sex with minors:

"The sex crimes inquiry deems it necessary for the 15 year age limit to be changed. The inquiry has considered the possibility of dispensing with an age limit and instead express the penalized act in terms of excesses but has found that this cannot be practically accomplished. Instead the inquiry proposes that the current age limit is lowered to 14 years and an option for courts to not pass judgement in **insignificant cases** is created."[1]

Hence, they wanted to make it legal for an adult to have a sexual intercourse with a child of any age, as long as the act couldn't be described as an excess, though this intent had to be dropped. The inquiry also called for the removal of incest as a crime. "The inquiry has found that the genetic and ethical reasons that are usually referred to to support the regulations on incest do not have any force to speak of." It's quite shocking how they can describe a case of child molestation as potentially insignificant. The age limit for the crime sexual exploitation of a minor was going to be lowered from 15 to 10; the term rape would be reserved for brutal cases of sexual assault, while the "woman gets drunk and loses her bearings" would count as a mild form of sexual coercion instead. Just about everything was going to be decriminalized unless it involved violence or coercion.

The gay lobby RFSL was a participant in this inquiry, and also a work group within the RFSL called *Pedofila Arbetsgruppen*, PAG, "the Paedophile Work Group."[2] The PAG referred to the proposed changes in legislation as "children's right to [their] sexuality," and if their suggestions had become law, no sexual intercourse between adults and children would have been illegal had it not involved violence or threats. Old men would have

1   SOU 1976:9, page 18

2   Riksföreningen stödcentrum mot incest

been allowed to approach children in playgrounds, offered them some candy and brought them home to their apartments to exploit.

Thankfully, this proposal wasn't received well at all by the people at large, it was widely protested and had to be entirely scrapped. This wasn't the only area in which Minister of Justice Geijer was a radical; he was an opponent of the use of incarceration as a punishment for crime in general, wanting to rehabilitate criminals instead. He felt just about all crime was the product of either psychological disorders or a bad upbringing. During his time as minister, 'open prisons' were introduced, that more resemble motels than penitentiaries, as well as half-time release into parole - convicts would only have to serve half their formal sentences. Geijer was a supporter of something called legal positivism, which unlike natural law gives society the right to legislate the way it sees fit, irrespective of any natural rights people might feel they're born with. This was manifested in the 1974 abortion law that made it possible to imprison doctors who refused to perform abortions; law was used to prevent conscientious objection instead of punishing actual crime.

Child molesters

Throughout the 1970's, child pornography had flourished in Sweden, being legally considered an essential part of society's freedom of speech. Magazines and movies of the Lolita sort depicted children having intercourse with adults, and if these productions were only sold in sex stores, they were indirectly promoted through regular pornography magazines in newspaper stands, magazines in which the child pornography was advertised. Sweden became such a centre for child pornography that a large portion of the world's consumption of this filth was imported from this country. The smut paradise the Social Democrats had erected wouldn't last forever, however - in 1976, a centrist Government took away power from the dominant party for the first time in 40

227

years, and they didn't share the sexual radicalism of the socialists. Eventually this led to legislation on child pornography, making production and distribution illegal from 1 January 1980, punishable with up to six months in prison. Possession of the same would remain legal for two more decades, however.

The new law drove the filth underground, though it certainly didn't kill it, especially since the VCR arrived during the 1980's, and it became possible for people to copy video tapes in their own homes, as well as shoot productions themselves if they afforded camcorders. In 1982, the Social Democrats regained power in the country, and the actual enforcement of the new law wasn't given much priority. American police requested Swedish authorities to do more about the matter, but they might as well have been speaking to a wall. In 1988, US authorities seized no less than 2,000 deliveries of child pornography from Sweden, but when Minister of Justice Laila Freivalds was asked about it, she felt the business was insignificant.

A favourite destination of the paedophiles was Thailand. Old Swedish men frequently went there with camcorders, paid children to engage them in sexual acts and taped the sessions. Then when they returned home, they made copies of the tapes and sold for profit to other paedophiles. Other countries had attempted to put an end to such activities through international law enforcement agencies such as the Interpol, but Swedish authorities weren't interested in participating. Swedish paedophiles on the other hand had well-developed networks across much of Europe, channels through which they distributed their productions, and also went on tours across Europe with their under-aged sex slaves, offering them to their associates. Unlike Sweden, these other countries did take advice from American police on how to combat child pornography, and as the 90's came, Sweden stood pretty much alone in its nonchalance towards the business.

Public opinion in Sweden did however manage to get the politicians involved eventually, especially after a couple of highly publicized busts of child pornography rings in the early 90's. The Social Democrats lost power once again in 1991, and the new centrist Government resumed work on the matter. It was as if society had stood still in the same spot as it was when the last centrist Government had left off when it lost power nine years earlier. The next couple of years saw grandstanding by politicians on both sides of the political spectrum, bickering over just which party was serious in its fight against child pornography. Little headway was made into establishing legislation to criminalize possession or allocating more police resources to the matter, however. It's somewhat hard to understand how the Social Democrats could criticize the Bildt Government, when they had had so much time earlier to do something about it. Nevertheless, the opportunity to change the protections the constitution granted possession of child pornography by 1995 was lost amidst quarrelling between the Social Democrats and the Government.

All that had been accomplished in the first half of the 1990's was a couple of internationally applauded announcements that Sweden would now spearhead the fight against child pornography. In typical Swedish manner, many words were spoken, but little action was made. The police authorities even avoided dealing seriously with the matter of sex tourism to Thailand, claiming cooperation with that country's authorities wasn't possible. Other European countries experienced no such obstacles on the other hand.

The state helps produce child pornography and then distributes it

A 57-year-old man had in 1985 become an assistant of the social services in a Stockholm suburb, helping out troubled families with their children. He's still young at heart, fond of movies and computer games, which in the eyes of the municipality had made him a suitable candidate for the task. The boys are very happy to spend time with him and play with his toys, and the old man is also openly intimate and cordial with the children that come into his home. The next couple of years, the municipality sends plenty of boys his way, and the man starts to produce child pornography with the sophisticated equipment he's got, selling it through postal orders to both Swedish and international customers.

Eventually another man joins his business venture - a man born in 1954, who worked as a youth leader and had earlier been convicted of sexual abuse against minors. This younger man is a globetrotter, frequenting orphanages in the third world and supplying children there with new clothes. He also seizes the opportunity to molest these children and record it. Now he had found a partner in crime to facilitate better distribution of his productions. These men were doing pretty fine in their business, able to have access to new children all the time. Something would thwart their plans, however; the German police had busted a man who had bought child pornography, and two of the sellers were Swedes. The Germans contact the Swedish police, who start an investigation.

In something that would later be called *Huddingehärvan*, directly translated as "the Huddinge skein," the two men are arrested in 1992 and their houses are searched. The police uncover 160 video tapes and movies along with equipment to copy and edit productions, as well as lists of customers and transactions. Now the police have a solid case on their hands. They find that the customers have been able to make requests for what kind of abuse the children was going to be put through. The younger man had plenty of photos of naked boys from his trips around the globe, apart from the produced video material.

In a sane society, the actions of these men would have earned them quite harsh sentences, but when they now go to court, the younger man is sentenced to four months in prison, while the older one is sentenced to six; there was naturally a public outrage about the sentences being too lenient, even if the older man got the maximum possible. A few years earlier, a man had received the same sentence, six months, for 'hate speech.' Naturally, expressing disrespect for another religion demands the same sentence as molesting children.

This wasn't the end of this affair, however. Under Swedish law, evidence used in courts has to be made available to the public unless the law specifically permits classifying the material. In this case, as the public learns that the evidence material consists of child pornography, journalists and paedophiles start requesting copies of the material. The standard fee is 500 crowns per video tape, or about $65, which is cheaper than the typical prices such productions are sold at.

Agnetha Almqvist at the Stockholm district court refuses to provide copies of the tapes, citing that the material could be spread even further if the court sold copies of it; a journalist named Robert Aschberg appeals this decision to an appeals court, *Svea hovrätt*, which states that the Stockholm district court has no legal right to keep the material classified, and orders it to comply with the requests.[1] Robert is the grandson of Olof Aschberg, a Jewish banker who helped finance the Russian revolution, and in his youth, Robert was a Maoist. Later in life he would be one of the founders of the 'anti-racist' Swedish magazine Expo, whose

---

1   Christina Hagner - Rätten att kränka ett barn, page 77

contributors have included several violent left-wing extremists.

But to return to the matter at hand. One company initially files a request for copies of all the video tapes involved in the case, but when the names of the people requesting copies are made public, the owner of the company takes back the request. Before it's all over, the court has received requests for copies from 169 different people, including incarcerated child molesters who would be able to watch the tapes on the VCR's in their prison cells. Overwhelmed by the unusual load of requests, the court decides it's going to display the tapes inside the actual courtroom, with free admission to anyone who wants to watch the material. On 17 May 1993, Sweden becomes most likely the only country in the world in which a judicial court has provided a screening of child pornography to the public. Demonstrators walk around with signs outside the courtroom, however, and few people actually enter the court to watch the tapes.

In this mess, sane voices within the Swedish legal system emerge - an inquiry is made into revising the regulation concerning secrecy which if hastily processed would let the court refuse to provide copies from 15 June and onwards. The police officers that have been given the task of producing the copies of the material intentionally procrastinate the work to make as few copies as possible, and by the time the date has hit 15 June, very few copies have been made. Paedophiles angrily protest to newspapers that they're going to molest new children instead now that they've been denied access to this material.

Possession of child pornography illegal... by 1999

Until 1 January 1995, the government could confiscate illegal weapons the police came across during house searches in other errands, but it couldn't confiscate child pornography. On several occasions, searching the homes of suspected drug

232

offenders uncovered such material, but the police wasn't legally allowed to seize it. The centrist government that lost power in 1994 had however left a bill that made confiscations possible by 1995, yet criminalizing possession would take another couple of years. This year, the term length for the parliament and Government had increased from three to four years, hence the next election wouldn't be until 1998. To change the constitution, majority votes in two different parliaments are required, and this meant that the earliest possible date to criminalize had now become 1 January 1999.

By now, the opinion was so outspoken against child pornography that the politicians couldn't quarrel any more, and the changes became law by that date. The new Social Democrat Government of '94 was still not all that keen on allocating resources for the new child pornography police unit, however, in spite of the arrival of the Internet and the expected rise in criminal activity. Due to a decision by Minister of Justice Laila Freivalds in 1995, the police had to make do with the limited resources at their disposal for some time more. By the time the afore-mentioned Örebro paedophile made the headlines, possession was still legal, but this case more than any other cemented public disgust with such activities that the authorities just couldn't dodge cooperating with international law enforcement any longer, and available resources seem adequate these days.

Prostitution and crime infiltrates government

By the 1970's, the capital of Stockholm alone had some 200 porn clubs and brothels, and since both buying and selling sex was legal, prostitution was open in the streets as well. Perhaps indicative of what a haven for prostitution the country had become is the fact that many young women, including under-aged ones, were trafficked to Sweden to walk the streets for their pimps. Functional police vice squads were but a memory - sex was seen as a commodity you traded like any other. Narcotics had become quite prevalent as well in a country that formerly had had a fierce anti-drug stance, rooted in Christian sobriety and the sports movement. Society was quickly going downhill as a consequence of liberal morality.

Some people had gotten started early in this. In 1958, Lennart Geijer, later Minister of Justice, was a lawyer in his late 40's at the trade union TCO and was also married. This marriage was somewhat open, and with the apparent consent of his wife, he started seeing an 18-year-old woman named Lillemor Östlin. Lillemor had dropped out of school after eight grade and her living conditions were questionable, supporting herself through drug sales and prostitution. Geijer helps support this woman in exchange for sexual services, in essence using her as a prostitute in a courtesan-like relationship. Lillemor also has a relationship with a drug-dealer at the same time, but this didn't appear to concern Geijer too much.

It does appear as if Geijer attempted to get Lillemor to stay out of trouble, but he would soon find himself in over his head with a woman who while writing her memoirs the other year, *Hinsehäxan*, bragged that she's spent more time behind bars than any other woman in Sweden, some 20 years. In August of 1967,

Lillemor was convicted of arbitrary conduct, forgery and cheque fraud and sentenced to a year in prison. Geijer attempts to use his influence, now as a minister without portfolio, in getting Lillemor paroled. He is however alone in having any sympathy for Lillemor and her case, and she's sent to prison. A year later, in September of 1968, Lillemor is convicted of drug crimes and fencing to one year and two months.

After getting out the next time, she's convicted of forgery and minor drug charges and sentenced to yet another ten months. By now, Geijer had become Minister of Justice, and his dealings with this woman became known to the police when they after searching her apartment in November of 1970 found a telephone book with his personal phone number. This matter reaches all the way to the top of *Rikspolisstyrelsen* (RPS), the Swedish equivalent of the FBI, which was founded in 1964 and had since then been headed by a man named Carl Persson.

Carl Persson was a man of firm convictions and a traditional view on crime prevention, which naturally put him on a collision course with his de facto boss - Geijer. Geijer had announced that the prisons were to be purged of all but the most dangerous inmates and replaced with rehabilitation programs. He's quoted as saying he wanted to bring the number of inmates down from 4,000 to about 700, and he wasn't that much of a friend of private property either - his view was that if someone needed something, that person could just steal it from someone who didn't need it.

This affair, brought to Persson's desk almost as soon as Geijer had taken office, would be the start of a sour relationship between him and Geijer. As a consequence of Geijer's dealings with this woman, Persson had sent a memo to Prime Minister Palme, describing Geijer as a security risk. For now, Geijer was forced to end the relationship with Lillemor, who had reached the age of 30 and was incarcerated most of the time. This would be far from the only time Geijer socialized with organized crime and society's outcasts.

Geijer and organized crime

If Geijer hadn't embarrassed himself enough through the affair with Lillemor, he'd now outdo himself. In 1974, a mother of two young children, let's call her Jane, had been employed as a secretary assistant at the same office where Geijer worked - *Statsrådsberedningen*, the Prime Minister's office. Apart from this, she was also working as a lay assessor for the Social Democrats in Södertälje, a politically appointed position, as well as teaching prison inmates job skills through the Swedish ABF - "the Workers' Educational Association." In this job, Jane came across hardened criminals, including a Baltic immigrant she'd fall madly in love with.

This man in his late 30's, whom I will refer to as John, had been convicted of crimes over and over ever since his teens and was incarcerated at Hall, one of Sweden's highest security prisons; yet now he had managed to impress the prison authorities that he had left his criminal life behind him and was doing academic studies inside the walls. He even held classes under the umbrella of the same ABF, where he met Jane. Though Jane was married, she now divorced her husband and moved in with John in August of 1975, shortly after he had been paroled from prison. Due to his good behaviour, the justice system had cut ten months off his sentence, ultimately approved by Minister of Justice Geijer. Back in 1973, he had been sentenced for forgery, fencing, illegal possession of weapons, attempted grand larceny and drug charges to two years and five months in prison.

When mass media learned that this John had a relationship with a secretary at Geijer's office, rumours started emerging that this connection had something to do with the parole. And John

236

would soon prove the trust of the justice system in him misplaced, as he went right back to crime as soon as he was released. That summer, John started smuggling large quantities of narcotics from continental Europe to Sweden, into a warehouse he presided over, to be distributed across the country from that location. The police monitor the activities and are shocked to learn that the culprit behind them is someone with connections in the Prime Minister's office. This web of drug smuggling with branches in several European countries wasn't just some insignificant tourism, and the police are confident that Jane must know what John is up to.

On 11 August 1976, the police finally attempt to bust John in the act of handing over roughly 50 kg of amphetamine at his warehouse, but he manages to escape them. The next day, Jane is arrested on suspicions of complicity in the drug trade. Her signature is on quite a few contracts for warehouses and car leases, and she's followed John on trips throughout Europe, though she maintains that both she and her fiancé are innocent. The arrest at the Prime Minister's office in the middle of the election campaign naturally makes headlines, and the right-wing opposition blasts the Government for allowing this to take place.

Somehow John mysteriously found reason to go into hiding the very day he was supposed to be arrested, and he eludes the police for a year or two before being incarcerated again. Olof Palme, Prime Minister at the time, would later relate how Jane had reached out to lots of people at this office to get John paroled, though Jane was ultimately freed of any wrongdoing and was given new employment by the party afterwards. Such is Swedish justice.

Doris Hopp, the lesbian brothel manager

Some time in the early 1960's, a woman named Doris Hopp had started organizing a call-girl enterprise through her connections with both young women at bars where she had worked and the more well-established members of society she had come into contact with from the rise in standing she had gone through as a consequence of a marriage with a German businessman; the affluent clients would contact her for their sexual needs, and she'd then call up a suitable woman that best matched their requests. Shortly after Hopp had married the businessman, he had passed away and left her with a sizeable inheritance. Though the enterprise often involved clients who were married with children, the authorities hardly bothered with it at all, due to the spirit of the time. The procuring part of the business was illegal, but neither selling nor buying sex from adults was.

For all of the 60's, her business went well, seemingly with little friction. She often went as far as to show off the prostitutes in her farm at nightclubs to attract customers. Eventually, however, some of her clients would request younger girls than what was legal. Though the legal age for intercourse was 15 years, you were charged with seduction of a minor if you purchased sex from someone below the age of 18. It never became known just how many girls under 18 she managed, but in 1974, she would take into her farm two girls who were even below the legal age of 15.

As the call-girl operation later came under police surveillance when the security police (SÄPO) learned that certain military officers made use of Hopp's enterprise, the communication between Hopp and both her prostitutes and clients was recorded on tape. These are two quite explicit phone calls she had with clients, discussing the girls in Hopp's farm:

D = Doris; C = Client (sound quality of the tapes was poor - my best attempt at interpreting)

D: She's younger than Martha and I think she looks like s***.

C: If she's that f***ing ugly I'm not going to f*** her.

D: She's no hooker either, eww... I've seen her naked, she looks like a plucked fowl.

C: I was about to say that, that it's a little like a newly shot crow.

D: Exactly - thin f***ing thighs and big knees. Well, you know - it's probably good with slender ones, but their flesh shouldn't be loose, that's what I hate the most.

If her extreme use of profanity wasn't bad enough, the objectification of the girls was unheard of, as she discussed them with her clients:

"D: I'll bring a small bag, I've got that here at home, but I had... Saga was with him last week.

C: Yeah.

D: And that was great. I like Saga in that way, you know. But you know, now I don't know how this one will do.

C: Yes, but Saga... Will Saga do then?

D: Yeah, I like that. I've told you before.

C: Yeah.

D: You know, I'm a lesbian, so I like her, you know.

C: Yeah, but does she like you?

D: F*** yeah! Yikes, she was in the shape of her life the other day, last week.

C: Oh s***.

D: It was at her house. But I don't think this will work just like that... I don't think, I don't know, you know. It's not my type. She's too young, you know.

C: So how old is she?

D: 17... 18. Large breasts, nice body and hips. But I don't really like that kid. I look at them, but... If I'm going to have a young girl it must be a really filthy chick. She can't look like a marzipan pig, you know, that's what I hate the most. You know, high cheeks and pink skin, that's what I hate the most.

C: She'd better know what it's about too.

D: They should have a bit of gypsy blood in them, you know... Somewhat filthy 17 or 16, that's nice.

C laughs

D: (inaudible) stand there jacking off while I talk"

(Doris was 45 years old at the time of these telephone conversations.)

It was never investigated just which people made use of the callgirl enterprise, though it's estimated that she had around 40 girls in her farm. The clients numbered in the hundreds, including military officers, employees of the justice system, business leaders and even ministers of Government. Hopp had two phones in her apartment - one for incoming calls from clients, and one for calling up the girls. The operation was a full-time job, though it appears to have been worth it in that it netted Hopp several million crowns between the early 60's and the time of her arrest in 1976. Sometimes she also took requests for lesbian action between herself and a girl in her farm, with the client sitting there watching and 'entertaining' himself.

240

Two 14-year-olds

A 13-year-old girl named Eva, whose parents had split up and were living in different parts of the country, had lived with her mother but not gotten along too well with her; she kept running away from home as well as arguing with teachers in early 1974, until the child welfare authorities put her in an orphanage on 17 June - *Ulvsunda*. Eva was quite messy and rebellious, lagging behind in emotional development for her age. People around her said she looked more like 12 than the 14 years she really was. Though she was hard to manage during daytime, the staff found that they could calm Eva down and get her to go to sleep without too much difficulty by reading her lullabies, which often made her suck her thumb. Eva was also fond of the stuffed animal toys she kept in her bed, and her contact at the authorities described her as precocious one moment, childish the next.

A month later, on 25 July, a cousin of hers arrives at the same orphanage and they naturally spend time together. Unlike Eva, her cousin would never make a public appearance, hence she won't be named here. Eva and the cousin are very different people - though about the same age, the cousin appears to be mature beyond her years instead. Both of them had in common that they were looking to see more of the world than the orphanage, and soon they discover the easiest way a young girl can earn herself quick cash - prostitution. Shortly after Eva had reached the age of 14, she offers her body in exchange for money, though any deeper significance of sexual intercourse eludes her - it's simply a way she can get the means to purchase expensive clothes for herself. Eva and her cousin both also start doing amphetamine some time during this period.

Soon enough, a man named Sigvard Hammar, a journalist

working for among other employers tabloid *Expressen* and the state TV, bought sexual services from the two. Hammar was also a client of Doris Hopp, and it was at Hammar's apartment that the two girls met the brothel mother. Hopp is overenthusiastic in getting them to join her farm and she offers them both cash and narcotics in exchange for serving the men she hooks them up with.

Now Eva and her cousin both have a sizeable regular income, though Hopp still tricks them away of most of the money. They don't save any of it, however, but instead go shopping every time they're able to. The staff at the orphanage soon become suspicious of how the girls can afford these things. When asked, they say it's from babysitting, and Hopp often calls the orphanage and asks for them - saying she's got 'babysitting' jobs for them. Hopp often arranges for a taxi to pick them up right at the orphanage, and the glamour of this isn't lost on the two girls who had never even been inside taxis before. The clients don't exactly mind Eva's young age - she's even showing them her public transport card that you got if you were under the age of 15, which Hopp had instructed her to do.

Eva does however start to feel dirty, the psychological impact of the prostitution is taking its toll on her. She tells Hopp that she wants to pull out of it, but Hopp doesn't want to let her go. As she tells *Sveriges Radio* later in life:

> "When you've taken a taxi you felt like you were a grown-up... but you knew where you were going, and it was terribly hard when you were getting off. You knew you were going to them. You didn't know who they were. You didn't know anything. You knew what you were going to do. It was incredibly hard... It was terrible."

> "It was a slippery slope you went into, it wasn't voluntary after that. It might have been the first one or two times, but then it wasn't."

"Only wanted to go home, wanted to forget it all. It was like a rat race, you couldn't get out, since she threatened you."

For now, the matter with these 14-year-olds was over since they were out of the picture when Hopp was arrested in 1976. Eva had been transferred to another orphanage by now - *Eknäs*. As the investigation into Hopp's enterprise was extended, they would return to the affair, however.

Doris Hopp is busted

During the cold war, the Eastern bloc often had an advantage as far as intelligence agencies went. While the Communists were more or less puritans and discipline in the matter of sexual relations was given, Western politicians and officials were often prone to decadence. In 1963, John Profumo, the then British Secretary State of War, had had an extramarital affair with a prostitute named Christian Kessler, who was also the mistress of a Russian spy. Hence it appeared as if the Soviets had been able to infiltrate the British government. As Britain was America's foremost ally within the NATO, this had caused the CIA great concern, and subsequently they had started monitoring the dealings politicians in Western Europe had with prostitution.

In the early 1970's, both the Swedish security service SÄPO and the CIA are alleged to have been witnessing the Eastern bloc countries sneaking young women into the prostitution business, with these women also regularly meeting up with their respective embassies. With the Profumo affair still fresh in memory, they naturally understood what was going on and began to keep track of just which people made use of the services of the prostitutes. To their shock, they found that prominent politicians and military officers were among the clients, including a certain Lennart Geijer.

One person seemed to be in a league of her own as far as the scale of the operation of this business was concerned - Doris Hopp. The way she ran her business, by simply hooking up clients and prostitutes and only occasionally providing quarters for the activity, meant it had gone below the radar for a long time, in spite of procuring being a crime. In 1976, the regular police had gotten wind of what was going on as well, and they started watching

Hopp's apartment as well as wire-tapping her phone calls. The two police officers assigned to the task, Ove Sjöstrand and Morgan Svensson, find that Hopp is on the phone almost 24/7, setting up meetings or simply having longer conversations with the clients.

It doesn't take long for the police to uncover evidence of illegal procuring, though they have to endure going through highly repulsive dialogues. On 11 May 1976, the police arrest Doris Hopp on strong suspicions and take her into custody. Sjöstrand and Svensson start interrogating Hopp, who's initially very accommodating and downplays the seriousness of her crimes. When Sjöstrand brings up the fact that her stable of prostitutes has included underage girls and that she's provided them with narcotics, the interrogation suddenly turns sour and Hopp isn't cooperative any more. Prosecutor Erik Östberg, who's in charge of the investigation, directs the police officers to only examine the procuring case, saying that's enough to reach a conviction. Östberg shows no interest in adding sexual exploitation of minors to the charges, and he also insists in a highly unusual move that the names of the clients won't be entered into the investigation, since that would reveal their identities to the public. The full names and contact details of the prostitutes are entered on the other hand. Sjöstrand and Svensson are told to rename the clients "client #1" and so on.

When Hopp is arrested, Östberg goes on sick leave and a prosecutor by the name of Torsten Wolff takes over, with Östberg now and then returning to dictate the way to deal with certain things. Some of the prostitutes stated that Östberg had been one of their clients, though this is never investigated.[1] During the time in custody, Hopp has been in high spirits, receiving flowers to her cell from all her acquaintances, and she also mentions that she's

_____

1   Source: *Makten, männen, mörkläggningen* page 151, as well as Carl Persson's memorandum to Olof Palme, 1976

going to publish her memoirs, mostly about her prostitution business, stretching some 500 pages. The prostitutes who testify aren't in very high spirits, on the other hand - as their personal identities are entered on the public record, they become the targets of anonymous threats and they're suddenly wary of revealing any more names.

On 26 June, the trial takes place with Wolff in charge of the prosecution. On 29 June, Hopp is sentenced for *gross procuring* to two years in prison and to a fine of 200,000 crowns. Through her lawyer Leif Silbersky, she appeals the verdict the next day in the hope of getting the charge changed to only *procuring* and having the sentence reduced. Now police officer Ove Sjöstrand locates the under-aged Eva at the orphanage where she lives and meets up with her. Up until this point, Eva hadn't been included in the investigation, and Sjöstrand is taken aback when he notices that she, in spite of having gone into prostitution as far back as two years earlier, still has no female forms and behaves like a child. Eva talks about the men she's served as a prostitute, and Sjöstrand is very surprised when he learns of one name in particular - Prime Minister Olof Palme. Since this information is simply too sensational and Eva is still only a child, he doesn't quite believe her but still attempts to be understanding in his dealings with her.

Through a bit of effort on the part of Sjöstrand, he manages to get now returned prosecutor Torsten Wolff to include fornication with minors in the charges, and the two 14-year-olds are called to testify. In the courtroom, one of them is cross-examined by Hopp's lawyer Silbersky, who alleges that she herself was the one that sought out Hopp due to requiring an income for her narcotics addiction. When Doris Hopp learns of the new charges and realizes she might face six years in prison, she drops her appeal and willingly starts serving her sentence, which the prosecution can't do anything about since this party hadn't appealed the original verdict. Due to the half-time release in effect

246

at this time, Hopp only has to suffer a year of incarceration.

When searching Hopp's home, the police had found a book with the names and phone numbers of all the prostitutes and plenty of clients. The names of the prostitutes have marks next to them signifying what kind of inclination they can satisfy. Hopp also kept a diary of all the occasions when she had met people in her house as a part of her enterprise, and for the period the prosecution covered, these numbered no less than 1,112. Nevertheless, prosecutor Östberg had not shown any interest in making anything out of this incriminating evidence.

Sigvard Hammar, who had hooked up the two 14-year-olds with Doris Hopp, is the only client that ever faces prosecution, being sentenced to six months probation for procuring. Though he admitted to having had sexual intercourse with Eva, he's not charged with fornication with minors since he declared he didn't know she was under the legal age of 15.

A scandal emerges, and a memorandum is written

The trial against Doris Hopp in 1976 becomes a hot topic in mass media at the same time as the political parties prepare for the autumn's election. Far from everything about the affair has reached the public eye, but what has, has sparked a seemingly insatiable demand to learn more, and there's plenty of gossip about just who has been a client of Hopp. Still at this time, the only name that has become public is Sigvard Hammar, and just about everyone is curious just who the rest are. Gossip magazines start offering the prostitutes money if they can reveal the identities of some of the clients, and Hopp herself makes it known that she will be quite candid in her memoirs. When Hopp drops the appeal of her sentence, curiosity reaches even new heights.

The security service SÄPO has also informed national police commissioner Carl Persson that some of the girls in Hopp's stable belong to the Polish intelligence service, and that they've been seen meeting up with foreign ambassadors. This apparently has Persson worried beyond belief, because in August of that year, he starts writing a memorandum he's going to hand over to Prime Minister Olof Palme about his concerns. Here he mentions that Hopp has claimed that Lennart Geijer has been one of her clients, and also lists several other names in politics and public administration, such as the leader of the Centre party, Thorbjörn Fälldin, as well as vice speaker of the parliament Cecilia Nettelbrandt, with which Hopp is alleged to have had a homosexual relationship. Persson fears that the dignitaries that have made use of the prostitutes could become victims of blackmail, considering this a security issue.

He also reports that Communist newspapers are hot on the trail, looking to unravel a scandal whose magnitude could

248

potentially put the country on the brink of revolution. He ends the memorandum by summarizing his information in ten statements, which include:

> "5) that for the sake of security, it must be made clear who within the National Police Board that's included among the clients

> 6) that the prosecutor who periodically has been in charge of the case but gone on sick leave afterwards appears to be among the clients

> 7) that the legal handling appears remarkable due to among other things that one hasn't specifically investigated and tried the matter of prosecution concerning the intercourse with the 14-year-olds"

Finally, Persson urges Palme to establish an investigative commission to examine the security issues and to review the legal handling of the case. The memorandum itself is signed 20 August 1976. By the end of August, the election campaign is in full swing, but when Persson contacts Palme to hand over the memorandum, he agrees to meet up with him swiftly, bringing his campaign director Thage Peterson with him. Palme now reads the document, but doesn't bother following Persson's suggestions. Instead he orders Peterson to make a quick investigation, which in a couple of days, as Palme would later state, proved that it was all 'nonsense.' The legal procedure when you receive a memorandum of this kind is to register it in the Prime Minister's office, but Palme doesn't acknowledge having been given it, merely storing it away in a locked safe there.

On 19 September 1976, the election is held and the Social Democrats lose power for the first time in 40 years. On 7 October, Thorbjörn Fälldin becomes the new Prime Minister, and Palme hands him the memorandum, hence it's now out of his hands. Neither Fälldin registers it, and the only action in what would later become known as the Geijer affair now takes place in mass media

249

- Hopp has started serving her sentence, and there's no further investigation into the matter.

The truth is out... and is denied

A journalist named Peter Bratt had back in 1973 exposed a covert Swedish intelligence agency called IB, the Information Bureau, which spied on the Swedish people and kept files over political sympathies, its operation very much in the hands of the Social Democrats. It turned out that IB was also cooperating with foreign intelligence agencies, and the people on which it kept files numbered in the hundreds of thousands. For disclosing this classified information, the government had convicted Bratt of espionage and he had spent a year in prison. Now in 1977 it was time for him to strike again. Bratt had recently been employed by *Dagens Nyheter*, and the newspaper was pressuring him to come up with a journalistic scoop.

Bratt had in conjunction with this employment taken a course in economic crime, and here he met Leif G.W. Persson, a young man about the same age who was working at the National Police Board. They had connected with each other and kept in touch even after this course, and during November of that year, this collaboration would result in a scandal of almost the same magnitude as the earlier IB affair. Bratt had started investigating the old Hopp affair, and was surprised that no one was charged with fornication with minors in spite of it being evident that some of the girls had been underage. At first he contacts prosecutor Wolff, but he's not interested in talking to Bratt, so next he turns to his friend Persson, to see what information he would be able to divulge.

In this, Bratt had hit jackpot, since Persson was a close associate of National Police Commissioner Carl Persson and had been present when he composed his memorandum. Still at this time, only a handful of people knew about the memorandum,

251

though this other Persson was almost eager to reveal its existence to a journalist. The accounts of Bratt and Persson about what happens next are in dispute, but after Bratt has called up Persson in the middle of November, 1977, Bratt is informed about the existence of the memorandum, and that Lennart Geijer is one of the names mentioned. Persson takes for granted that his anonymity is respected when he's talking to this journalist, but soon he would find himself in the crossfire from having divulged this information.

Persson now walks over to his boss Carl Persson and tells him that Bratt somehow knows about the memorandum, which comes as a shock to him; Bratt on the other hand starts working on a newspaper article from the limited information he's got and has his editor-in-chief somewhat reluctantly approve it. Bratt calls up Persson once again too, to confirm the validity of what he's writing in the article. Then he can't wait to tell the other staff at DN that his source stood right next to National Police Commissioner Carl Persson as he confirmed it all.

On 18 November, *Dagens Nyheter* publishes Bratt's article, and the cat is out of the bag. Here he makes the claim that in a memorandum from Carl Persson to Palme, six names had been listed as suspected of having made use of the services of prostitutes, and that now former Minister of Justice Lennart Geijer was one of them; he also alleges that Persson had warned Palme about Geijer's dealing with prostitutes already back in 1969. The article generates enormous controversy, and both other mass media and the political establishment ask the questions: What does Bratt know, and how does he know it?

Olof Palme responds in the same newspaper on 20 November, calling the information "Loose gossip, supplemented with distortions, insinuations, lies and damned fiction," as well as saying that he never received any such memorandum. As for Bratt,

Palme refers to journalists of his kind as "mange-infested rats with yellow tusks and naked tails." The tabloids *Aftonbladet* and *Expressen* also interview officials that had been involved in the investigation and deny all the claims. Peter Bratt and DN suddenly find themselves under a heavy barrage.

Without any evidence to back up the article, DN quickly surrenders to the pressure and apologizes to Geijer as well as offering 50,000 crowns in damages. Geijer is repeatedly interviewed about the matter and laments what a shock the accusations had been, but that it now seemed to be over. Even though Bratt and DN have both been publicly embarassed at this point, this is not enough for some people; now they go after whoever leaked the information. *Aftonbladet* in particular puts effort into this task and assigns Jan Guillou to it. Guillou had just like Bratt also been imprisoned over the earlier IB affair, and he believes he can get Bratt to reveal his source.

After the article was published, establishment media has argued that this story has its origins in Carl Persson and his ideological differences with Geijer. They say that this was rumour-mongering on his part, to smear Geijer's good name. This is also the angle from which Guillou goes to work on Bratt. Both of them belonging on the far-left, Guillou tries to convince Bratt that he's been had by right-wingers, that they've used him to publish a fabricated story in order to ruin Geijer's reputation. Bratt starts to believe this, and now he contacts his friend Leif G.W. Persson again, the source for the article, with a tape recorder running. He discretely attempts to get Persson to acknowledge that he's the source, but Persson starts to become suspicious and Bratt doesn't get anything of value recorded after a 30 minutes long conversation. Still, he has mentioned to Guillou that Persson is the source, and now Guillou contacts him instead, trying to get him to spill the beans.

Guillou never finds any proof, so *Aftonbladet* is left with publicly calling for DN to reveal the source. At this time, DN is very much on the retreat, and soon enough the newspaper names Persson as the source. Due to Palme's strong influence in society even after not being Prime Minister any more, the pressure is strong on Carl Persson to resign as Palme accuses him of having disseminated rumours through his associate. Carl Persson is shocked at being treated this way after 35 years of loyal service in the justice system, and in December of 1977, he leaves his post vacant; Leif G.W. Persson is outright fired on the other hand.

It's not over just yet

On 3 May 1978, the story is revisited on the TV show *Studio S*, after among others a man named Janne Mattsson had researched the story and found out that most of Bratt's 1977 article was true, and that there had indeed been a memorandum. Mattsson would many years later also co-write a book about the Geijer affair. The parliament is once again called on to answer the accusations, and now for the first time they face critics with solid information. A week after the TV show, they assemble in the parliament to discuss this matter.

The parliamentary debate on 9 May 1978 started with the chairman of the Communist party, Carl-Henrik Hermansson, grilling Prime Minister Thorbjörn Fälldin and former Social Democratic leaders for taking part in the Bilderberg conferences. Then the main focus of the day is brought up: (What follows are only excerpts, though the portions between quotation marks are intact.)

"§ 7 About an investigation concerning the dealings of leading politicians with organized prostitution etc."

"Prime Minister THORBJÖRN FÄLLDIN:"

"It is true that then national police commissioner Carl Persson had delivered a memorandum on the subject to then Prime Minister Olof Palme. Concerning this matter, Olof Palme has spoken in an article on 20 November 1977 in *Dagens Nyheter*. In the article, one is reminded that, in connection to the police investigation concerning the so called brothel mom in Stockholm, there had flourished rumours about a number of well-known Swedes - among others government officials, ministers and prominent members of parliament - being clients of the brothel."

"It was at the time of the change of government that Olof Palme

255

handed over the memorandum in question to me. He told me at the same time that he had carried out certain research related to the memorandum and that he had concluded that there existed no basis for proceeding with the matter in the form of a special commission.

I - and afterwards also Minister of Justice Sven Romanus - partook of the contents of the memorandum. In a passage there was stated that the brothel mom had reported names of famous clients that she supposedly had had. A couple of examples were given. I could straight up establish a direct lie. You see, I found my own name included among the reported clients. I would here like to interject that I have no intention of contributing to improper spreading of rumours by reporting any of the other names."

"Our view became the same one as that of earlier Olof Palme: there was for the Government no basis for proceeding with the matter in the form of a special commission. In agreement herewith our view was that there was no need - to relate to Gunilla André's second question - for further investigation into the matter in accordance with statements made in mass media."

"OLOF PALME (s):

On Sunday 22 August 1976, then minister Thage Peterson and I were visited by national police commissioner Carl Persson and director general Åke Magnusson. That Sunday we held election campaign rallies in various parts of the country but headed to Stockholm for this urgent meeting. The national police commissioner then handed over to me the memorandum mentioned by Thorbjörn Fälldin and included a couple of comments as well. After the representatives of the police had dispersed, we made certain decisions.

Firstly we decided to keep the memorandum and its contents strictly confidential and inform at most an additional one or two people. The reason is obvious - certainly the statements didn't appear very credible, but if they emerged in the middle of an election campaign, they would have great political explosive power. Thorbjörn Fälldin has himself mentioned that he, when he was leader of the Opposition, was one of the names in the memorandum. We assessed it as such that he in the final stage of the election campaign wouldn't stand a chance of finding the time to dodge the accusations and rumours, no matter how unfounded they were. We didn't want to win any elections on such terms, we wanted the election campaign to be about the political issues."

I wonder if any politicians anywhere have made claims that were anywhere close to being this preposterous - who would believe that a politician wouldn't seize the opportunity to smash his opponent when he's given the chance? One is more likely to suspect that this had more to do with the rest of the memorandum, but at the time Palme spoke these words, the only validated information the public had was Fälldin's own admission about being on the list.

"If it is of any value, I can based on that completely exonerate Thorbjörn Fälldin from the accusations of collaboration with organized prostitution."

It's quite a wonder that in the last weeks of an election campaign, in spite of the memorandum supposedly only containing information that would hurt the Opposition, one would let one's own campaigning efforts be distracted? What jury would believe such a testimony? Also worth mentioning is the fact that Thage Peterson was named by some of the prostitutes as having been a client of theirs, perhaps not a very fit person to hold an investigation if so.

"One can, Mr Speaker, ask the question how rumours of this kind can emerge. [...] Unfortunately there's always a soil for malicious rumours. This is unfortunately nothing new either. There's always those who are willing to run with gossipy mouths, pretend to have special insight, make themselves special to their peers. Especially

257

pronounced is the preoccupation when it's about liquor, drugs, sexuality and financial improprieties. 'Have you heard?' they say. 'Have you heard that this one or that one has taken to the bottle, shot himself up, moved out and lives with someone else, cooked the books?' And then the lies are cemented in wider circles, and then the stench of ignorance and malice is spread."

A critical voice from the Communist party then questions Palme and Fälldin.

"JÖRN SVENSSON (vpk):

Mr Speaker! The Leftwing party the Communists is not interested in digging into personal gossip or private tragedies that lack personal relevance. To the extent such things exist we see it more as the consequence of bourgeois double-standards and a dishonest view of sexuality in society. What it now is about is the trust in government officials and politicians, in the workings of the justice system, in equality before the law and the chance for the common man to get his justice."

"Firstly: Top politicians should not only talk about spreading of rumours and how objectionable this is. They've known that this affair started surfacing already around 1970. Neither Olof Palme or Thorbjörn Fälldin have previously done anything to bring clarity."

"Both the criminal police and the security police have conducted extensive surveillance work. One has had the opportunity to elucidate all direct personal relationships. One has monitored locations. Can then, I ask, the relationships in all the 200 cases in circulation only be lies and slander? Can all the 70 people whose names have appeared in connection with the exploitation of under-age girls only be innocent victims of malicious rumours?"

"Fourthly: Why the secrecy around certain well-established people? The prostitutes for example aren't awarded the same concern. They're there for the public to see."

Per Gahrton, at the time of the Liberal People's Party, also offers critical words:

"PER GAHRTON (fp):

Mr Speaker! I was not going to speak my mind in this debate. Certainly, I feel very much sympathy for Thorbjörn Fälldin in his cornered position. But I'm also deeply disappointed in the debate in the way it's been done, and I simply consider it my duty as elected by a portion of the Swedish people to react."

"And in there lies the fundamental shortcoming in this way to put an end to the rumours. You can't validate yourself. You can't be the judge who judges himself innocent - no matter how certain you are of your own innocence. Therefore I'm deeply disappointed, because I had taken for granted that one from the side of the Prime Minister and the Government today would have informed us that one intended to undertake some form of impartial investigation of these accusations, which I certainly personally assume are untrue."

"All of the police and the security police have been on the case, and the police commissioner - no matter how you view him - has compiled a memorandum and delivered it. Then Thage Peterson from the campaign headquarters of the Social Democrats has made an investigation, and then one fully expects the Swedish people to believe that the matter is sufficiently investigated and made clear!"

Next, Olof Palme answers his critics:

"OLOF PALME (s):"

"I've never been afraid of taking such a responsibility. Therefore there's no reason to attack the police just because its commissioner walks over and delivers this memorandum. Then you've got to review this memorandum, and both Mr Thage Peterson and I are fully qualified to do this. When you then look at it and find that nothing in there is supported, but that it's only malicious rumours, one shouldn't out of some kind of cowardice and fear launch grand investigations and citizens' commissions. Snuff is snuff and nonsense is nonsense, even if in police memorandums - that is the simple truth.

Hence we found, after carefully examining the material, no reason whatsoever to give way. I consider it quite a crude attempt by people, associated with organized crime, to get away from their cornered position by spreading rumours around them - and then there will always be some Svenssons and Gahrtons who to the point of damnation stand up and say: "What if, there really is something to it! What if, the trust of the citizens demands an investigation!" Then they continue pushing the insinuations onwards to attempt to establish one commission after another. Then we need politicians who will put their feet down and say that this is nonsense and remains nonsense."

Some more speeches back and forth, then followed by a final speech by Palme:

"OLOF PALME (s):

Mr Speaker! For the sake or order I would like to once again point out that I already from the start distanced myself from the idea of a citizens' commission. It sure would have looked like something, if we one week before the election had established a citizens' commission relating to the spread of rumours concerning the leader of the Opposition. But completely disregarding this there was no factual basis for establishing any such thing, and if there's no factual basis, then you shouldn't."

"When push comes to shove, what this is about is trust. I'm not accused of anything here - on the contrary, it's my political opponents that are severely accused, and I have no ties whatsoever to them in this case - but I would still like to say that I'm disgusted by the ones who use the spreading of rumours and suspicions as a political weapon."

At this time, no one had verified that Lennart Geijer was on the list, and it would remain that way until the memorandum was declassified in 1991, hence Palme could take for granted that people would believe him when he said this. Palme most definitely had ties to his Minister of Justice Lennart Geijer, and in the speeches here, he keeps on lying.

> "When I said that the gentlemen are in possession of the matter, I forgot that the national police commissioner has retracted his memorandum... This special matter doesn't exist any more - that's correct. But I am, with my knowledge of human nature, convinced that new trash-talkers, new tell-tales and new rumour-mongers will appear. Rumours will be spread about if not this person, then that person. Then one has to keep one's head cool, reviewing what's actually been said and put one's foot down if it involves malice and shameful rumours and not facts."

I bet he could take for granted that new "rumours" would appear with all the things Palme had attempted to keep out of the public eye. Perhaps Palme's speeches could be better understood if you viewed the word rumour as codeword for "what I know but that I don't want you to know?"

As the debate had ended, the momentum had once again died down with the whole establishment still rallying behind the accused parties. Party leaders Gösta Bohman from the Moderates and Ola Ullsten from the Liberal People's party had both denounced the memorandum as hogwash and also expressed their support for Palme in spite of them being right-wingers and him being the number one Socialist fiend in the country. The only members of parliament that hadn't contented themselves with the explanations given were Per Gahrton and Jörn Svensson, still quite lone voices. No citizens' commission is established even now, and for the third time, this affair appears to be over.

Former National Police Commissioner Carl Persson is saddened by this last verbal exchange; even though he's now entrusted with the position of head of the Interpol, the Swedish political establishment still dismisses his memorandum as 'rubbish.' Already the day after the debate, mass media also stands up for Fälldin and Palme as well as accuses Persson of having attempted to divert the public's attention from the real issues during the election towards personal matters. *Aftonbladet* asks the question:

> "Why wasn't Carl Persson immediately fired after his blunder in forwarding unfounded gossip to the Prime Minister? Why hasn't a police authority that preoccupies itself with lies and malicious rumours instead of for example major economic crime been investigated and reorganized?"

Expressen has an editorial the same day entitled "Carl Persson, it was rubbish."

Reading these articles, Carl Persson the same day decides he's got only one way left to clear his name; he files a complaint against himself with the Chancellor of Justice (JK), to let this official determine if he has been guilty of any wrongdoing in his job. This post is held by Ingvar Gullnäs, who swiftly goes to work with the task, calling up all the parties that have been involved in the police investigation and reading their reports as well as the actual memorandum.

On 11 May, after mass media learns of the JK becoming involved, they make demands on his investigation. *Aftonbladet* even turns the idea of a citizens' commission around against Persson himself: "The demand for a citizens' commission, which in a more comprehensive way reviews the work of the police force, becomes dependent on the JK:s examination of Carl Persson's actions." Carl Persson has at this point for some time been the target of many vicious attacks on his name and reputation, and it had taken its toll on family life as well.

On 1 June 1978, Gullnäs produces his 40-page verdict, ruling very much in Persson's favour. Gullnäs states that it was apparent due to the many sources pointing out Geijer as a client of Doris Hopp that it was credible information. He also criticizes Palme for not registering the memorandum when he received it. As far as the security concern goes, Gullnäs writes:

"Taking into consideration the position and functions in society of the accused individuals there was therefore, still under the condition that the information met the above stated demand, good reason to inform the Government."

"I can therefore not find any reason for criticism of the measure to inform the Government about the uncovered information regarding the contacts between famous individuals and prostitutes."

Mass media now reports that the JK has cleared Persson's name, but is reluctant to disclose any more information about the JK verdict. Naturally, not too many people request personal copies of it either, and the affair goes into hibernation for more than two decades with brief interludes. Peter Bratt attempts to convince his newspaper DN to point out that they were right all along, but his editor-in-chief has lost his fighting spirit and lets it go. Eva and the other prostitutes live waning existences on the margins of society, and the clients all remain in their well-established positions in society.

The aftermath

In 1991, Carl Persson's memorandum was finally declassified and *Svenska Dagbladet* published an article about it: "Olof Palme lied about the Geijer affair." By now, Palme is dead, having been assassinated in 1986, his dirty deeds never having been exposed in public while he was still alive. *Dagens Nyheter* also publishes an article, but soon the affair dies down yet again without any investigation done - the only additional person apart from Sigvard Hammar who has been exposed as a probable client of Doris Hopp is Lennart Geijer. So it remains even to this day, with the police investigation records from the original prosecution still classified.

At the start of the 21th century, it was once again time for the affair to resurface. A former social worker by the name of Deanne Rauscher, who had been in contact with Doris Hopp during the 1980's, had decided to do some digging into the matter, to see what more could be uncovered. She teams up with Janne Mattson, who was one of the people behind the 1978 TV show *Studio S*, and they start gathering material. They go through the publicly available tapes of the recorded conversations between Doris Hopp and her clients and prostitutes, as well as interview police officers and alleged clients. After three years of work they come up with a 380 page book that is published in 2004, entitled *Makten, männen, mörkläggningen* - "The power, the men, the cover-up."

Though the journalistic value of covering ground that few people have wanted to tread is immense, a good portion of it consists of unsubstantiated rumour-mongering, dropping famous names left and right and alleging them to have been clients of Hopp. At this time, Eva Bengtsson has still not gone public as a former prostitute, and she and her cousin are referred to as Liv and Emelie in the book. This book is the first time these two get to tell their story, at least indirectly, though only Eva is really interested in relating her experiences. The story of her childhood and placement at an orphanage is told by her and her contact person at this institution, and with the publication of this book, the affair is once again alive.

The first attention the book gets is the reaction from the politicians who with little evidence provided are described as clients in the book. Olof Johansson of the Centre party slams her for defaming his name, though neither he nor anyone else actually file criminal charges. There is little hard evidence provided in the book, and beyond the heated exchange caused by the name-dropping, society once again seems to take only a mild interest in the affair.

In 2006, Christian news site *Världen idag*, owned by the *Livets Ord* church, picked up the story as well, interviewing Eva Bengtsson and publishing a series of articles. *Världen idag* makes the sensational claim that Palme was indeed one of the clients, based on the testimony of Eva. They publish a lengthy interview with her where she talks about the rough life she's had when no one has wanted to believe her and the cover-up has never ended, as well as talking to her cousin, who also drops a number of famous names. After receiving support from this news agency, Eva finally gets the courage to step out and go public. She decides she's going to examine whether she can get any compensation for what she's gone through, and in December of 2007, she files a complaint with Chancellor of Justice Göran Lambertz through the law agency Lawhouse:

> "The police under the administration of the prosecutor had completely adequate material to proceed in the matter with a prosecution. In spite of the investigation material there has been a cover-up, in order to protect the criminals due to them belonging

to the elite of politics, government and business. The rights of the girls as citizens and crime victims have been violated when the state in spite of its knowledge of the crimes has neglected to take legal measures against the crimes and prosecute the men that have molested them. Terms such as abuse of power and corrupt legal practice have rarely, if ever, been as appropriate as in this case. The betrayal of the girls on the part of the state has resulted in mental anguish that constantly torments them and has deformed their lives.

Eva Bengtsson and her cousin demand an apology from the Swedish state and one million crowns each in damages as compensation. I will assume that the state does not invoke limitation since it would be exceptionally offensive for the general sense of justice."

On 26 February 2008, Lambertz produces his verdict:

"Demands for compensation referring to the handling of the so called brothel matter

Date of decision   2008-02-26
Registration number   8235-07-40"

Excerpts from the report (the JK's italics):

"*Is it clear that Eva Bengtsson and her cousin have been subjected to a serious damage-liable wrongdoing through police and prosecutor neglecting to prosecute sex crimes they had been subjected to, and if so, have they suffered greatly from this wrongdoing?* I have considered myself meant to investigate the matter as far as that I after a reasonable investment of time and work can judge whether the stated requirement has been met.

With the indicated starting point I have had no reason to attempt to investigate which people were clients of the girls."

(The JK's cursive.)

"The investigation shows according to my view that there's no reason to doubt that Eva Bengtsson and her cousin were subjected to a large number of sex crimes. Eva Bengtsson was only 14 years old when the excesses began and hence was subjected to the crime that was then called fornication with minors."

"I have thus concluded that the state should not abstain from invoking limitation. With this assessment I lack reason to go into the matter of which injury has been suffered by Eva Bengtsson or her cousin, as well as into the matter of whether any misconduct has taken place that would constitute a right to compensation for violation."

"Eva Bengtsson's and her cousin's demands have been limited. It can't be said with certainty that any serious wrongdoings have been committed against her or the cousin. The Chancellor of Justice then has no reason to abstain from invoking limitation. The damage claims will hence be rejected."

No compensation...

"*The request for an apology*

Eva Bengtsson and her cousin have demanded an apology for what the authorities have subjected them to."

"The Chancellor of Justice should in any case not apologize on behalf of the state when it comes to events that haven't been able to have been investigated with a sufficient degree of certainty."

... and no apology.

"Decision by the Chancellor of Justice

The Chancellor of Justice refuses, referring to limitation, Eva Bengtsson's and her cousin's demand for compensation from the state."

And this last verdict by JK Göran Lambertz is where Swedish society stands today - still no consequences for the child molesters, and still no compensation for the victims - no clarity on just what took place either.

Children are still in demand

Though the attitudes in society have changed somewhat since the 1970's and child molesters aren't very popular figures, the fight isn't won just yet. Now and then paedophiles in prominent places are exposed, quite often as part of the gay rights movement, and there are still activists who attempt to get society to see paedophilia as something natural. There's a website at *pedofil.se* downplaying the seriousness of the problem and even alleging that the acceptance for paedophiles as people who just like homosexuals supposedly can't control the sexual drive they're born with, is growing. From the website:

> "The acceptance of paedophiles has increased dramatically the last couple of years, it's because people have asked themselves a very simple question. Why are homosexuals accepted but not paedophiles?

> "What sets present day apart from history is that today we have a completely different knowledge about sexual minorities and we know that no person chooses his orientation or can be blamed for it. We also know that there aren't any inherent problems that automatically lead to a certain kind of behaviour. All people are unique individuals no matter orientation and there is no longer any 'sin' or other reason to despise them."

Under a call for "a united struggle for freedom," the need to accept paedophiles as well is urged, lamenting that homosexual activists have dropped their former co-partners as they've reached mainstream circles, and the viewer of the website is encouraged to step out and fight for their emancipation through participation in the public debate.

Under a section entitled "Research and knowledge about

paedophilia," it's alleged that 'consensual' intercourse between an adult and a child isn't psychologically harmful. The children are portrayed as actively seeking this intimacy with adults, and there being nothing wrong in the adults responding. A couple of alleged case studies are cited where pre-teen boys actually insist on their adult partners having intercourse with them.

It's quite absurd that material such as this is allowed under the freedom of speech, while explaining what the Bible has to say about such behaviour can get you sentenced to prison - see the Åke Green case.

. . . .

THE SOCIAL DEMOCRATS

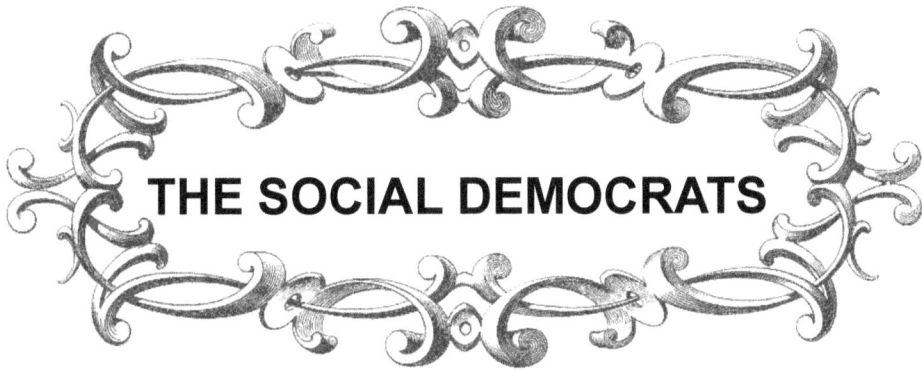

"Jag ska be att få sjunga en sång som kritiserar samhället...

Här i Sverige är politikerna inte kloka
för de har ingenting i sina huvuden
jag ska nu beskriva
på ett jätteintelligent sätt
vad det är för fel på de jävlarna

Ingvar Carlsson, han är inte klok
Bengt Westerberg är heller inte klok
vad Werner inte är, det kan ni kanske gissa
och de andra, de är samma idioter"

"May I ask to be able to sing a song that criticizes society...

Here in Sweden, the politicians are out of their minds
because they've got nothing in their heads
I would now like to describe
in a very intelligent manner
what's wrong with those f***ers

Ingvar Carlsson, he's out of his mind
Bengt Westerberg is also out of his mind
what Werner isn't, well take a guess
and for the others, they're the same idiots"

*Eddie Meduza - Dom e kueksuegere - "They're c***suckers"*

The Werner mentioned is Lars Werner, former chairman of the Communist party, with a known drinking problem. Other works of social commentary by Eddie Meduza include songs which translated into English become:

"Olof Palme was an idiot"

"More nuclear power"

"Göran Persson up my a**hole"

Ok, a great deal of time could be spent elaborating on the specifics as to why the policies the Social Democrats adhere to are flawed and how their party structure and political outlook is outright totalitarian. However, in this book I will not go there, but will let the arguments stated above by Eddie Meduza suffice. I'm sometimes amazed at his ability of summarizing complicated political discourse into a few select words, whose essence contain everything needed to be said about this party that's ruled Sweden for most of the last century. For people who are interested in learning more about one of their greatest scandals, look up *IB-affären*, the IB affair, the political registration that had hundreds of thousands of Swedes go into government files, resulting in their exclusion from the job market. *Folket i Bild/Kulturfront* and Dennis Töllborg have covered this matter quite well.

With this over with, now for the next chapter.

LGBT NATION

Only a century or two ago, virtually the whole world condemned homosexuality and other deviant sexual practices. It's forbidden in various well-known passages in the Bible, forming the foundation of the Christian and Jewish perspective on the matter, and the same goes for the Koran. Less well known is that Buddhism condemns it, and the old Egyptian Book of the dead, with the ceremonies to be performed in preparation for the afterlife, had you make this pledge (Spell 125b):

> "O backward-facer who came forth from the tomb-pit, I have not done wrong sexually, I have not practised homosexuality."

Sweden is possibly the country in the world that has moved the farthest away from this perspective, with regular gay pride parades where politicians and celebrities participate, and even a special LGBT group in the parliament, formed in 1998, with a large number of openly homosexual members. According to its own statements, this lobby had around 60 members in 2006. The typical chant of this crowd is that they're simply looking for equal rights, yet this next section might make you ask yourself if they will be content with remaining equals with the rest of society - it appears instead that they're aiming for queer domination. A search for parliamentary bills with the acronym LGBT (HBT in Swedish) in the title yields the following results - my translation of excerpts from the bills (I beg your pardon if you find the bills outright nuts – I do too):

"LGBT and sports"

2009/10:Kr311

"We know that discrimination and unequal treatment doesn't just go away."

"We know that for vulnerable groups, legislation is required, since the vulnerability is so all-encompassing."

No belief in achieving any understanding spontaneously, obviously.

"Sometimes the sports movement is considered to be lagging behind when it comes to fighting homophobia. Sometimes they dodge these matters."

"There is reason to raise our voices **against** the sports movement. The sports movement is one of the largest recipients of grants of all the social movements in Sweden. That's the way it should be, but if sports federations continue to not take the issue of homophobia seriously, there is reason to consider the important fostering spirit it has. In the end, this could lead to society not wanting to support the sports movement in the clear way it does today."

(My bold emphasis.)

The Swedish sports movement has been of tremendous value in teaching growing Swedish generations sound values and sound lifestyles, and its history goes back over a century, long before it became glamorous showing an interest in sexual intercourse with your own gender. You can tell what great respect these activists have for this movement when they use this language and also threaten it with withdrawn funds if it doesn't comply with their demands. I've personally been active in five different sports within the sports movement, and nowhere have I encountered this supposed 'homophobia.' Some of the values this movement has stressed have been fair play and showing respect

273

for your fellow man. Perhaps these values are simply incompatible with the spirit of the LGBT activists?

"The health of young LGBT people"

2009/10:Kr298

"The establishment of an interdisciplinary expert team with researchers from different branches in the LGBT sphere and other experts - to for example carry out continual, national summaries of the knowledge within the LGBT sphere."

"an LGBT knowledge centre as a resource for authorities and organizations in their work to integrate the LGBT perspective into their respective activities."

Or in other words, government jobs for LGBT people.

"LGBT in the world"

2009/10:U343

"EU is the world's greatest aid donor and it's therefore important that Sweden, in accordance with our international policy documents for developmental co-ordination that include the rights of LGBT people, works to make the EU member countries prioritize in a similar way in their aid sexual and reproductive health and rights."

"Officially it's said that Sweden in that manner can influence these states to change their attitude towards LGBT people. In practice however, nothing or very little is done, to make these for trade policy important countries respect the human rights of LGBT people. This is not acceptable and here Sweden must work more firmly to use its influence within the realms of trade policy."

So... Trade embargoes for countries that don't accommodate LGBT people enough?

"The LGBT work of SIDA"

2009/10:U240

(SIDA is the Swedish government agency for foreign aid.)

"Unfortunately only a fraction of SIDA's budget today goes to LGBT work. Equally regrettable is that the cutback in the number of recipient countries for Swedish aid that has taken place probably hasn't taken into account the work with the LGBT issue."

"The foreign aid work can't focus only on the worst catastrophes in the world."

"Sweden should reconsider the grounds for its foreign aid work and then bring up the matter of the situation of sexual minorities."

Something tells me that perhaps this work has something to do with members of parliament wanting to make sure there are gay bars to hang out at in these countries when they visit them. Zimbabwe and Uganda are specified as countries requiring the most work. Perhaps a regional fetish wanting to establish LGBT activities there? Or maybe there are real homophobes there that they want to associate their political opponents with by sharing victimhood with people who want to be gay in "repressive" third world countries?

"LGBT and the educational system"
2009/10:Ub503

"There is a need for education concerning matters of homo- and bisexuals and trans people. As a pupil in mandatory schooling you shouldn't have to face staff with a negative attitude towards or lacking knowledge and understanding about homo- and bisexuals or trans people. To this should be added that at for example religious private schools, so called confessional schools, there's often a down-prioritizing of education in these matters. This is unacceptable, and this should be included when a new school law is worked on."

"There are families where the parents are of the same sex, but the teachers don't have the tools they need to meet the different families. The consequence can be that some teachers today work on matters concerning sex and social life and teach about these matters without education and knowledge about LGBT matters. This is absurd and it's necessary that the LGBT knowledge of teachers is increased. Therefore it's important to work towards teachers getting education on the living conditions of homosexuals, bisexuals and trans people."

Or in other words... LGBT people getting paid with tax payer money to teach people about these very LGBT people.

"The aspiring teachers should learn to deal with the most common prejudices about homo- and bisexuality. Society's view on homo- and bisexual love as equal to heterosexual love is the view teachers are expected to express. Therefore knowledge about the forms of coexistence of homo- and bisexuals should be included as a part of the teacher's examination."

"Hence the knowledge about the situation of lgbt people must increase. A clarification of the examination ordinance in the college ordinance should therefore be made for the following professional degrees: midwife degree, child- and youth pedagogical degree, medical, psychological, psychotherapeutic and nursing degrees, degrees in social care and social studies, grade school and high school teaching degrees, police degrees along with candidate of law and candidate of theology."

You know society has strayed far from God when homosexual activists demand to dictate what's taught in theology classes, the studies aspiring ministers have to attend. On paper, Sweden has freedom of religion, but in practice, this is hardly worth the paper it's printed on.

"Surely there are other areas as well that especially need proficiency in the situation of lgbt people."

What could be more important than going through all of

society to find areas where people lack 'LGBT proficiency?'

"Elderly LGBT people"

2009/10:So604

"The understanding of homo- and bisexual relations within elder care is today no matter-of-course. On the contrary, heterosexuality is the norm, and sexuality is made invisible for lgbt people in particular. For an older lgbt person it can for example be very rewarding to receive help acquiring newspapers by and for homosexuals or gain support by visiting other homosexuals."

"Then the right of the individual to [be shown] respect for his or her sexual preference should be a matter-of-course. To achieve this, society's elder care needs to increase its knowledge on the needs of homo- and bisexuals and trans people."

"The optimally best for elder homo- and bisexuals in need of elder housing such as service flats, nursing homes and similar would be if special collective housing for homo- and bisexuals was offered to the ones that so request."

"Asylum for homo- and bisexuals along with trans people (lgbt)"

2009/10:Sf380

"It's also common that lgbt refugees upon arrival in Sweden don't dare to reveal their sexual preference, but these circumstances appear later on in the process."

Hmm, my application for asylum was rejected, what do I do... I know - I've understood now that these Swedes are all crazy about sexual deviants and offer that as a valid reason for asylum. There was this girl back in high school that I kissed, and I didn't feel a thing back then... That must mean I'm really a homosexual! The marriage I've had during my adult life has only been a cover for my secret queer life. Yep, that's it.

Hey, this might be something for Americans too. In the

USA, it's not quite as easy living off welfare all your life as it is in Sweden. So, Americans that want to do that might come to the realization that they're homosexuals too. How about this for a background story. "I tried to live as a homosexual in the USA, but then suddenly these weirdoes with neon signs appeared, saying God hates people like me. After that, I've always been on the run from these people. The Westboro Baptist Church has been chasing me all across America with their picket signs, which is why you Swedes must grant me asylum because of my sexuality. I'm a victim of persecution!"

> "The Government decided in the yearly ordinance for the year 2007 that the department of migration should raise its lgbt proficiency."

> "To be sure, the department of migration has decided during the autumn to launch a special lgbt project. This is a praiseworthy initiative that arrives too late, however, and doesn't meet the demand for lgbt proficiency there is among the staff."

> "One way of letting lgbt applications receive a more fair treatment is to always let staff with lgbt proficiency take part in processing and decision in these matters, at least as long as the deficiencies are as serious as they are today."

For the past few decades, far-left political organizations have actively recruited members among refugees that have just arrived. Perhaps the LGBT people are doing the same thing now?

"LGBT and culture"

2009/10:Kr310

A fairly long bill suggesting the government should spend more time promoting the cultural contributions of LGBT people. As if mass media wasn't doing that enough already. Maybe the person that came up with this bill had completely talentless hacks in mind? The kind that wouldn't even be accepted by today's

278

Hollywood.

"LGBT matters"

2003/04:So568

"... single women should have the same right to artificial insemination as women in couple relationships."

"... launch an inquiry with the purpose of reconsidering the family law so that children can have more than two guardians."

"... demands should be put on the national sports federations to account for how they're fighting homophobia and discrimination to qualify for state funds."

"... gender identity should be grounds for discrimination [lawsuits]"

And to think you considered yourself privileged enough to be able to go to your job without having to have a drag queen around...

"... launch an inquiry with the purpose of reviewing the naming law."

Ah, the important things these politicians fight for... The right for men to have names such as Lisa.

"Culture and sports from an LGBT perspective"

2006/07:Kr308

"We want a special LGBT museum to be prioritized. Such ones exist in other European countries with the *Schwule* museum in Berlin as model. A Swedish LGBT museum should not depend on private donations but should instead be included in established framework for the cultural grants and as a special assignment for perhaps the Nordic museum."

"LGBT in Scandinavia, the EU and the world"

2005/06:U368

"A first step would be for Sida to receive the assignment to introduce an LGBT perspective into **every foreign aid activity** Sweden is a participant of."

Jobs for LGBT people... It's pretty well-acknowledged that the generous 1% of the country's GDP that Sweden spends on foreign aid is a goldmine for profiteers wanting to finance their own projects.

"LGBT people and education"

2005/06:Ub572

"The result might be that some teachers today work with issues concerning sex and social life and teach about these matters without education and knowledge in LGBT matters. This is absurd."

"The Government should therefore push for the national school board and other affected departments and institutions requiring that teachers are educated on the living conditions of homosexuals, bisexuals and trans people."

"Culture for equal worth regarding homosexuals, bisexuals and trans people (LGBT)"

2002/03:Kr339

"... work towards prioritizing public cultural grants to the cultural activities that aim to influence the attitudes towards and counteract prejudice against LGBT people."

"The parliament demands that the Government in contract negotiations with the public TV and radio brings up the LGBT issues."

"... The national sports federation, to be able to enjoy public grants, must also be asked to present a plan for how to resolve the negative attitudes towards homosexuals and LGBT people that are present within the sports movement."

Enough with the sports movement already... Ever wondered if the reason you guys had a hard time with the sports movement was because you played like sissies and were cut from your teams for that reason?

"LGBT education at colleges"

2002/03:Ub303

"International work concerning LGBT"

2002/03:U287

"Family law concerning LGBT"

2002/03:L254

"LGBT people with immigrant backgrounds"

2003/04:Sf296

"LGBT education in hygiene and health care"

2009/10:So456

"LGBT proficiency among public employees"

2009/10:A250

"LGBT and economic growth"

2008/09:N419

"LGBT in the labour market"

2008/09:A391

"Some constitutional matters concerning LGBT people"

2008/09:K389

"National strategy to improve the mental health of LGBT youth"

2008/09:So273

"Equal rights for LGBT people"

2005/06:L342

"Open community participation for everyone - bill on LGBT matters"

2005/06:L341

"LGBT people and elder housing"

2005/06:So683

"Education of nursing staff in LGBT matters"

2005/06:So262

"The image of LGBT in textbooks"

2006/07:Ub325

Ok, me commenting on every single silly bill would be too much. All in all, as of April 2010, 79 parliamentary bills have been introduced with the acronym LGBT (HBT in Swedish) in the title, all of these bills demanding better adherence to the interests of LGBT people. This is to be compared with the 36 bills with Christian in the title since 1990, some of which are complaints about too much Christian influence in society. For the search function to browse these bills online, go to the Swedish parliament website at *http://www.riksdagen.se/Webbnav/index.aspx?nid=400*.

EDUCATION OR INDOCTRINATION?

As many people who have followed the news lately are aware of, homeschooling is pretty much illegal in Sweden. Earlier, there existed slight loopholes that let you homeschool your children if you were able to get a permit, which you had to renew every year. Yet in the new school law introduced in 2010, that option was entirely shut down, and now all children have to enroll in a school whose curriculum is determined by the state. So, what are the pupils taught at Swedish schools? As we will see in this section, not much worthwhile. Whatever the school authorities decide shall be taught in school becomes mandatory for the pupils to attend; you can't opt out of anything due to your own personal beliefs or morals.

LGBT education as a part of the curriculum

A program on the state TV called *Skolfront* on 19 March 2009 focused on the topic of supposed homophobia at schools and what the education system was doing to fight it. They had interviewed a member of the gay lobby RFSL who as an adult 'realized' he was a homosexual after feeling different in some inexplicable way during his school years.

> "The last three years, Fredrik has visited hundreds of Schools in Norrland [the sparsely populated northern part of the country] to instruct in LGBT matters."

That's just a part of the country... Hence he probably was invited to just about every single school there and most likely received honorarium as well. I wonder how long it took him to go from finding out he's gay to turning it into a business holding these seminars? In the show, it's lamented that the education system doesn't invest enough money in LGBT education in spite of everyone that's invited him. After that, a female teacher named Greta Björklund was introduced:

> "But there are teachers who take LGBT issues seriously. Greta teaches Swedish to the industrial program at Strömbacka high school in Piteå."

(Greta welcomes in the fourteen students of her all male class into the classroom and walks up to the black board.)

(G = Greta; S = Student)

G: What's so nice and what feels so good about being in love?
S: Intimacy!
G: Intimacy, ok! [she writes it on the black board]
S: ... when you watch a movie or hug and cuddle.
S: Yeah, when you feel a bit lonely without that person.

G: We've talked a little about feelings between a girl and a boy, a love relationship. But what if it's Billy and Tom, two guys.
S: Yeah, there are still feelings.
G: Then I'll draw a green arrow, in the homosexual relationship there are also feelings.

S: They might not dare to hold hands while walking across town, do stuff together and show that they're homosexuals.
S: Death threats just because they're different.
G: Yes, and who are the ones making the threats?
S: Usually heterosexuals.

I think it's safe to assume that to the extent they suffer death threats, it's more likely their ex-partners behind them, either ones obsessed about them not responding to their 'love,' or them fed up with their ex-partners stalking them.

G: The ones that consider themselves normal. And who are the ones that consider themselves normal?
S: Usually heterosexuals.

Strange, I've not seen a single heterosexual trying to convince me of just how normal he is... I often see deviants doing it though.

G: Hey, do we have the right to judge?
S: No.

At this point I'm a bit disturbed at how the class is feeling obliged to respond in the expected way, hence being conditioned - or in other words, actively indoctrinated.

(Now followed more of the interview with the RFSL representative.)

"The goal for today is to make the school realize the responsibility they've got, that they're required to have a norm-breaking education, to for example in math have examples where two guys buy a car they purchase on credit because they're going

285

to have children. To introduce this norm-breaking (aspect) into the education. If you don't change the education, you won't change the students either."

(Back to the school and teacher Greta.)

G: Sit down for a while and think for yourself or with a friend, out of which perspective I should write this poem about homosexual or bisexual love?

(The students get started with the assignment while the teacher goes to another room and speaks to the TV team.)

G: They've been assigned to freely write love poems, and then it was a lot about heterosexual love, some wrote from a homosexual perspective...

Oh no, a majority prefers being attracted to the opposite sex - naturally in the name of equality they must then be indoctrinated until at least half embrace their own sex.

G: ... and I want everyone to try doing it - change their thoughts - switch glasses, when thinking about love.

(Greta sits down with two students.)

G: What was on your mind, what did you want to express with the poem?
S1: ... a girl who was a lesbian.
S2: It's a lesbian girl who wants to have sex with another girl...

Whew... At least one sign of sanity - they refrain from identifying with a person of their own sex practising homosexuality. Though on the other hand - there is of course the risk that these boys don't need to be instructed to fantasize about lesbian love since a lot of them probably do it while connected to the Internet anyway.

S2: ... that she doesn't know if she's a lesbian or not.

(The teacher reads the poem aloud, which has one short sentence per line.)

G: Hello.
G: I like you.
G: You're the girl of my dreams.
G: I think dirty thoughts about you.
G: Do you have the hots for me?
G: I'm a girl as well.
G: But I want you.
G: Can you do me?
G: I can do you!
G: Do you even want me?

Seriously... this stuff belongs among the cream of modern LGBT fiction.

(Now the teacher sits down with two other boys; one of them reads their poem.)

S: My life is wonderful, when I was yours.

Ok, I'm not supposed to act teacher here... But different tenses? I don't get why their teacher didn't remark about this. Maybe actual language skills don't matter in school any more these days.

S: But now it's over. You said 'goodbye, Erik.' It felt like I fell back to my limited life I lived before. Life was so wonderful when you were mine.

Afterwards, the RFSL representative praises the teacher:

"We realize what a huge work effort she puts in, just by being a regular teacher and teach Swedish... She makes classes that at first might have been the typical rough boys to become very... wise"

Yeah, that's surely to be praised, turning boys into sissies.

On top of writing the poems in class, they're also to be published in a book as a class assignment, all part of the regular school activities. If you think you'd be able to opt out, here's what 3 § 11 of the school law in effect at the time said:

> "Every child, who fulfills compulsory school attendance within the public school system for children and youth or in any other way, shall take part in the activity that is arranged to grant the designated education [program], if the child isn't ill or has other valid reason to fail to come."

Naturally, boys have to be forced to write gay poems and publish them as part of their education. I'm reminded of how in admittedly totalitarian states, students were sometimes required to write hymns to their leaders; this is gay fascism at its finest.

HATE LAWS AND CENSORSHIP

"The Government cannot be concerned any longer with outmoded penological theories. Cram criminals together and see what happens. You get concentrated criminality, crime in the midst of punishment. Soon we may be needing all our prison space for political offenders."

Anthony Burgess 1962, "A clockwork orange"

In a certain country, they've got a thing called the First Amendment, which guarantees its citizens that the government can't restrict their freedom of speech, and though there are some limited exceptions as to what can be said in the form of harassment, the government of said country has no means whatsoever whereby it can imprison political dissidents or forbid the free practise of religion.

Swedes are not so lucky.

The laws regulating speech in Sweden are mainly *Tryckfrihetsförordningen* (TF, the Freedom of the Press Act) and *Yttrandefrihetsgrundlagen* (YGL, the Fundamental Law on Freedom of Expression), setting the limits for the rights granted in 2 § 1 of *Regeringsformen* (RF, the Instrument of Government). TF regulates printed material such as books and newspapers, while YGL regulates statements in radio, TV and over the Internet. With no less than two basic laws and a constitution assuring you you have the right to speak your mind, I guess you think you'd be in free speech heaven? The actual contents of these laws will give you a completely different idea. Though legal quotations may not be interesting to read, they're necessary in order to understand the hate speech cases that will be described later on. First to cover excerpts from TF – my own unofficial translation:

The Freedom of the Press Act

(Emphasis in quotes is mine.)

1 § 1:

"With freedom of the press is understood the right of every Swedish citizen to, without any by public authority or other public body in advance introduced obstacles, publish writings, to afterwards only in front of a legal court **be held responsible** for their contents, and to not in any other case **be punished therefore**, than if this content violates distinct law, introduced to maintain public order, without restraining public information."

You know you're in for a ride when the first paragraph of the 'Freedom of the Press Act' mentions punishment. How about this for a wording that more clearly states what this paragraph means:

"As part of the Swedish freedom of the press, you may publish anything you want without review beforehand, but afterwards you may be held responsible in front of a legal court, and punished if your views have been banned."

1 § 3:

"For abuse of the freedom of the press **or complicity therein**, no one in any other order or in other case than this ordinance may be prosecuted or be held accountable or liable for damages or have the publication confiscated or seized."

Ah, it's comforting to know that I can't be fined, imprisoned

290

or have my publications seized unless there is some clause in this 10,000 word ordinance that provides for it. I guess I also have to watch out so I don't assist someone else in expressing any inappropriate views, or I might face the same consequences. You do wonder, however, why they don't reword it in a more honest way:

"If in writing you express a view we disagree with, or help someone else in doing this, this ordinance specifies the grounds on which you can be prosecuted, be held accountable, liable for damages or have the publication confiscated or seized. So don't even think about trying to express a dissenting opinion."

7 § 1

"With breach of the press law is in this ordinance understood to be the actions noted in 4 and 5 §§."

Paragraph 4 has 18 different crimes, paragraph 3 has three.

7 § 4

"11. agitation against ethnic group, whereby someone threatens or expresses contempt for (an) ethnic group or other such group of people alluding to race, colour of skin, national or ethnic origin, creed or sexual orientation;"

(Translation remark: The Swedish wording is *hotar eller uttrycker missaktning*, which directly translates into "threatens or expresses disrespect." For some reason, the official English translation is the incorrect word "contempt," which doesn't reveal just how restrictive the law is on free speech.)

This is the version in this ordinance of the crime listed in 16 § 8 of *Brottsbalken* (The Penal Code, official translation for the first paragraph):

"A person who, in a disseminated statement or communication, threatens or expresses contempt for a national, ethnic or other such group of persons with allusion to race, colour, national or ethnic origin or religious belief shall, be sentenced for agitation against a national or ethnic group to imprisonment for at most two years or, if the crime is petty, to a fine.

If the crime is gross [the person] is sentenced to prison for at least six months and at most four years. When considering if the crime is gross, special consideration shall be taken to if the message has had an especially threatening or violating content and has been disseminated to a large number of people in a way that has been meant to create considerable attention."

This is the law that people are sentenced to prison under in Swedish courts since 2003; before this, the maximum sentence was two years, and sexual orientation wasn't included. For an interesting comparison, note that you can theoretically serve as much time in prison for first degree murder as for 'hate speech.' The minimum sentence for murder in the international meaning is six years, and with the 2/3-rule, this becomes four years. Hence if a 'hate speech' offender has to serve his full four year sentence due to having attempted to escape prison, he can serve the same term as a murderer. Now where is the justice?

7 § 7

"Printed writing, which contains a breach of the press law, may be confiscated. Confiscation of printed writing means that all copies designated for distribution shall be destroyed and that molds, stones, stereotypes, plates and other similar, exclusively for the printing of the writing usable materials, shall be dealt with so that abuse thereby cannot take place."

Complicated language for saying the state will not only destroy the printed material, but the means with which to print it too.

9 § 2

"The Chancellor of Justice [JK, *Justitiekanslern*] is sole prosecutor in cases concerning breaches of the press law. No one else but the Chancellor of Justice may initiate preliminary investigation concerning breach of the press law. Only the Chancellor of Justice and the court has the right to decide on forced measures based on suspicion of such a crime, **if nothing else** is provided for in this ordinance."

There's that 1984 language again... Only the JK can put you in prison for expressing your views. Now, naturally, you need a law to specify that only a government representative can do it and not that guy at your job who disagrees with your views. But just to be safe, let's not be too definitive - without the "if nothing else," this clause might have invalidated some other one. How about this wording instead:

"The JK can prosecute people for breaches of the press law. The JK may initiate preliminary investigation concerning breaches of the press law. The JK and the courts have the right to decide on forced measures based on suspicion of such a crime. There might be other clauses in this ordinance that limit your freedom of speech even further, too."

10 § 1

"If there is justification that a publication because of a breach of the press law can be confiscated, the publication may be seized awaiting a decision thereon."

Let's not wait for the rule of law to have its course when we can seize the material immediately. The least you could expect the authorities to do is to make a copy of the publication and return it as soon as possible. Then again, if they decide to seize the publication, they most likely have a copy of it already. For abuse of this clause, see the 'hate speech' cases to come.

10 § 2

"Before press law charges are raised or an application at a court has been made for the confiscation of the publication, if the crime belongs under a public trial, assignment in accordance with §1

293

about seizure and ban on publication may be delivered by the Chancellor of Justice. In law, it may be provided that a public prosecutor as well can deliver assignment on seizure within his field of activity."

Let's not even inform the suspects ahead of time that they're about to be prosecuted for hate speech... Nothing like an early morning house search by a squad of police officers to convince you you're living in a 'democracy.'

10 § 7

"Assignment to confiscate shall by police authority be immediately executed. Concerning ban on distribution of printed writing, that has been confiscated, is regulated in chapter 6."

A certain Gestapo comes to mind here.

13 § 2

"Writing, that has been printed outside Sweden, shall be considered published here when it in the way stated in chapter 1 § 6 has been delivered for distribution within Sweden."

I remember reading about the Soviet Union seizing Bibles that American missionaries tried to smuggle into the country. I guess the same thing will be possible in Sweden in a not too distant future.

14 § 5

"In everything whereupon regulation has not been communicated in this ordinance or in a special law, which is issued with support thereof, what is elsewhere regulated in law or statute applies. A foreigner is, if nothing else follows from this ordinance or other law, equated with a Swedish citizen."

That's the last paragraph of the ordinance. I guess it can be nice for foreigners visiting Sweden to know that they're entitled to the same 'rights' as Swedish citizens, and not any more limited in their freedom of speech. Who knows, maybe otherwise they could be as restricted by censorship as people in North Korea. That's about the only country I can think of that truly has less freedom of speech than Sweden does.

You can't but help to wonder how the people who wrote this "Freedom of the Press Act" in 1949 thought. "Hmm, we don't really like freedom of speech, this idea could give an opportunity for our dissidents to freely express their thoughts. Let's fill up an ordinance with 10,000 words and make it sound as if it grants people rights when in reality it only limits them."

The Fundamental Law on Freedom of Expression (*Yttrandefrihetsgrundlagen*) has similar provisions for the media it covers, though since one paragraph is not too infrequently used against Internet dissidents, I will quote it here:

5 § 6

"A technical recording that contains a breach of the press law may be confiscated. [...] During confiscation, all copies meant for distribution shall be destroyed. Additionally it shall be ensured that objects that can be used specifically to duplicate the technical recording can't be used to produce additional copies."

Bye bye your PC you uploaded your controversial webpage with.

The statutes on liberties in the constitution - the Instrument of Government - are eerily similar to the ones found in the Soviet constitution from 1936, also seemingly granting free speech:

"ARTICLE 125. In conformity with the interests of the working people, and in order to strengthen the socialist system, the citizens of the U.S.S.R. are guaranteed by law:

a. freedom of speech;
b. freedom of the press;
c. freedom of assembly, including the holding of mass meetings;

d. freedom of street processions and demonstrations.

These civil rights are ensured by placing at the disposal of the working people and their organizations printing presses, stocks of paper, public buildings, the streets, communications facilities and other material requisites for the exercise of these rights."[1]

This is 2 § 1 of the Swedish Instrument of Government:

"Every citizen is versus the community ensured

1. freedom of speech: freedom to in speech, writing or picture or in other way transmit information and express thoughts, views and feelings,

2. freedom of information: freedom to obtain and receive information and otherwise share in the expressions of others,

3. freedom of assembly: freedom to stage and attend gathering for information, expression of opinion or other similar purpose or for delivery of an artistic work,

4. freedom of demonstration: freedom to stage and take part in demonstration on public property,"

Others similarities between the Swedish and Soviet constitutions are these ones (my bold emphasis for comparison):

"ARTICLE 3. **In the U.S.S.R. all power** belongs to **the working people** of town and country as represented by the Soviets of Working People's Deputies."[2]

1 § 1 of the Swedish Instrument of Government:

"**All public power in Sweden** emanates from **the people**. The Swedish democracy is founded on the free forming of opinion and

_____

1
http://www.departments.bucknell.edu/russian/const/36cons04.html
2
http://www.departments.bucknell.edu/russian/const/36cons01.html

296

on **universal and equal suffrage**. It's realized through a representative and parliamentarian form of government and through municipal autonomy."

"ARTICLE 134. Members of all Soviets [specifics cut]--are chosen by the electors on the basis of **universal, direct and equal suffrage** by secret ballot."

On top of this, 1 § 2 of the same Swedish document states that "It shall particularly fall on the community [*det allmänna* in Swedish - the public sector] to ensure the right to health, work, residence and education and to work for social care and security," words that have obvious counterparts in the old Soviet constitution.

With the actual law covered, let's look at cases of people being sent to prison over 'hate speech.' But first an observation found in a government report on the development of the application of the HMF law:

> "Before the 1990's there were only a couple of verdicts per year, but several of these have come to play an important role in how the law on agitation against ethnic group is applied today. The verdicts concerning the period from 1948 to the early 1980's generally concern people who have run a substantial publishing effort, in contrast with the verdicts during the 1990's."[1]

Now to briefly cover the last two decades of imprisoning political dissidents in this country.

---

1 Hets mot folkgrupp - BRÅ-rapport 2001:7

Ahmed Rami - political refugee turned political prisoner

Some time during the mid 1940's, a man was born into a family belonging to a Berber tribe in Morocco, working the land for their livelihood. He's given the name Ahmed, though the date of his birth is uncertain since births aren't registered in this area at this time. As he reaches adolescence, he moves into the city of Casablanca, where he goes to school and eventually also becomes a teacher. Already during his teen years, he's a political agitator as well, though he still joins the military as an adult.

Rami is unhappy with king Hassan II, the ruler of Morocco during his time here, regarding his regime as corrupt and Hassan himself as a puppet of Western colonial powers. In 1972, Rami takes part in a botched attempt at a revolt against king Hassan, and becomes a refugee. Making his way through France at first, he then finds his way to Sweden in 1973.

Arriving in Sweden, he's warmly greeted, describing in detail the story of his immigration to the country in his self-biography. Left-wing political activists are overjoyed when they learn that a man has sought refuge in Sweden after having attempted to overthrow a "capitalist dictatorship," and he's featured on the state TV during prime-time hours; he's quickly granted a residence permit even before the year 1973 has ended.

During the 70's, he's a darling of the political and cultural establishment in Sweden while also attempting to help organize Moroccan resistance from abroad. Rami expresses sincere gratitude over the freedom he enjoys in his new country, at least relative to that in Morocco, though eventually he would find that this honeymoon isn't unconditional, when he starts speaking out on matters in Swedish society as well.

His coming activism during the 80's sees him make assorted international Islamic connections, having a meeting with Ayatollah Khomeini among others. He visits Israel in 1982 and becomes familiar with the plight of the Palestinians under the occupation; he's bothered at the negative way some Swedish mass media comments on Islam, and identifies Jewish organizations and activists as the source for this stigmatization. In 1988, Salman Rushdie publishes his novel "The Satanic Verses," a work that's condemned in the Islamic world, where it's considered blasphemy. In Sweden, the work is highly featured. The year before, in 1987, Rami had launched a radio station where he talks mostly about the Israel-Palestine conflict, portraying it as being caused by Jewish racism - Zionism.

The year this novel is published, Rami publishes a work of his own in Swedish - *Vad är Israel?*, "What is Israel?" Questions asked in this book include such ones as:

"Is Zionism 'Jewish Nazism'? Is there a Jewish mafia? Is Israel a fraud? Is USA run by the Jewish lobby and Israel?"

"Why does democratic and freedom-loving Sweden hold on to the right of the Zionistic conquest- and oppressor state to exist as a 'Jewish state' in the old land of the Palestinians, when a unanimous opinion in Sweden condemned other colonialist states and powerfully condemns racist South Africa as an unjust regime that must be abolished?"

Of the 100,000 words in the book, these are some of the most commonly occurring, amounting to one in 50 all in all:

'judarnas' 64 times '(of) the Jews'
'judarna' 289 times 'the Jews'
'judiska' 550 times '(the) Jewish'
'judar' 434 times 'Jews'
'juden' 23 times 'the Jew'
'jude' 55 times '(a) Jew'
'sionisternas' 38 times '(of) the Zionists'

'*sionisterna*' 205 times 'the Zionists'
'*sionistiska*' 322 times '(the) Zionistic'

Later on he would also refer to the Chancellor of Justice (*Justitiekanslern* in Swedish) who prosecuted him as *Judekanslern*, the Jew Chancellor.

Jewish circles in Sweden are now very unhappy with Rami's activism and start exploring the legal options available for silencing him. In 1988, the Swedish Committee Against Anti-semitism files a complaint with the Chancellor of Justice, who prosecutes Rami the following year. As the case garners attention, he's described as an "Anti-semite" in tabloid *Expressen*, though isn't given room to defend himself. On 5 September 1989, a trial is held at Stockholm district court, and on 14 November, the verdict is delivered where he's sentenced to six months in prison under the HMF law for his book and his radio broadcasts.

He appeals the verdict, but in Svea Court of Appeal, the same sentence is handed out the coming year. This verdict is sets a precedent, and from now on, people will be sentenced to prison under the HMF law on looser grounds than before. Though before this, HMF trials had been a rarity, they would become quite common during the next two decades.

While the legal proceedings go on, Rami writes no less than three books - his autobiography in 1989, *Ett liv för frihet*, "A life for freedom;" *Israels makt i Sverige*, "Israel's power in Sweden" in 1989, and *Judisk häxprocess i Sverige*, "Jewish witch trial in Sweden" in 1990. All of them would see complaints about them filed with the Chancellor of Justice, though only "What is Israel" ever brought criminal charges.

Following the conviction, his licence to broadcast radio is suspended for a year, but after that he returns to this activism of his, discussing the same topics. He likes reading works aloud that show how the world has viewed the Jews throughout the ages. In

1991, criminal charges would be raised again over his portrayal of "Jewishness."

> "Jew, Jewishness: In the major languages of the world there are a collection of words, that describe a particular kind of fraudulent conduct. In English we have the verb 'Jew,' 'to Jew somebody' which means to fool, scam or trick someone. Equivalent expression in the German language is the verb 'jüdeln.' With 'zu jüdeln' is meant to haggle and commit usury. In French we have the noun 'juif' meaning usurer. Hence the great languages of culture have related expressions for a behaviour targeted at the righteous congregation."

> "Our weaknesses: The Jewish force gains power over its victim by appealing to and conjuring up its weakness. We all have major or minor flaws, and this is what makes us men, and divides us from the divine. We're cowardly, spiritually wavering, desiring pleasure and enjoyment. We have limited intelligence and so on. A sterling man must have an inner softness too, a compassion towards other people, an aim for what's fair and beautiful, the ability to love. It's this weakness of ours, the frail and soft within us, that supplies the nourishment for the Jewish power. Nature doesn't lack examples, just think of the ichneumon fly [*parasitstekel* in Swedish], which plants its eggs in the body of the host creature. The soft internal parts of the helpless victim then become food for the crawling parasite worm."

> "If we move on to later ages, to our century, we find that just about all more or less perverted sexual theories have been introduced by and are advanced by predominantly Jews"

> "Violence, pornography and sex trade is indeed the mark of organized crime. It's an indisputable fact that the Jewish documents, Torah and Talmud, are literally teeming with expressions of bestial violence and perverted sexuality. This fixation on violence and sexuality is indeed repeated as a theme among many later Jews."

In 1992, Rami is convicted due to the radio statements

above, and the same year he's also fired as a French teacher from the negative publicity he's gained for himself. In 1993, the new Chancellor of Justice, Johan Hirschfeldt, briefly investigates a flyer Rami has been distributing - "Facts instead of Jewish propaganda." This is the end of his radio days, but in 1996, a new chapter of his activism begins, when he launches a website with the same name as the radio station - Radio Islam, at www.radioislam.org .

On this website, available in many different languages, one can read such articles as "USA's Rulers - All Are Jews!' and 'Jewish Power in Russia.' The webpage also features an extensive list of Jews in prominent positions in Swedish society, which upsets these circles. It doesn't take long before this webpage as well becomes a criminal matter under the HMF law; in 1998, after a complaint by the Swedish Committee against Anti-semitism, prosecutor Tora Holst orders the police to search Rami's home since he's suspected of being behind the webpage, but an 18 year-old-woman steps up and takes responsibility for the contents, and the investigation is dropped.

Meanwhile, Rami is interviewed by National Socialist magazine Nordland, where he says that "Hitler's mistake was that he was too humane." He also makes the ADL (Anti-Defamation League) list of anti-semites on the Internet.

In 2002, Rami encounters the fourth Chancellor of Justice to investigate his activism, this time newly appointed Göran Lambertz. In September of 2002, the police raid Rami's home again, seizing three computers as well as assorted digital media, looking for evidence that he's behind the website. Tora Holst says to a newspaper that before the house search, "certain surveillance had yielded results," in their investigation, possibly referring to the extensive monitoring of Internet traffic by the police.

Some time later, in 2003, Rami is declared a suspect of

having breached laws of the freedom of the press with his website, though after the prosecution fails to uncover any court-admissible evidence, Rami's personal belongings are returned in June of 2004. Though these investigations have been a considerable nuisance for Rami with the seized personal belongings, neither in 1998 nor in 2002 was anything more than the willingness of the Chancellor of Justice to prosecute required to go ahead. You'd think that it should be established beforehand that a 'crime' (in the Swedish meaning) had actually taken place, by having a legal consensus that the material constituted hate speech, before intrusive house searches are performed. But, perhaps it comes in quite handy for the thought police being able to raid people's homes and keep their computers confiscated for years, constituting an effective extra-judicial form of punishment. What ultimately made prosecution impossible was the fact that Rami kept his homepage on American servers, in a country where they actually enjoy freedom of speech. And American companies fortunately don't let socialist dictatorships tell them what clients to keep.

Though freedom of speech is sometimes debated in Sweden, the symposiums on this matter usually don't have the country's own dissidents invited. Starting on 11 February 2009, an exhibition was held at the Nobel museum with the name *Yttrandefrihet - var går gränsen?* "Freedom of speech - where is the limit drawn?" Following Sweden's great modern tradition of never entertaining any criticism towards itself, none of the victims of its own limitations on free speech were featured. Instead, Salman Rushdie was portrayed as the greatest martyr of them all. In connection to this, a man writing books about the mafia influence in southern Italy was also invited to talk about this topic on the state TV.

Since this topic had been brought up, students at Linköping University did however invite one of society's pariahs to discuss the matter - Ahmed Rami. Even though he was only invited to discuss free speech and not his own views, they could probably never have anticipated the controversy this would generate. The students are condemned by mass media and have to defend themselves in countless interviews about the matter.

On 22 May, *Dagens Nyheter*, one of the largest newspapers in the country, has an editorial with the title "Keep racism on a leash," where this self-defeating argument is presented:

> "The invitation gives the impression that Rami has something important to add to the debate on freedom of speech. But shouldn't the fact that he's severely misused freedom of speech for his own ends, that is spreading lies and prejudice about the Jewish people, have disqualified or at least made him fairly unappealing in such a discussion?"

The newspaper resorts to lies of its own too:

> "It also isn't a matter-of-course that people with racist views should be given the opportunity to spread their views at Swedish universities."

Only thing is, he was only there to talk about freedom of speech, not his own 'racist' views.

Östgöta Correspondenten also has an editorial of its own on the following day, titled "Hatred of Jews shouldn't be legitimized at Linköping University." This editorial as well offers quite self-defeating arguments.

> "Freedom of speech exists to protect the one who has inconvenient or controversial views. The purpose is to make national debate as free as possible."

> "Inviting Ahmed Rami to a debate on freedom of speech is therefore a little like inviting a serial rapist to a debate on men's violence towards women. Can you see anything constructive in such a provocation? That's highly doubtful."

In this author's opinion, the fact that Rami has been reported to the Chancellor of Justice over at least nine different 'hate speech' offences makes him more suitable than anyone else to comment on freedom of speech in the country. As of 2010, public debate in Sweden has returned to "normal." In the blogs of politicians such as Jan Björklund, head of the Liberal People's party, the country's own dissidents remain a pariah. In a newsletter from 10 March 2010, entitled "Now it's about our freedom of speech," Björklund acts all high and mighty about the need to support people who defame Islam in provocative ways and are physically attacked over it, yet doesn't mention a single person convicted for 'hate speech' in Sweden. But of course, he mentions Salman Rushdie.

One man - twelve hate speech trials and counting

At what point can you truly consider yourself an enemy of the state? Do you have to be on the run from government assassins? Or is it simply enough to have to gone to court no less than twelve times over "hate speech?" Björn Björkqvist, born in 1979 and former member of the National Socialist Front, has faced criminal charges at least twelve times for the opinions he's expressed in speech and in writing. It all began on 30 November 1995 when he was walking Visby town in his mid teens, wearing an assortment of badges on his clothes. These featured old Norse symbols that are usually associated with nationalist sentiment, though didn't include an actual swastika. For this he was charged with violating the HMF law along with an offence for disorderly conduct called *förargelseväckande beteende*; the police seize the badges from his clothes and he's scheduled to appear in court.

On 29 March 1996, he's sentenced to a 3000 kr ($400) fine by Gotland district court, along with forfeiture of the badges. He appeals the verdict.

On 11 June 1996, Svea Court of Appeal repeats the same verdict, though drops the disorderly conduct charge. Björkqvist appeals to the Supreme court.

On 17 October 1996, the Supreme Court repeats the original verdict as well.

This verdict would set a precedent and make it a criminal offence carrying any out of a large numbers of traditional symbols as a political statement.

The next couple of years he gets more involved in Sweden's nationalist movement, referred to as *nationella rörelsen* in Swedish, including joining the National Socialist Front, a Nazi

306

party looking to participate in the parliamentary elections of the 'democratic' system. He would find that political activism can be quite hampered by hate speech laws, however.

On 5 October 2002, NSF held a rally in the town of Borås, where Björkqvist was speaking. In a fiery tone, he railed against the Social Democrats for having brought about the multi-cultural society with the problems it's meant for Sweden. The authorities would have a say in this matter; after the speech, he once again faces criminal charges for the views he's expressed. A particular line that the prosecution bases its case on is this one: "I don't think I'm alone in feeling bad when Swedish girls are being raped by immigrant hordes." In the district court he's acquitted, however, on 11 September 2003.

The prosecution appeals the verdict, and on 25 May 2004, he's sentenced to two months in prison; the court describes the offence as "far from insignificant."

By now, Chancellor of Justice Göran Lambertz has set his sights on him, the sole prosecutor for offences relating to the freedom of the press - now he gets criminal charges for just about everything he does.

A year or two earlier, his party NSF had published a book titled *Judefrågan*, "The Jewish question" in English. The publisher had been sentenced to six months in prison for this in 2002. Björkqvist had written a preface to this book, however, where he describes Jews as "lying and manipulative." For this, he as well receives a prison sentence; on 16 December 2002, he's sentenced to eight months, though when he appeals the sentence, it's reduced to four months instead.

Apart from this he would also face charges for something his party had kept up on its webpage, for which he was the person in charge; during 2002, two different pages had featured swastikas, illegal under Swedish law, along with a caricature of a

Jew. This saw him face two more prosecutions as well.

On 19 November 2002, an article had been posted on the party webpage criticizing another nationalist party for not having a racial perspective. To support the need for such a perspective, the article had alleged that Africa's poverty was due to racial qualities. To quote the most controversial part of the article:

> "Marxists like to claim that negroes have low IQ because they have a bad economy, not that they've got a bad economy because their IQ is low. However, by comparison with negroes who thanks to the work efforts of white people have a relatively good socio-economic situation, with negroes whose situation is worse they still have an equivalent IQ."

On 4 December 2003, Lambertz starts an investigation into this matter, and on 20 February 2004, he files charges against Björkqvist yet again, since he was implicitly responsible for the website's contents.

On 12 July 2005, Björkqvist is sentenced to two months in prison for expressing contempt for another race. He appeals the verdict, and in the Court of Appeal for Skåne and Blekinge, he gets the same sentence on 31 October 2006.

Sweden celebrates its national day on the 6th of June, and in 2006, Björkqvist was invited to speak in front of an audience of about a thousand people in Stockholm. He addresses the topics at heart for him - immigration, race and such, and also talks about his earlier convictions. To quote a portion of the speech, delivered in a merry manner:

> "I got two months in prison for the crime agitation against ethnic group because I had said this at an earlier demonstration, and now I'm quoting. I'm not saying in any way that I mean this now, but then I said that **I don't think I'm alone in feeling bad when I read about how Swedish girls have been raped by immigrant hordes**. Two months in prison is what I got for that, for the crime

agitation against ethnic group, and for the ones not familiar with the law, it means so to say, and now I'm quoting again, that you express contempt for an ethnic group or other such group of people alluding to race, skin colour, national or ethnic origin, creed or sexual orientation. And that was I did when I said that I feel bad, or... **I don't think I'm alone in feeling bad when Swedish girls are being raped by immigrant hordes.**"

(Discussing the importance of race)

"[Negroes]... they can get various diseases... that white people can get too. But then when you provide them with medicines it turns out that if you give this negro the same medicine as for a white person, well then the negro dies"

(At this point portions of the audience burst out in laughter.)

"and that's pretty negative actually... well, for that negro."

(Some more laughter from the audience.)

This time around the police are already waiting to pick him up, standing next to the podium while he holds his speech. As he finishes, they quickly grab him and throw him into their car, saying he's suspected of hate speech, though the exact details of what parts of the speech would be considered criminal were going to be sorted out later on. He's brought to the station and interrogated, being kept in custody for the next few days. On the 15th, he writes an article about his arrest and subsequent treatment at the hands of the police, posting it on his party's website. He also expresses fear about the degradation of free speech in the country.

"At about 11:00, the custody negotiations started and not until now the prosecutor explained what he considered to be agitation against ethnic group. In spite of the seriousness of the situation, I had to restrain myself from laughing when the charges were brought up. Among other things, the prosecutor felt I should be sentenced for quoting what I had been sentenced for earlier," he writes.

309

On 10 September 2007, Björkqvist is sentenced to two months in prison, though on 26 February 2008, after he's appealed the verdict, Svea Court of Appeal acquits him.

Hence between 1996 and 2008, Björkqvist was in court no less than twelve times for "hate speech," as well as suffering numerous house searches and confiscations of property by the police in connection with the criminal investigations. Today he has left the NSF behind and is instead running a publishing house for controversial literature, together with afore-mentioned Ahmed Rami - www.logik.se.

Academic freedom?

On 5 December 1997, an unspeakable event took place at Umeå University, the repercussions of which would shape public debate for years to come. In front of a handful of people in a room at the university on a Friday evening, a young man with National Socialist convictions held a lecture on the topic "What do the Nazis want?" The man's name was Dan Berner and he was 22 years old. Berner had been invited to speak by a research student in sociology at the university, Karolina Matti, who had received a B.A. degree from this academic institution. Her duties at the university included being a coordinator for the UFÅ, the Young Researcher's Association, which meant inviting thought-provoking lectures to be held here. She had felt this lecture in particular would be suitable for the purpose.

Before this evening, Berner was an unfamiliar name outside National Socialist circles in the country, but the speech he held would generate some major controversy as well as legal consequences. Matti had looked around for someone who could hold a speech for her project called "National dissidents," which would cover the perspectives of this group in society, and she had come across Berner on online discussion forums and writing for the National Socialist magazine Nordland. Matti invited him to come up there, and on 5 December, they were standing in an auditorium before a small crowd of people.

Berner now held the speech he had come for, after which the audience would be allowed to ask questions. Portions of the lecture for which he would be subsequently prosecuted included these lines:

"Our women are being raped by cultural enrichers of other races."

"Multi-cultural youth gangs spread fear around them."

311

The entirety of the lecture isn't publicly available, unfortunately, after a court determined it to be 'hate speech.' In August of 2000, a man was convicted of having reproduced Berner's lecture online, being found guilty as well of the same crime. This is an interesting contrast to when in 1993, the court in the Huddinge child pornography case disseminated such movies on request because they were evidence in the case. Apparently it's more important keeping people from accessing National Socialist agitation than from child porn.

After the lecture was over, it was time for the audience to ask questions, and the answers he provided would become additional charges against him.

> "If we compare ourselves to Africans, these have never managed to create a civilization at all."

> "Ridding the country of immigrants won't be a comfortable undertaking."

The coming days, when the university administration and mass media learn of the lecture that has been held, there is quite an outcry. How could something as atrocious as a speech by a National Socialist have taken place at Umeå University? Though a criminal investigation is swiftly underway, sanctions against research student Karolina Matti are delivered even faster. Days after the lecture, she's interrogated by her superiors at the university and required to make a statement that she distances herself from National Socialist ideology, something she refuses to do, citing how the constitution protects one's right not to answer such questions. Matti is now suspended from her position at the university, and the case garners national media attention.

Berner's speech wouldn't mean legal consequences only for him, but for Matti as well; she's charged with being an accomplice in Berner's unlawful lecture. Both of them go through police interrogations and face trials during the coming year. On 16 June 1998, the verdict is delivered. The district court writes:

> "Dan Berner's lecture, whether you consider the now commented particularities or when considered in its entirety, is not an insert in a factual discussion concerning immigrants or other ethnic groups or in some other way social problems with or without relation to the immigration to Sweden. The lecture is instead a propaganda address for an ideology based on racist ideas."

> "Neither Dan Berner or Karolina Matti have been - as far as is known - previously convicted of crimes. The investigation doesn't reveal anything else than that their living conditions are in order. Agitation against ethnic group is a crime of the sort where prison should follow. When it comes to Dan Berner there has been no circumstance that gives reason to abstain from this. Hence the sanction shall be determined as prison.

> When it comes to Karolina Matti there is well-founded reason to assume that her options to gain further employment at Umeå University are just about non-existent. In practice the same ought to apply to her options to at the university conduct research. Taking these conditions into consideration, the sanction for Karolina Matti applying chap 29 §5 1 of the penal code [*brottsbalken*] [leniency in sentencing due to other sustained injury] should be determined as probation along with a fine."

Berner is sentenced to a month in prison for HMF, and Matti is sentenced to probation and a fine for *medhjälp till hets mot folkgrupp*, complicity in agitation against ethnic group. Both the defendants and the prosecutor appeal the verdict.

In the appeals court on 7 december 1998, Berner's sentence is increased to two months, while Matti's remains the same. One of the judges has a dissenting opinion in Matti's sentence this time, arguing that she should be sentenced to prison as well - one month.

The defendants appeal the verdict to the Supreme Court, and

313

on 7 July 2000, this court establishes the verdict of the previous court.

Unexpected friends

Berner and Matti suffered quite a bit of persecution following this matter and have today changed their identities to get away from both mass media and left-wing terrorists. One of these terrorists even vandalized the home of Berner's father, in spite of this man being a Communist. Both the university administration and the political establishment have put their feet down in the matter and declared that people with these ideologies can't be allowed to express them, not even at universities. Prefect Sten Höglund at Umeå University, with a background as a revolutionary Communist, who when his own free speech came into question stressed how important freedom of the press was to society, now told a TV audience that Nazis can't be invited to speak since you can't "rein them in," the audience might not be prepared for their propaganda.

Another man who stated his support for the ban was minister of education Carl Tham, with a background in Sweden's far-left, who declared that people with "violent ideologies" have no place in universities. One could ask how many of his own comrades have agitated for the violent overthrowing of the democratic order at some point? Minister Tham was a peculiar man to grandstand on this matter, considering his own lack of respect for liberty.

During his time as minister of education 1994-1998, Tham was notorious for steam-rolling his critics in the academic world, who were outright hostile to his plans for their domain. He established quotas for the minimum number of women to become professors, cutting down on research in general though financially supporting gender research; he also attempted to establish a program for 9000 people of the right backgrounds ages 25-45 to get paid a decent salary while they read at universities, which infuriated the regular students. His totalitarian way of running the education ministry saw many petitions filed against him - the paid student positions resulted in nearly 40,000 students signing a protest.

You can't but help noticing that the people who have the least respect for other people's rights are the ones the most prone to call for forceful measures to be taken against people of other totalitarian inclinations. Though it was dangerous to oppose the establishment in the Berner/Matti matter, there were still people that did. A member of *Lärarförbundet*, the Teacher's Association, posted an article denouncing this Mccarthyism, ending with the question, "The question is in what tradition job exclusion [*yrkesförbud* in Swedish, *Berufsverbot* in German] for 'personal antidemocratic values' belong: in that of a police state or that of a civil democratic society?"

Most surprising in the ones to come to the couple's defence was however *Folket i Bild / Kulturfront*, an independent political magazine that's generally left-leaning, though open for anyone who can't find any other outlet to express their views. In a display of true noble spirit, Hans Beukes, born in Namibia as a black man, had in a letter protested Umeå University's decision to suspend Matti because of the lecture as soon as he had heard of the measure.

Beukes relates how when he had arrived in Sweden in 1960, he had been invited to debate Per Engdahl, the leader of a fascist movement called *Nysvenska Rörelsen*, which during World War II had supported Nazi Germany, though as an organization never actually considered itself National Socialist. The topic of discussion was the apartheid policy in South Africa. A portion of the attendees at Gothenburg University, where the debate was to be held, had opposed letting Engdahl speak there. Though after a vote by the people present, it was settled that he should be given the right to speak. This pleased Beukes, who wanted a debate and not merely hold a lecture. Many of the objectors walked out in protest when Engdahl spoke, however.

Now in 1997, Beukes called on Umeå University to reverse their decision to suspend Matti. He would be joined by the rest of the FiB/K establishment, which was outraged especially at the way Matti had been treated, though they supported Berner's right to speak too. They even filed criminal charges against the university for suspending Matti, though the police quickly dismissed this complaint.

Today, Karolina Matti, new name unknown, has stated to media that she wants to put this affair behind her. Dan Berner on the other hand appears to have become more radicalized, not getting a public venue to speak, though not wavering in his activism and apparent desire to overthrow the state by any means necessary.

Brottby - Mass arrests at a White Power concert

During the 1990's, following the explosion in the immigration of asylum seekers in the first years of the decade, the common man began to regard this 'refugee' (the actual asylum need of the people coming to the country was highly doubtful) immigration as a serious problem. Though the average Swede wasn't too vocal about the issue, especially since it's not in the spirit of the Swedish people to oppose established authority and its policies, there started emerging an underground nationalism. This nationalism became quite popular among the youth, in particular due to white power bands such as *Pluton Svea*, *Midgårds söner*, *Division S* and similar, whose music inspired them. One could even say it became trendy being a racial nationalist, and this counter-culture seemed to emerge as a threat to the continued reception of 'refugees' to the country - people just didn't want them to come in the large numbers that were arriving.

The later part of the 90's saw many white power concerts staged, which attracted crowds in the hundreds, in spite of the covert nature of the arrangements. The lyrics expressed by the bands at these concerts were often in violation of the HMF law, which meant they had to remain an underground phenomenon. In mass media, and in the tabloid *Aftonbladet* in particular, the political establishment started lamenting the existence of these 'racist' concerts, calling for something to be done about them. Soon enough, the national police was tasked with disrupting them. The police attempted to find out where the concerts were going to be held, while the concert organizers attempted to keep them a secret - for some time, it appeared to be a never-ending cat-and-mouse game.

At the end of 1997, the cat was about to seriously escalate

317

this game. The police had caught rumours of a large concert that was going to be held during the first days of January the coming year, though the authorities didn't know yet just where it would be held. As the concert date was approaching, they found out it was going to be somewhere near Stockholm on the 3rd of January. The police had at this time quite a few people in the nationalist movement on its watch list, and they followed these individuals, stopping to search them for tickets as well as confiscating clothes with print that was deemed racial agitation. On top of this, they also stopped buses the organizers had hired to shuttle the concert-goers to the gig, frisking every single person on these buses. From the tickets, they learn about the actual location - *Brottby*, a small town some 30 km from Stockholm City. As they now have information about the destination, they undertake quite a large-scale operation to stop people from going to the concert, which includes telling the state railway company SJ to not let them on board the trains.

Eventually when the police has done the best they could to prevent people from going to the concert house, hundreds of them gather outside this building with riot gear while the concert is going on. They send officers in civilian clothing inside to document what's taking place. Halfway through the concert, the people present realize that these police officers intend to have them arrested. The exits to the building are barricaded, and preparations are made to confront the police. Soon enough, the armed police officers storm the premises and fill up the room with tear gas, flailing their nightsticks around while getting everyone present down on the floor.

The concert-goers soon learn that everyone that was present that night would be booked for suspicions of racial agitation simply for being there, and they're detained by the police; no less than 314 people all in all, including an American band called Max Resist that was playing at the gig. The next couple of hours, the police check the ID's of the detained people and let them out one by one after they're on the books. For some of them, criminal charges would await; for every single one, political registration became a reality as the suspicions of racial agitation were entered on their public record. One could say that this was a devious way by the police to punish in an extra-judicial way anyone that had been present at the concert, even though they would never be declared guilty in an actual court since they hadn't broken any laws.

After the concert, 27 people would be prosecuted and 15 were eventually found guilty under the HMF law or for other charges such as resisting arrest. The sentences delivered were an extreme break from normal Swedish norm in that teenagers without previous convictions were sentenced to prison for nothing more than Nazi salutes, while typically it takes several normal crimes before you have to face such a sanction. Four American citizens were among the ones sentenced to prison - one of the two being the singer of Max Resist, Shawn Sugg, who got a month of incarceration.

Two of the Americans challenge their sentences through the Swedish legal system all the way to the European Court of Human Rights, but alas they stand through every instance. In front of the ECHR, the Americans state their complaints that they couldn't know that their salutes were criminal offences, due to the general wording of the HMF law and that they had only arrived in Sweden some twelve hours earlier. They also bring up the fact that one of the lay assessors was a politically appointed Social Democrat, which they felt made him biased towards them. The court strikes down both claims as as invalid and declares the application inadmissible, citing Sweden's right to regulate speech through law, and the requirement of anyone residing in the EU (including merely visiting) to know the laws of the country they reside in. For more information on their case, see *Sugg and Dobbs v.*

Sweden.

Following the concert, left-wing extremists happily send requests for personal information about the people detained at the concert to the authorities, such as passport pictures, adding them to their political files. For some, this political registration meant loss of jobs or trade unions blocking companies from employing them.

The unexpected repression by the state scared people away from the established nationalist movement, and successful record companies such as Nordland died soon afterwards. If you think you live in a democracy, you're simply not prepared for suddenly facing a clampdown of this nature.

The 21st century - Freedom of speech goes down the drain

On 1 October 2001, the Government appoints a new man as Chancellor of Justice - Göran Lambertz, with a background in the Social Democratic party. This Lambertz would escalate the already vigilant application of the HMF law and tread new ground in what would be considered agitation. And unlike the men who had preceded him on this post, he would turn himself into quite a public figure, causing spectacles along the way. Lambertz introduces a special policy for dealing with mass media into an office that was formerly rarely discussed among wider circles, pushing himself into the limelight. Already when assuming the office, he was critical of the police force, yet as we will see in later sections, he would be quite happy in making use of their services in searching the homes of political dissidents. During these searches, political material is seized that would be offered to certain journalists for research on "right-wing extremism."

Swedes need not apply for protection

Far from all Swedes are aware of it, but the HMF law defines a hate crime as something a "majority group" commits against a "minority group." Cases of minorities attacking other minorities have occasionally been prosecuted too. "Majority groups" are not afforded protection, however. In essence, only two "majority groups" exist - Swedes and Christians. The latter is somewhat curious due to the few Swedes that actually consider themselves Christians - far less than an actual majority of the population. A group of immigrants raping a Swedish woman while screaming national insults against her isn't a "hate crime," but a Swede making a derogatory comment about a certain race or ethnic group, even while not in the presence of anyone belonging to that group, is.

Now and then, Swedes have filed complaints under the HMF law and attempted to have people prosecuted for agitation against Swedes, only to be reminded of this law not applying to such expressions. In 1986, a band called *Stockholms Negrer*, "Stockholm Negroes," consisting of immigrants, had written quite offensive song lyrics against Swedes. The contents of the lyrics included these lines:

> "Death to all blonde, proper f***ing Vikings!"

> "[About Swedes] You will suffer a terror, a terror that will terrify you, and you will witness more than death!"

A Swedish man reported this to the Chancellor of Justice at the time, but was told on 3 December that year that it wasn't considered agitation. The singer of this band, Michael Alonzo, was later put in a prominent position by the Government when he became the head of *Ungdom mot rasism*, "Youth against racism," and was given millions of crowns in taxpayer money to "fight racism." He was invited to debate shows on the state TV frequently, but never had to answer for his own racism.

Another similar case was Tobias Hübinette, a man of Korean descent, who for a short period when he took a break from his regular career of violent crime, had started an organization called *Expo*, whose aim it was to "educate the public on racism and xenophobia." Hübinette's record sheet includes damaging property, sabotage, agitation, verbal assault (death threats) and arson (against his former girlfriend). His own views obviously made him a perfect candidate for the job of fighting racism, since he in 1996 in a magazine called *Creol* had written this about white people:

> "To feel that or even think that the white race is inferior in every way imaginable is natural considering its history and present

322

actions. Let the Western world of the white race perish in blood and suffering."

But that was apparently not agitation either according to Swedish law. Is it just me, or does the term "anti-racist" instead appear to be a codeword for "anti-white," even if this doesn't necessarily means being against racism in general?

In 2003, Göran Lambertz was faced with another of these HMF lawsuits on behalf of a majority group:

"The contents of a letter to a editor has not been viewed as constituting agitation against ethnic group in relation to Swedes

Date of decision   2003-11-05
Registration number   3217-03-30"

"The article has been attached to the report. In the letter to the editor in question, with the headline "Original Swedes [are] the most simple [people] I've met," it says among other things that "Original Swedes are the most boring, simple, mean and stupid people I've ever met."

The public prosecutor of Stockholm, the City chamber, has handed the report to the Chancellor of Justice for trial."

Reading Lambertz' answers, I'm a little bit envious of him being able to refer to himself in third person, especially with a fancy title. Something tells me he gets off on it. "Don't you forget that I'm the Chancellor of Justice, bitch!" Neither the title of king or prime minister is capitalized in Sweden today, yet when this man refers to himself in his writs, he capitalizes his own title. I'm almost surprised he doesn't add a bold typeface and large font to the documents.

"Assessment by the Chancellor of Justice"

"The purpose during the coming into being of the penalization of agitation against ethnic group was to ensure minority groups of different compositions and adherents of different creeds a certain legal protection. The case that someone expresses criticism towards Swedes doesn't appear to have been intended to be targeted by the penalization. Already due to what now has been said the contents of the letter to the editor can't be considered to constitute agitation against ethnic group. I therefore take no further measure due to the report."

The HMF law is expanded

The surge in expressions of nationalist sentiment during the 1990's such as White Power concerts had caused concern among the political establishment, and though even teenagers had been sentenced to prison for Nazi salutes at the concert in *Brottby*, it was felt that the current HMF law wasn't enough to deal with the problem; legislators set to work on a new law that would give the state greater authority and also expand what groups would be protected under the law. On 20 August 1998, about half a year after the afore-mentioned concert, the Government appointed a committee to examine what could be done about this problem; one of the intents was to see whether mere membership of "criminal organizations" could become a crime in itself - the "crime" in question being of a non-violent political nature.

In October of 2000, an initial investigation titled "Organized crime, agitation against ethnic group, agitation against homosexuals etc. - the scope of culpability" (SOU 2000:88) is released. When describing "Xenophobic and racist associations," the legislators have extensive material at their disposal due to the efforts the security police has made of monitoring these organizations. There's some lamentation about the emergence of a new distribution media for material that the government wants banned:

"There aren't only upsides to the opportunities towards communication and distribution of information that the Internet brings. The computer network has become a channel for the distribution of racist, xenophobic, Nazi and antisemitic propaganda. Activists can also make connections with like-minded people and offer products for sale through postal order. It has proven itself hard to create any effective legislation against the **abuse of the Internet**."

You'd expect only countries like China and North Korea to use such terms as "abuse of the Internet" for anything but spam, but evidently the Swedish state does as well. This government investigation also discusses previous attempts at criminalizing membership of "racist organizations," finding that though many other legal ways of attacking the problem have been introduced, mere membership has so far not been successfully criminalized. With this new investigation, the scope isn't confined only to "racist organizations," but from what could be read into this next passage - possibly churches as well:

"First and foremost the assignment is limited in the way that we're meant to investigate matters about culpability for taking part in organizations that deal with criminal enterprise and certain other matters of criminal law in connection therewith (among other things the regulation on agitation against ethnic group and criminalization of agitation against homosexuals)."[1]

The suggestion of Chancellor of Justice Hans Regner that a new form of the criminal offence HMF should be introduced is also quoted;

"That the undertaking has a large extent or otherwise stands out as especially serious indeed appears to be taken into consideration already when determining the sanction. With a maximum penalty of two years in prison it is however far from certain that adequate respect is taken to circumstances of this nature when the sanction is determined. No matter what the state of these things is, the Chancellor of Justice feels a special penalty scale is justified for

---

1   SOU 2000:88, page 113

serious offences."[1]

The investigation shares the notion that a higher sentencing guideline than the one in place is required. The initial draft of the offence specification, and the one that would remain, is called *grov hets mot folkgrupp*, "gross agitation against ethnic group," with a sentence of between six months and four years in prison. Cases of what should be considered to fall under the more serious offence are mentioned:

> "The racist gatherings that we've seen in this country haven't been of the the really large kind, but the type of manifestations that the Brottby concert are examples of are very disturbing and alarming."[2]

I wonder if legislators will ever describe actual violent crime as "disturbing and alarming," and not only thought crime?

> "It can't be ruled out that we'll see even larger gatherings of this kind in the future. Whoever stages and leads such a gathering makes himself guilty of a form of agitation against ethnic group (possibly instigation to such a crime) that has a greater sentencing guideline. If such a gathering would additionally be part of a more systematic racist campaign, it is a type of criminality that there are good reasons to classify as gross and for which a greater sentencing guideline than the current one ought to exist."

I so wish Swedish legislators would make such effort as this to fight real crime as well; it's unbelievable what an uproar among the political elite the *Brottby* concert seems to have created.

> "Preparation for or instigation to agitation against ethnic group that is gross is therefore according to our view a kind of action that is worthy of punishment and we therefore propose that it's criminalized."

---

1 SOU 2000:88, page 206

2 SOU 2000:88, page 216

If this suggestion had become law, it would have been a crime to simply prepare "racist" propaganda for distribution even if you hadn't actually spread it. Thankfully, this part never became law.

The report also quotes earlier unsuccessful attempts at outlawing agitation against homosexuals, which found the laws protecting an individual from defamation and verbal assault enough since everyone no matter sexuality is protected by them. This time around, the legislators wanted to make sure that statements about homosexuals as a group are criminalized, however. The gay lobby RFSL is involved already in the beginning of drafting the intended legislation, and its representatives are unanimous in their call to add homosexuals to the groups protected by the HMF law. The investigation has quite a peculiar view on what is freedom of speech:

> "A limitation on freedom of speech may not extend so far as to endanger the free forming of opinion. We can't see that a criminalization of agitation against homosexuals generally speaking jeopardizes the free forming of opinion. Threats against or insulting opinions about homosexuals can, viewed generally, hardly be seen as the expression of a certain view."[1]

> "We therefore propose that agitation against homosexuals as a group shall be criminalized."

When the specifics of what kind of sexuality should be protected by the new law are worked on, the legislators are reluctant to include protection for heterosexuals:

> "The question is however whether there are reasons to extend the new criminalization to anything else than agitation against homosexuals. Heterosexuals constitute a majority of the population and it appears quite far-fetched that anyone would pursue agitation towards this portion of the population."

---

1   SOU 2000:88, page 240

I beg to differ - gay rallies quite often feature quite virulent attacks on heterosexuality using such terms as the "hetero norm" and the nuclear family, institutions being assaulted by the activists; the implicit attack on normal heterosexuality is quite evident. On 28 August 2010, "the queer institute of Gothenburg" held something called *Heterohatets dag*, "the day of Hetero hatred," pretty much an assault on everything good and decent in society. During an earlier gay pride parade that summer, activists had shouted the English phrase "We're here, we're queer, we're gonna f*** your children" over and over when they passed a stand that the Christian church *Livets Ord* had set up along the path of the parade. The *Livets Ord* members did nothing whatsoever to provoke the activists, yet their stand was assaulted by masked individuals. Ripping apart the billboards of the Christians with the message "God loves you," the activists also chanted "Fags hate God," a phrase possibly taken from the Westboro Baptist Church, who's not only used the well-known phrase "God hates fags," but that one as well. As the gay activists are making fools of themselves, they're being recorded on camera, which doesn't seem to do anything to discourage them from embarrassing themselves. For video footage, look up "Livets ord-medlemmar attackeras i Göteborg" on Youtube.

But to return to the legislation - "majority groups" without protection now numbered three: Swedes, Christians and heterosexuals. Though only unofficially designated, three minority groups awarded special protection now also existed: Jews, Muslims and homosexuals.

The following years, this report is sent around for circulation to a large numbers of courts, legal instances, government departments, trade unions and non-government organizations (including the national councils of both Jews and Muslims) to form a consensus; 24 organizations invited to have a say don't bother adding anything to the matter, among them a taxpayer-funded special interest group with the somewhat comical name *Afrosvenskarnas riksförbund*, "The national league of Afro Swedes."

Though this organization of African immigrants didn't add anything to the actual discussion about the legislation when it took place, they've been quite happy in attempting to exploit the hate laws; in 2007, they supported a lawsuit against the re-publisher of the old cartoon Tintin because of the way it portrayed Africans, and have also taken to the streets describing all of Sweden as a giant den of racists. In 2009, they protested the name of a Stockholm residential block named *Negern*, "The Negro," a name given to it in 1866, though mostly only used by city planners. Now ARS got the name changed by claiming they were offended by how the word had been used during earlier centuries. Organizations such as these know from experience that staging activities of this sort usually earns them a bit extra taxpayer money, and are necessary to not fade into obscurity.

Another of the organizations listed as declining to respond was *Svenska kommittén för antisemitism*, the "the Swedish Committee For Antisemitism;" something tells me they really mean "the Swedish Committee Against Antisemitism." Or might it actually be a discrete jab at an organization whose activities, calling people 'antisemites' left and right, rather contributes to antisemitism? Who knows, but this is a digression.

Most prominent among the parties discussing the change in legislation would of course be the gay lobby RFSL. On 22 November 2001, the final government bill is produced to the public, a bill that sets 1 January 2003 as the date for when the new law would take effect.[1] The feedback from the various organizations is presented along with responses from the Government. Most of the suggestions are intact, but the aim to

---

1   Proposition 2001/02:59 Hets mot folkgrupp, m.m.

attempt to criminalize membership of racist organizations has been scrapped.

Initially, the protection for homosexuals was going to be added as a special case of the law, not listed under ethnic group, but the RFSL and other organizations feared that that might make homosexuals appear to be a group awarded too much special protection, and the legislators instead settle on the term "sexual orientation" as one of the forms of ethnic groups. Somehow you wonder how homosexuals could be considered an ethnic group - don't you have to be able to reproduce and have children to constitute such a group? The RFSL also wants cross-dressers protected, but the Government isn't interested in this, referring them to the protection granted them as individuals instead, though still assuring them that this doesn't mean that they're less worthy of protection than other groups.

Following this government bill, portions of the parliament attempt to block the expansion to cover homosexuals as a group.

In bill 2001/02:K29, ten members of the Moderate party attempt to stop this portion of the government bill, but their bill is voted down.

In bill 2001/02:K26, ten members of the Christian Democrats express their support for the new law and its protection of homosexuals, but ask for clarification on just what expressions concerning sexuality are being criminalized - this is also voted down.

In bill 2001/02:K27, three members of the Liberal People's Party lament among other things that cross-dressers aren't covered by the law; their bill is voted down as well.

The last bill to be voted down is 2001/02:K28, by three Moderate members of parliament, calling for the new legislation to be scrapped, citing what it would do to restrict freedom of speech.

Hence on 1 January 2003, thanks to Göran Persson's Government, Sweden has its new law criminalizing threats or expressions of disrespect towards homosexuals as a group, as well as raising the maximum sentence from two to four years.

Ban the Bible!

Some actions just make you wonder about the hubris of the people behind them. As the newly expanded HMF law had been enacted, a man identified by the initials TB had immediately filed a complaint with the Chancellor of Justice, to see whether the contents of the foundation of Western civilization, the Bible, would fall under the jurisdiction of this new law. A new Swedish translation of the Bible had recently been issued, Bibel 2000, and already at that time there were talks among society's 'intellectuals' about banning this book; now this man was investigating whether it could be banned because of what it had to say on the topic of homosexuality.

On 21 January 2003, the Chancellor of Justice answered the complaint.

"Question whether certain texts in the Bible can be considered agitation against ethnic group

Date of decision 2003-01-21
Registration number 16-03-30"

"The matter

TB has in a writ here reported certain religious texts in among other works the Bible to try if a breach of the freedom of the press in the form of agitation against ethnic group (HMF) has been committed. He has referenced the circumstance that the direction about agitation against ethnic group these days also includes attacks on groups related to sexual orientation."

"Assessment by the Chancellor of Justice"

"On the topic of whether certain Bible texts might include agitation against homosexuals, there has occurred a certain debate in among other places the media. From among other sources legal

332

science there has occurred statements with the implication that certain passages in the Bible will be criminal when new prints are released. Not the least for that reason I feel I should make my position known. I would like to point out that certain **changes in the texts** could lead to another position and therefore limit my current considerations to the versions that have been subject to official translation into Swedish."

So... Maybe the Bible should be rewritten to better fit contemporary Swedish law? Then it would be entirely safe from being banned? Thank God that you give us this assessment, oh dear Chancellor of Justice, so that we may know whether this old tome of no real significance to anyone should still be permitted in today's Swedish society. Naturally, such a decision should fall upon one man, with no respect shown to the people who want to preserve it in its traditional form.

"Does the Bible contain agitation against homosexuals?

There exists statements in the Bible whose content in themselves are such that the statements, were they to be viewed in isolation, could be considered to include agitation towards homosexuals (see for example Leviticus 18:22 and 29, Romans 1:15-32 and 1 Corinth 6:9-10)."

You didn't do your homework, mister Chancellor of Justice, you really overlooked Leviticus 20:13 and Revelation 21:8. I'm also a bit curious as to how Leviticus 18:29, if viewed in isolation from 18:22, could be considered agitation against homosexuals. "For whosoever shall commit any of these abominations, even the souls that commit them shall be cut off from among their people."

"It could be considered agitation against homosexuals if the statements were raised today and expressly cited in a derogatory manner against a homosexual lifestyle. But already the circumstance that the statements exist in the Bible can't be be considered any such threat or any such expression of contempt that make them criminal.

Hereby the case is closed."

"Decision by the Chancellor of Justice

The Chancellor of Justice doesn't proceed with the matter.

The Chancellor of Justice states that new prints of the Bible can't be considered to contain the freedom of the press offence agitation against ethnic group. The statement concerns the versions of the Bible that have been subject to official translations into Swedish."

Hence, to summarize: While you can still distribute the Bible, preaching its message just might get you imprisoned. On another note, I sure as hell hope that the person referred to as TB here isn't the T.B. behind the many complaints to the JO for what he had to 'suffer' through while incarcerated. This author has no further information about the identity of the people filing these complaints than the initials; it would simply be too much if a convicted sex offender complaining about everything also tried to have the Bible banned.

Christians start to bite the dust

Åke Green - the first man in modern times on trial for preaching the Bible

Few people could have missed the trial against Christian pastor Åke Green. Searching his name on Google, you get over 35,000 hits, with roughly 10% being in English. American churches in particular brought it to the world's attention when they heard of the guilty verdict and his subsequent prison sentence. An organization called the Alliance Defense Fund even stepped in and assisted in the pastor's legal defence after he had appealed the first verdict.

On 20 July 2003, pastor Green had held a sermon at his local church on the topic of homosexuality, with an audience of some 75 people. Little did he know that this sermon in the least religious country on the planet would become a world affair. Green explained the Bible's view on homosexuality, quoting relevant passages, and also expressing his fear that homosexuality would destroy Sweden; he described it by saying that "sexual abnormalities are a deep cancerous tumour on the entire society," though he ended the exposition with the words "it is by showing all people grace and mercy that we can win them for Christ. We never win anyone by giving them the cold shoulder." The full sermon can be found online, even translated into English.

After the sermon, a representative of the gay lobby RFSL filed a complaint with the police, citing the HMF law, and a legal process began. The RFSL representative explained to mass media that he felt the sermon "legitimized threats, violence and violations against LGBT people."

A year later, on 29 June 2004, the district court of Kalmar found him guilty and sentenced him to a month in prison. Both parties appeal the verdict, and in the appeals court, the prosecutor demands at least six months for Green, a view seconded by the RFSL. This time the courtroom is teeming with media, however - plenty of international reporters have shown up apart from the Swedish reporters, attention that might have influenced the court. Though the worldwide condemnation of the guilty verdict was diverse, Swedish media and the state TV preferred to focus on what the not too popular Westboro Baptist Church had stated, essentially associating Green with this church. The appeals court actually acquits Green on 11 February 2005, and the prosecution appeals the verdict to the supreme court, which on 29 November also acquits him, stating that even though he's to be held responsible under Swedish law, the precedents set by the European Court of Human Rights make it a violation of his rights to sentence him.

The RFSL and other gay activists are very unhappy with the verdict, and quite a lot of discussion ensues with them claiming that society still overlooks their rights. My, it's so unusual hearing such complaints coming from this crowd. In particular, they argue that if Green had expressed himself in the same way about actual ethnic or religious groups, he wouldn't have been acquitted. An academic thesis by a student at the faculty of law at Lund University with the initials J.M. from 2005 deals with Green's prosecution; in the essay, the author contrasts the verdict with one received by Ahmed Rami for what he had stated about Jews, pointing out that Rami was punished much more severely. To quote the essay:

> "It appears obvious that the courts put more energy into investigating the case where the Jewish people are subjected to insulting remarks than when homosexuals are the exposed group."

"Taken together, the message becomes that homosexual individuals have to accept having to put up with a bit more than Jews are forced to do. Why is this so?"

Ah, the competition for victim status... "They're more established as victims than we are, it's not fair!" To quote *Animal Farm* - "All animals are equal, but some animals are more equal than others."

Christianity = Nazism?

Though you'd expect people to show more respect for Christianity than to directly associate it with the most controversial political ideology there is, that's not the case in Sweden. After Åke Green had held his sermon, a homosexual activist of an 'artist' called Elisabeth Ohlson-Wallin made an exhibition called "In hate we trust," where one of the pieces is a picture of a church congregation where the parishioners raise their arms in Nazi salutes, with what appears to be Åke Green standing on the pulpit holding a sermon. Former head of the Swedish church, K.G. Hammar, felt she had a point in linking Christianity with Nazism.

This exhibition isn't the only attack she's made on Christianity; in 1998, she had made another exhibition - a compilation of photographs of Jesus surrounded by gay men in different positions, called *Ecce Homo*. There was one where Jesus was baptised by John, with genitalia showing. One where a group of leathermen looked up to Jesus. And naturally one of the most frequent targets of anti-Christian attacks: The last supper. Except here, the apostles were men in women's clothes.

Though the exhibition was a very clear affront to Christian faith, the then still head of the Swedish church, K.G. Hammar, embraced it as a positive contribution to society's debate. In fact, he even blessed the display of the exhibition in Uppsala cathedral,

337

one of the churches where not even children were spared the sight. This blasphemy saw the pope cancel the Swedish arch bishop's visit to the Vatican that year. *Ecce Homo* was also brought up for display inside the Swedish parliament.

A wolf in sheep's clothing

But who was the man who had started the whole legal process against Åke Green? Fredrik Johansson, then head of the Kalmar local chapter of the gay lobby RFSL, had spent much of his 20's devoted to gay activism, identifying discrimination against LGBT people all across society, especially against himself - a professional victim. In a 2003 interview with tabloid *Aftonbladet*, he laments that the police don't take his complaints seriously when he claims he receives threatening phone calls every week as well as being regularly assaulted in broad daylight - he describes himself as subjected to systematic terror. When asked the question "It sounds like a rough life?" he responds "Yes, it's turned into a lot, it drains one's energy. But I don't bow to **people's** threats."

Though the standard drill of these activists is to describe their persecutors as consisting of 'Nazis' and 'homophobes,' this word might be a telling Freudian slip in how he relates to the world – all of it is an enemy in his eyes. Fredrik had received enormous media coverage for his various projects, supposedly aimed at fighting "homophobia" and enabling LGBT people to participate in mainstream society - though you'd be hard-pressed to find someone that was actually prevented from doing it even before his arrival.

Not only did he file hate speech charges against Green, but also against *Ölandsbladet*, a perfectly conventional mainstream newspaper, portraying it as a haven for bigotry. He was also a paid associate of the notorious organization Sweden's United Gay Students (*Sveriges Förenade Gaystudenter*), which a couple of years back had managed to get a university lecturer fired from his job over a "homophobic" statement he had made. It turned out that this statement was him arguing that you should meet dissidents with dialogue, not with censorship, and the lecturer hadn't been given the right to even defend himself against the charge; the university authorities feared too much standing in the way of the gay lobby to question them and simply terminated his employment.

Johansson's projects, for which he was granted plenty of government funds, were exposed as nothing more than money-making schemes on his part. When his affairs were eventually scrutinized, an almost Machiavellian plot emerged; while working with these "projects," he had also claimed unemployment benefits, and on top of that he had applied for and received welfare checks, payouts that over a four year period had netted him a fortune of almost a million Swedish crowns, or about $100,000. He even requested the government to pay for him and his friends travelling to Greece to lecture the Greeks on HIV (and if I know these people, probably also helped spread it too).

This became a police matter, and on 26 September 2007, he was sentenced to ten months in prison for fraud. During the concluding speech of the trial, prosecutor Bo Svensson had this to say:

> "We have before us a very peculiar man. I'm certainly no psychologist, but to me it seems as if the 29-year-old has psychopathic traits. He doesn't answer a single question in a straight and clear manner, but we see here a person who exploited the country's welfare system so that he in a couple of years could amass a private fortune of 750,000 crowns."

Though his activism had been considering a blessing to the RFSL before, now they expelled him, and the national chairman of the organization referred to Johansson as a disgrace to their community. This organization has gone through many such disgraces over the years; among others one in 2003, when Mattias Helander, then head of the RFSL youth organization, was convicted of having lured two young boys, ages 13 and 14, to his home to sexually exploit them. Helander was however spared incarceration, only being sentenced to community service. As is the case with almost all of these gay activists, he as well had been paid taxpayer money to promote his own causes.

The following years saw additional ostracism of pastor Åke Green; though few homosexuals were particularly active in the Swedish sobriety organization IOGT-NTO, through outside pressure they were able to get Green expelled on 30 January 2008. At least a thousand Christians quickly left the organization in protest.

No Christians allowed?

During the autumn of 2008, one of the most renowned academic institutions in Sweden, Lund University, was in the process of appointing a new principal - rector being the title for the position. After some deliberation, eventually a man named Per Eriksson was selected by the university committee on 26 September 2008, who's a professor in signal processing and was the principal of Blekinge Institute of Technology between 1989 and 2000. Initially his religious background, being a former member of a Pentecostal congregation, wouldn't be a problem, but when seven teachers at the science faculty learned of this, they sent a protest letter to the university committee. Interviewed by media, one of these teachers, Cecilia Hägerhäll, has this to say.

> "He belonged to a movement where they feel the Bible is the word of God, and that's that. And the Pentecostal pastor Åke Green says homosexuality is a sin. That's not the kind of person that's fit to be rector. The Pentecostal church is a pretty extreme anti-science movement. If he had been a buddhist, it would have

been far less controversial."

Challenged by this criticism, Eriksson presents the university with an open letter on the 5 October, attempting to dispel the concerns his Christian faith had raised, where he touches specifically on the topics of homosexuality and stem cell research:

"When it comes to specific issues that have been discussed such as my attitude towards homosexuals and stem cell research, I would like to refer to the values expressed in the strategic plan and my own positive experience of qualified co-workers with another sexuality than my own. When it comes to the ethical problems that may arise within research, in stem cell research among other areas, this research is tested by a specific public authority, *Etikprövningsnämnden* [The ethics testing board], in accordance with the legislation that applies to the field. The decision of this board guides me as well as all researchers, financiers of research and heads of universities."

Hence, he's coerced into stating that he doesn't have a problem with homosexuality or stem cell research.

The matter raises quite a bit of discussion in society, and a Christian member of parliament named Lennart Sacredeus even expresses concern that this has been an outbreak of christophobia, irrational fear of Christianity. However, on 23 October, the Government confirms his appointment and he becomes rector, starting on 1 January 2009.

Homosexuals impaled on stakes?

The Åke Green affair wasn't the only crackdown Swedish Christians suffered at the hands of the state; early in the morning on 30 June 2004, four police officers pay Leif Liljeström a visit on similar charges. He's awoken to them banging on his door and is taken to the station for an interrogation, while two officers stay behind in his apartment to seize his computer, personal notes and various CD's and floppy disks in his possession. The day before this, Åke Green had been sentenced to prison, and Leif now faced the same prospect because of his website www.bibeltemplet.net.

He's not told what it's about until he reaches the station and the interrogation has started; he's then informed he's suspected of having violated the HMF law because of the writings he's had up on his website on the topic of homosexuality. Leif goes through a 1.5 hour long interrogation where he admits he's responsible for the content on the site, but defends his right to express these views. When he learns his computer has been seized, he pleads with the authorities for a swift process in this matter, but is told that him getting it back may take some time.

The criminal investigation had started in 2003, when law student Jonas Eklund had come across the site and reported it to the police as hate speech, citing what Leif had written about homosexuality giving rise to the AIDS epidemic. The authorities are initially somewhat reluctant to go through with the errand, but in 2004, a public prosecutor picks it up and initiates the process. The activity on the site in question is quite limited, with about 50 people a month visiting it, out of which only three or four actually write anything.

On 26 April 2005, the district court sentences him to two months in prison and orders his computer destroyed, since Leif admits that he will go back to writing in the same manner if he gets it back. This is Liljeström's second HMF conviction, having been convicted in November of 2000 as well for what he wrote about Islam back then. He appeals the verdict, and on 18 May 2006, he's only sentenced to one month in prison; this time for *medhjälp till hets mot folkgrupp*, complicity in agitation against ethnic group, for what another man had written in his guestbook. This appeals court clears him of the original charge.

This man, using the name Karl-Göran, had argued that homosexuals ought to be put to death, in what appeared to be a somewhat jokingly manner.

> "The ones that can't live by Leviticus 18:22, they should naturally receive help - help to stop them from sinning. This is done through implementing Leviticus 20:13."

> "The men who can't muster the power to abstain from intercourse with other men they should be punished by death through being impaled on stakes in the town square. That way they're saved from continued sin while other sodomists [sic] are given a valuable warning."

Leif is held responsible for these statements since he hadn't deleted them, but only distanced himself from them, saying he doesn't want any violence against homosexuals. Almost two years after the initial seizure of his computer, the seizure is lifted and the computer is returned to him. The verdict is appealed again, and in the Supreme Court on 7 November 2007, he's acquitted of all charges. Though not becoming quite as big a matter as the Green trial, it still receives a bit of international attention, covered in the British magazine Times Online. "Christian web editor in gay row wins appeal."

So much for tolerance

"HomoSexuellt.com - we publish facts, research and critical studies about homosexuality and the gay movement."

In 2002, there appeared a critical information resource on homosexuality called homosexuellt.com. On it, you could find a compilation of scientific studies on the link between homosexuality and STD's, child abuse, heredity etc. The site had a very serious appearance, though it wasn't threatening or towards individuals, but merely discussing this topic. There were articles such as "The negative health effects of homosexuality," "Gay-To-Straight Research, "The Gay Gene?" and similar. The site also featured a forum, where people were allowed to discuss the contents of the site, including a section specifically on the topic of what is to be considered homophobia. "Here you can discuss agitation against homosexuals. What can be considered agitation. Is this website agitation?"

The existence of the site naturally caused an outrage among LGBT activists, whose lifestyle was being questioned. The administrator of the site was very happy to receive letters, answer them and have a dialogue with people who might disagree with the available material. You'd think this would be an excellent way for these people to present their grievances, yet they showed little interest in this. Instead they turned to legal action and disruptions to achieve their aims. In January of 2003, gay communities on the Internet decided they were going to crash the site and spam the administrator's E-mail; one invitation on the gay site qx.se read as follows: "This campaign is in full swing. Join in you too! Soon they'll receive hundreds of thousands of mails per day! Send new mails every day!"

An apparently technically very proficient man working at

RFSL Borås sent him 60 identical mails over a period of four minutes. This makes one every four seconds, about the time you could expect it to take for someone to repeatedly back up in his mail client or web browser to send the same message again. Wonder if he ever heard of more automated ways of spamming than clicking a button over and over?

On top of this, member of parliament Fredrick Federley reported the site to HomO, the Ombudsman against discrimination based on sexual orientation, to investigate whether it could be prosecuted under the recently expanded hate laws. To the dismay of these activists, the contents could however not be argued to qualify for prosecution, and no trial was held. So, the activists moved on to physical intimidation instead. After the site had become quite well-known, the administrator started touring Sweden to spread information material in paper and electronic form. He announced ahead of time where he would be, and the activists would then often show up to meet him. At one time his car was smashed, and another time he was assaulted by a large mob who destroyed what they could of the material he kept in his car. He details his travels on his new site emaso.com.

The gay lobby

The largest homosexual activist group in Sweden is the RFSL, an acronym initially formed by the words National League for Sexual Equality. Though having 5000 members doesn't make it too large an organization, their media presence is enormous; it's even received awards for being Sweden's most prominent lobby organization. While the RFSL claims to fight for equal rights for their members, they've been very active in attempting to censor their opponents - people who don't agree with their activism.

In 2007, an organization called *Bevara Äktenskapet*, Preserve Marriage, ran an advertisement campaign with the motto "Preserve marriage - mum dad children." This saw a furious response from the RFSL, which felt this campaign was offensive to LGBT people, that it would even lead to oppression of and violence against them. The campaign had a website up where you could sign your name to support the message, and some 50,000 people signed it. Nevertheless, the campaign encountered destructive retaliation; the posters were torn down, they received hateful phone calls and E-mails, and the website was attacked and shut down.

RFSL members were interviewed in mass media about the campaign, and one of them had this to say: "I don't want to have to see homophobic and socially conservative messages in the public arena."

The RFSL is dominated by men, and an article in a feminist newspaper complained about how the organization ignores the topics at heart for them, such as putting an end to pornography. I guess the gay lobby ought to get a "Lesbians need not apply" sign.

346

Stockholm pride

Every summer, Stockholm is host to one of the largest gay pride festivals in the world - *Stockholm pride*. The attendants of this event usually number close to 50,000 and has an audience of almost half a million watching it in the streets. It's even gotten to the point where all the major institutions of society and all political parties are expected to have official representation. The military (marching as individuals in their uniforms), trade unions, student organizations, *Regeringskansliet* (which in Sweden is what the White House is to the USA) and most of society's establishment.

When I was a child, people would show up in large numbers to see the royal family when they visited your town, with older generations being completely enthralled with their lives. These days it looks like the torch has passed to the LGBT movement. If a famous homosexual has a quarrel with his or her partner, naturally it has to be splattered all across national newspapers, and every little statement they make about anything has to be covered as if it was a divine revelation - the LGBT people are the new royalty.

The festival is usually initiated with a celebrity holding a speech. Over the years, the speakers have included these people:

2001, Wanja Lundby-Wedin, head of LO, Sweden's largest conglomerate of trade unions.

2003, current (not in 2003) prime minister Fredrik Reinfeldt. His centrist political stance made certain famous LGBT activists refuse to listen to his speech, however - Elisabeth Ohlson-Wallin, the 'artist' behind an exhibition called *Ecce Homo* portraying Jesus as a homosexual, being one of them.

2004, bishop of Stockholm, Caroline Krook, discussing marriage.

2005, head of Stockholm police, Carin Götblad, discussing 'hate crimes.'

During the election campaign of 2006, the leaders of the political parties, even the Christian Democrats, participated in a debate during the festival, where 'heteronormativity' was the topic of discussion, and all the participants were required to describe how heteronormativity had affected them personally. They were also asked to respond to certain questions by placing themselves on a scale from 1 to 5 based on their approval of said questions. One of them was, "I would let my seven-year-old son wear a skirt to school," and none of them picked the 1 of complete disapproval. The left-wing parties generally responded with 5 to everything, complete approval. "Children ought to be allowed to have more than two guardians" being one.

During the 2010 election campaign, all of the parties in the parliament were invited again to what's become one of the most important debates of the election cycle. This time the Christian Democrats passed on the invitation, and the Sweden Democrats complained about not being invited in spite of having a shot at entering parliament this election. The leader of islamophobic SD feels he's got something important to add in talking about how Islam views homosexuality, but the gay activists aren't interested. I just don't get how they willingly crawl before the activists... In a sane society, a debate held by sexual deviants would be boycotted instead.

In spite of the overwhelming support for the festival, with ticket prices averaging $100 or so, along with heavy taxpayer funding, the festival has recently faced financial difficulties. In March of 2010, the association reported a loss of some two million crowns. The chairman of the association had this to say: "The revenue side adds up, but somewhere the costs have escalated. We don't know just why yet." Perhaps he and the other members of the board ought to have a look in their own wallets? It's far from the only time funds in LGBT organizations have mysteriously disappeared.

Yet another Bible preacher is targeted

Ulf Ekman is the founder of a Swedish church called *Livets Ord*, the "Word of Life," which to an English-speaking person would best be described as a part of the charismatic movement. On 31 July 2004, Ekman, due to the uproar that the guilty verdict against pastor Åke Green had caused, had held a sermon on the same topic as Green - homosexuality. He quotes the usual Bible passages and declares that he stands by these passages, in defiance of the HMF law, and also declares his support for Green and condemns Green's sentence. This saw him become yet another one of the ministers investigated for hate speech, and the matter arrives at the desk of Chancellor of Justice Lambertz. However, in this case, Lambertz decides not to press charges, stating in his decision on 20 August the same year (registration number 2900-04-31) that Ekman in Lambertz' view was not guilty of agitation against homosexuals.

The affair surrounding his sermon wouldn't be the only breach of his civil liberties that Ekman would have to suffer, however; during the summer of 2008, it was revealed that the National Defence Radio Establishment (FRA in Swedish), dealing with signals intelligence, had eavesdropped on about a hundred people who had done business in Russia during the 1990's, which in Ekman's case consisted of his missionary work in this country. The public learned that telephone and Internet traffic in Sweden had also been broadly monitored, and the information gathered was stored no less than 18 months after its acquisition. Ekman wasn't notified even afterwards of this eavesdropping, but only now when a whistleblower had produced an excerpt of the names of people specifically monitored did he learn that the state had listened in on his traffic.

Sometimes I wonder if preachers in the old Soviet Union were put through as much trouble as the ones in today's Sweden.

Addressing the gay lobby

When 'right-wing extremists' visit schools to distribute information material, there is usually quite an outcry. When revolutionary Marxists do the same, there is none. The fliers handed out at *Staffanskolan* in *Söderhamn* on 10 December 2004 would even result in criminal lawsuits for all the seven young men responsible. National Socialist organization the Swedish Resistance Movement had this day visited this high school to spread their fliers on the topic of homosexuality, where they described it as destructive and argued that the gay lobby had too much power. As they arrive, Mattias Harlin meets up with the school principal and asks if they can get an invitation to stand at the school. The principal furiously rejects the idea and drives them out of the building, but before they had gone up to him, they had put fliers in a couple of school lockers.

As is always the case in contemporary Sweden when dissidents have been able to express their views, another HMF investigation is swiftly underway. Within 18 days, on 28 December, Chancellor of Justice Lambertz has stated that the contents of the flier aren't covered by the freedom of the press. Harlin is interrogated by the police and explains that they had visited the school to spark a debate about the lack of objectivity in Swedish schools on this matter, with one-sided teaching on the part of the education system. He states that the purpose wasn't to disrespect homosexuals as a group, but only to discuss what's being taught in school.

The prosecutor in this trial at the Bollnäs district court argued that the following passages constituted 'hate speech' and should be considered criminal:

"Homo sex propaganda

Society has in a few decades turned around from a dismissal of homosexuality and other sexual perversions to an embracing of this deviating sexual inclination. Your anti-Swedish teacher knows very well that homosexuality has a morally destructive effect on the national body and will readily try to present it as something normal and good.

Point out to your teacher that there has been a law in Sweden that outlawed homosexuality, but which under the first half of the 20th century was revoked. Tell him that HIV and AIDS appeared early among the homosexuals and that their promiscous lifestyle has been one of the main reasons that this modern plague has taken hold. Also tell him that it was because of this that the now repealed "sauna club law" was introduced to prevent the spread of this disease. Tell him that the homo sex lobby with its agencies is also attempting to dedramatize paedophilia and ask him if this sexual perversion should be legalized."

On 11 July 2005, Harlin and another man are each sentenced to two months in prison for the flier; another man receives probation and a fine while the fourth man is sentenced to 40 hours of community service.

All four of the defendants appeal the verdict, and so does the prosecutor as well against three of them. The defendants want the charges dropped, while the prosecutor wants the three charged with *grov hets mot folkgrupp* instead, something that could be seen as 'major hate speech,' and is punishable with up to four years in prison instead of the two for the ordinary HMF offence.

On 14 December 2005, the appeals court, in a complete reversal of the previous verdict, states that the defendants have spread the fliers with the aim of sparking a debate, and acquits all of them.

The prosecution appeals this verdict to the Supreme Court,

calling for it to return to the verdict of the district court. On 6 July 2006, three of the men are sentenced to probation and fines – 19,000 crowns for Harlin, or about $2,500. The fourth man is sentenced to probation.

On the SMR webpage, the verdicts are described as a miscarriage of justice, and they declare they will appeal to the European Court of Human Rights, though these plans are never carried out and the case ends here.

There can be other downsides in becoming known as a speech offender as well, apparently; in April of 2008, without any advance warning, the police search the apartment of one of the four men, confiscating the four rifles and the pistol he was registered as owning. He was left with this notice:

> "It has been brought to the attention of the police that you because of your conduct can no longer be considered fit to own firearms. You see, it's been claimed that you have had dealings with people and organizations that can be linked to crimes as listed: public order, the constitution and national security."

The Sweden Democrats taunt Muslims - The Swedish Government apologizes

On 30 September 2005, the Danish newspaper *Jyllands-Posten* had published caricatures of Islam's prophet Muhammed, defaming him and the Islamic religion. This had caused quite a lot of controversy, with Muslims at first demanding that the newspaper apologized for publishing them, followed by calls by ambassadors from Muslim countries to discuss the matter with the Danish Prime Minister. The following months saw violent protests against the publication around the world, which turned *Jyllands-Posten* into a household name across the planet.

A small nationalist party called the Sweden Democrats (SD), which hadn't been able to get enough votes to qualify for entering parliament under the 4% requirement, was intrigued by the development. Looking to garner itself some recognition, albeit in the same reprehensible way as the Danish newspaper, they announce a caricature contest of their own in their party paper in January of 2006, encouraging their readers to send in their own. For now, not much is happening, but things would heat up the coming month.

On 2 February, the youth organization of this party publishes the *Jyllands-Posten* caricatures on its webpage, and the coming day, they start publishing their reader's contributions as well. The Swedish ministry for foreign affairs had for the last few months attempted damage control in the Danish affair to avoid having Swedish interests harmed, and minister for foreign affairs Laila Freivalds is now dismayed to learn that the same publication has taken place in Sweden as well.

The coming days, Arab countries learn of the Swedish contest and it's mentioned in their mass media. Freivalds realizes

Sweden might have a crisis on its hands, and in a complete breach of the legislation concerning censorship, on 8 February she sends an employee to the Internet provider Levonline that's hosting the webpage of the Sweden Democrats, to inform this ISP about what the publication might mean to Swedish international relations. The security police (SÄPO) visits the ISP as well. Freivalds never makes any attempt to speak directly to the Sweden Democrats, however. The following day, the ISP takes the domain of the Sweden Democrats offline, and Freivalds is in a radio debate with the leader of SD, calling for him to stop the publication of the caricatures. The security police are on 9 and 10 February in individual talks with prominent Sweden Democrats about the problems the publication is causing.

Freivalds also starts apologizing to the Arab world for the actions of SD, sending a letter to among others the Yemen foreign ministry that includes these paragraphs (my emphasis):

"However, a small extreme right wing, and xenophobic group – *Sverigedemokraterna* – has launched a cartoon contest regarding **the Prophet Mohammed** on its web site. It is a provocation, with the sole aim of creating reactions which may serve this group's own sombre aims all of which lack support in Swedish society. I find this act to be disgraceful and insulting. I am ashamed and **I apologize** that in my country there are individuals who are disrespectful and inconsiderate and who abuse the freedom of expression to manifest such kind of views with a malicious intent. I will always under all circumstances defend the freedom of expression but from this manifestation I disassociate myself. We take this very seriously. Sweden's Attorney General and the police are closely following developments."

Two days later, on 11 February, the Swedish ministry for foreign affairs informs Yemen that the webpage has been shut down. The apology is made public the following days - an article by the Yemen Observer from 15 February has the headline "Swedes Write to Yemen after closing Website Showing Cartoons."

That same day, on 9 February, Freivalds writes a directive to the Swedish embassies in all Muslim countries in the Middle East and North Africa, calling on them to make conciliatory measures, adding that the personal message from the minister for foreign affairs

"... can be presented to the authorities in your country/countries of employment. A direct reference to the minister for foreign affairs shall be made. The head of the authority decides based on his own judgement if this should be done actively or be used if/when opportunity is given. Under all circumstances, the message should be presented on a suitable level."

Hence she makes sure that the Arab countries understand that this is an official apology on the part of the Swedish Government.

On 10 February, SD files complaints with the Parliamentary Ombudsman (JO) and the Chancellor of Justice (JK) about the actions of the ministry for foreign affairs and the security police; a member of parliament also files a complaint against Laila Freivalds with the Committee on the Constitution (KU). The opposition parties in the parliament criticize Freivalds and Prime Minister Göran Persson for the shutdown of the webpage. Ultimately Freivalds is forced to resign on 21 March due to lack of support. Persson disclaims all personal responsibility, and Freivalds becomes the sole scapegoat to take the blame.

On 24 March, Chancellor of Justice Lambertz delivers a nine page response to the complaint:

"QUESTION WHETHER THE SECURITY POLICE OR THE MINISTRY FOR FOREIGN AFFAIRS HAVE ACTED IN VIOLATION OF THE PROHIBITION AGAINST

CENSORSHIP OF THE FUNDAMENTAL LAW ON FREEDOM OF EXPRESSION"

"Have representatives of the Ministry for Foreign Affairs violated the prohibition against censorship?"

"No violation of the prohibition against censorship can therefore be considered to have taken place through the contacts that an employee of the ministry for foreign affairs had with Levonline."

"Has the Security Police been guilty of crimes against the prohibition against censorship?"

"Even when taking into consideration what representatives of the Sweden Democrats have stated, it's clear that the Security Police can't be considered to have taken any measures that mean that one has "prevented" publication. Hence no crimes against the prohibition against censorship have been committed by the Security Police."

"Decision of the Chancellor of Justice

The Chancellor of Justice establishes that the questioned actions haven't meant any crimes against the prohibition against censorship of the fundamental law on freedom of expression and that from what's been learned, there exists no reason to criticize the Security Police or the affected employee of the Ministry for Foreign Affairs."

Mobster tactics involving implicit threats apparently work well when used by authorities against their subjects - the threat is there, but you don't have to actually do or say anything that would incriminate you.

The slippery slope of criminalizing speech

Though the chronology of this chapter may seem somewhat awkward, this section will be a summary of the development from the enactment of the law until the present day, and what restricting free speech has meant for society and public debate.

In the first half of the 20th century, freedom of speech in Sweden was quite unregulated, and the promises in the constitution held up quite well. Well, with the exception of the World War 2 period, when the state directly censored newspapers in order to avoid having media aggravate Germany, with the risk of invasion it meant for Sweden. The powers that be naturally have always desired to imprison dissidents, but about the only applicable law they could use was the one called *förargelesväckande beteende*, disorderly conduct, though this couldn't be used against the printed word due to its nature.

The political activism of one man would cause the state to react in such a way as to take the first shovel full in what would become the almost complete abolishment of free speech. On 20 April 1890, exactly one year after Adolf Hitler was born, a man named Einar Åberg entered the world. Åberg would follow in Hitler's footsteps and assume the same views as his, adopting an antisemitic world view in 1922 and eventually becoming a world-renowned publicist.

Einar Åberg looking serious.

Åberg would truly start making his mark on history from the 1940's and onwards, when he became possibly the world's leading antisemite outside of Germany. In 1941, Åberg had set up a book store in Stockholm for antisemitic literature, even adorning it with the same sign as many German shops at the time employed: "Jews and half-Jews not allowed." This led to friction with the surrounding community, however, and Åberg was sentenced to a fine for disorderly conduct as well as being forced to take down the sign. Åberg doesn't give up that easily though, putting up many similar signs on his shop, which caused quite a bit of melee to erupt outside.

Shortly after setting up the store, still in 1941, Åberg also formed *Sveriges antijudiska kampförbund*, "the Anti-Jewish Action League of Sweden." Its stated goal was "the total annihilation of Jewry in Sweden," and all members had to declare upon their honour as Swedes to remain in the organization until the goal was achieved.

In the year 1941, Åberg also launches a tirade of publishing antisemitic pamphlets of his own, disseminating them both in Sweden and the English-speaking world. This propaganda distribution was what ultimately would force the Swedish authorities to act, enacting a new law called *Hets mot folkgrupp*, HMF. These were some of his publications:

Jews and Morals (Swedish, 1941)

The Jew is the master of lies! : How can anyone say something of this sort? : Read the following pages! (Swedish, 1944)

Exposed Jewry (Swedish, 1945)

Who's to blame for the war, world Jewry or Germany? (Swedish, 1945)

The war criminals (English, 1945)

"God's chosen people" (Swedish, 1946)

Why I am anti-Jewish (English, 1951)

A collection of anti-Jewish pamphlets published by E. Åberg (English, 1958)

Initially, his agitation upsets only Jewish congregations in Sweden, but when he distributes his material on an international scale, both the American Jewish Committee and the World Jewish Congress start pressuring the Swedish government directly to do something about it. There are calls for a law for the specific purpose of outlawing Åberg's activities, and the new law would sometimes to be referred to as Lex Åberg - The Åberg law.

Though Jewish groups are very anxious to see immediate

action, the law takes several years to sort out, but eventually it's enacted on 30 June 1948, in force from 1 January 1949 and onwards. The new law was placed under the "Crimes against public order" section of *Strafflagen*, the law code that preceded *Brottsbalken*, the Penal Code. Chapter 11, paragraph 7, of *Strafflagen* now read as follows:

> "If anyone in public threatens, defames or reviles an ethnic group with a certain descent or religious belief, (he's) sentenced for agitation against (an) ethnic group to a fine or prison."

Åberg is naturally the first one to be convicted under this law, and he's sentenced to a fine on 25 August 1949. Before his death in 1970, Åberg would be convicted five more times under the HMF law, even though he contested the notion that his propaganda really fell under the new law.

Even in spite of the convictions, Åberg proceeds with his agitation, to the dismay of the World Jewish Congress. Then general secretary Siegfried Roth had this to say to Swedish newspaper *Göteborgs Handelstidning* on 13 July 1954:

> "The antisemitic propaganda, which the Swede Einar Åberg in his pamphlets spreads across the world is one of the greatest problems there is for Jews today. There has to be some way for the Swedish Government to put an end to his activities."

By 1964, bad health was taking its toll on Åberg and his propaganda came to an end. The HMF law would live on, however, eventually becoming the tool of censorship it is today through various revisions. In 1965, *Strafflagen* was transformed into *Brottsbalken* as the bulk of Swedish law, and the law was moved to chapter 16, paragraph 8, where it still remains today. Ah, if only someone instead had 'accidentally' deleted it discretely during this transition.

In 1970, the wording was changed, and "threatens, defames

or reviles" was changed to "threatens or expresses contempt." (Well, the Swedish word *missaktning* better translates into disrespect, but the official translation is the word contempt.)

In 1982, the law was revised again, and the new wording of *Brottsbalken* 16 § 8 became:

> "A person who, in public or otherwise in a statement or other communication that is disseminated among the public, threatens or expresses contempt for a national, ethnic or other such group of persons with allusion to race, colour, national or ethnic origin or religious belief[...]"

The 1988 HMF revision

Until the late 80's, roughly one person a year was convicted of HMF, the law didn't see much use in the country. In the mid 80's, the Government started working on yet another revision of the HMF law, however, one that would enable much more liberal use. Quite a few people would find themselves imprisoned under the revised law during the coming two decades, even though their activities wouldn't have been anywhere close to being prosecutable under the original law.

The discussion on the further extension of the HMF law resulted in a government bill (proposition 1986/87:151 - "concerning changes in the Freedom of the Press Act etc").

To quote portions of the discussion in this bill:

> "My suggestion: In order to prevent activity of racist organizations, the liability regulation concerning agitation against ethnic group shall be raised. Thus it shall no longer be required for a statement to be made in public or disseminated among the public to be punishable. As per the proposal, it's enough that the statement is disseminated within for example an organization. No special exception for statements that can be seen as justified when taking into consideration freedom of speech or other circumstances is introduced. Any direct ban on racist

362

organizations as such shall neither be introduced."[1]

Here, freedom of speech takes yet another plunge downwards. This move makes it apparent that it's not about preventing people from being exposed to hurtful statements, since this will include groups of like-minded people speaking amongst themselves. It's about limiting one's right to express certain views even to people who share them.

> "It is however obvious that the criminalization shouldn't go as far as to include statements within the completely private sphere. It should still for example be exempt for punishment to in front of a close relative express an otherwise injurious opinion. Anything else would mean a much too far-reaching curtailment of freedom of speech and also be impossible to monitor in any fairly reasonable way."[2]

Oh, thank you, my enlightened guardians, for letting me speak my mind in my own home, and that you don't consider it realistic wire-tapping every personal residence. The next three sentences in the discussion have a completely different tone, however:

> "Outside this private sphere it should in my view not be permitted to disseminate statements that express threats or disrespect against an ethnic group because of race or similar. This can become so, if the requirement that the statement has to be made in public or be disseminated to the public is removed. Dissemination of racist and similar statements within an association would hereby be punishable as well."

> "To sum up, I feel that one should remove the requirement entirely on a statement to be made in public or disseminated among the public. It shall be enough that the statement is disseminated. Society would thereby establish that statements that

---

1   Proposition 1986/87:151, page 104

2   Proposition 1986/87:151, page 109

express racial contempt are unacceptable as soon as they appear outside the completely private sphere."

The constitution was also modified - the following text was added to the regulations on the freedom of association in 2 § 14 of the Instrument of Government (*Regeringsformen*):

"The freedom of association may be limited only as far as associations whose work is of a military or similar disposition or involves persecution of (an) ethnic group of certain race, with certain colour of skin or of certain ethnic origin go."

Hence now it was open to though not outright ban "racist organizations," still legally restrict their activities. The actual application of this practice today usually has the police show up to harass and intimidate alleged racist organizations if they stage public manifestations, attempting to chase away the participants.

Some parties invited for comment also called for gender to be included in the legislation to be able to ban degrading pornography, but the lawmakers working on the bill weren't interested:

"To begin with, the so called influence research when it comes to pornographic representations is very sparse. Additionally it ought to be hard to scientifically prove that there is a connection between consumption of pornography and for example the proneness to resort to sexual violence. Yet greater are of course the difficulties in exploring what mental effects pornographic representations may have on the observer."

This government bill became law in 1988 under Prime Minister Ingvar Carlsson, and was binding from 1 January 1989. The HMF law now had the form it would have until 2003:

"A person who, in a disseminated statement or communication, threatens or expresses contempt for a national, ethnic or other such group of persons with allusion to race, colour, national or ethnic origin or religious belief shall, be sentenced for agitation against a national or ethnic group to imprisonment for at most two years or, if the crime is petty, to a fine. (Law 1988:835)"

The later development of the law was covered in an earlier section, which in 2003 meant the inclusion of homosexuals under ethnic group, and the increase from two to four years as the maximum possible sentence.

There's a famous parable about a frog put in initially cold water that's not harmful to him, but which is heated and gradually becomes warmer until the frog finds himself in boiling water, never having noticed just how hot it has become and not jumping out; this is called *the parable of the boiling frog*. Through various revisions, the HMF law has been gradually extended, when it initially posed little threat against free speech, while it today means a serious limitation on what views you can express. Though this author might have missed minor revisions, the major changes have occurred at five different occasions: 1948, 1970, 1982, 1988 and 2003. A formerly free people that suddenly found the 2003 law thrust upon itself would protest, but the extension of the law has taken place gradually with little in the way of actual protest in mainstream media.

The state teaches the people fascism; portions of the people embrace it

The limited legal means people have at their disposal for criticizing immigration policies and similar have caused some youth to forget about achieving any change through democratic means. The ones that have grown up watching people being sentenced to prison because of their views have learned that there's no point in attempting to discuss such topics as part of society's debate. Instead the hate laws have given rise to political violence, involving the far end of both sides of the political spectrum. Though these activists do read ideological literature, they rarely participate in discussions with their opponents, preferring violence as a means instead.

It's an interesting development that both sides have become involved, and if my analysing abilities don't fail me, this is how I believe it's become this way: For the Marxists, whose ideological opponents have been more or less banned, about the only reason they haven't been being due to the lack of practical means to institute such a ban - these Marxists see themselves as justified in their hatred of these opponents. Since the nationalists are 'supposed' to be banned, the Marxists take it upon themselves to be judges and executioners, identifying 'Nazis' and attacking them. They take for granted that they have a right not to be exposed to the message of their opponents, and hence if they spot them, it becomes a knee-jerk reaction to attack.

For the nationalists, whose freedom of speech is curtailed, street activism and fighting become the only means left under these circumstances. Successfully fending off the Marxists while holding your banner high is a way to show your strength, and propaganda becomes second nature. When you win the street clashes, you attract followers. About the only thing you can safely write about in your propaganda is your public events, since it can become a case for the legal system if you simply make a statement in favour of your ideology.

If you take mass media at face value, there is a lot of 'Nazi violence,' though these cases, if not outright made up, usually have Marxists attacking the public events of the nationalists and then suffering injuries in the process. The heavy infiltration of Marxist militants into established mass media helps skew the reporting in this regard as well, with these people giving their own version of events they themselves have been involved in.

It's even reached the point where women enter the fray as well, at least if armed with some form of weapon. On the national day 6 June 2009, Martin Kinnunen, press secretary of the Sweden Democrats, as well as his girlfriend were attacked by a Marxist mob on a subway station in Stockholm. At first he's assaulted by men smashing him with bottles while chanting 'Nazi pig!' He outruns these men, but a little later he's jumped by three young women armed with knuckle dusters with which they repeatedly hit the two in the head, and start kicking them as they fall to the ground. The assault goes on until patrolmen intervene, and then one of the crazed women attack these as well, but the three are soon overpowered and detained. The events are all captured on surveillance cameras.

The Sweden Democrats condemn political violence, their members have not been involved in any such thing, and they clearly distance themselves from National Socialism. From an international perspective, their politics are quite conventional populist right, and to make the 'Nazi' accusation even more absurd - they're strong supporters of the state of Israel. This man and his girlfriend found himself assaulted in broad daylight by what has to be described as terrorists, going after him because of his participation in the democratic process. The three women are all sentenced to prison for about a year each for aggravated assault, though who knows what would have happened with their two victims if the patrolmen hadn't showed up soon enough.

On 10 September 2010, nine days before the election, it was time again for an armed assault on a member of the Sweden Democrats. At his apartment in Malmö, David von Arnold Antoni was jumped by two masked men armed with knives, who forced their way into his home. Inside, one of the men allegedly carves a swastika into the man's forehead, and then they make off with his laptop computer and some cash. While leaving, the two men spray "racist pig" outside Antoni's home. The Sweden Democrat political secretary Erik Almqvist declares the assault to be politically motivated, and the police charge the unidentified perpetrators with suspicions of *unlawful deprivation of liberty*, aggravated assault, *gross theft* and *unlawful threat*.

At the end May of 2010, at a house party in the province of Skåne one Saturday night, two men in their late teens had showed up wearing clothes that to some of the other young men present at the party made them appear to be 'Nazis;' Some of them rush out and smash the car of the newcomers to then assault them with hammers and knives because of this. A 21-year-old who had arrived at the party earlier attempts to protect the two men but he's assaulted as well in the process. The attacking party leaves the scene for now, fearing the police might show up, and the 21-year-old and the two men move into a nearby forest to recover. A little later these three return to the house, but then the attacking party returns, and now the 21-year-old is the main target, and the 23-year-old resident of the house joins in. They beat him down and kick him while he's on the ground, and the 17-year-old that started the original assault now takes out a knife and cuts the 21-year-old open. At this point, the man is no longer conscious, yet they keep hitting him and jumping on his head. The 21-year amazingly survives the ordeal, and at the hospital he later receives no less than 166 stitches in a life or death situation, nearly going into cardiac arrest as the doctors sew him together. His jaw was also kicked loose during the assault.

During the subsequent trial, it becomes clear that the alleged 'Nazis' weren't Nazis at all. And in spite of the 21-year-old nearly dying, none of the four defendants are charged with anything more than aggravated assault. On 26 August 2010, as a juvenile offender, the 17-year-old is sentenced to ten months of *secure youth care* (LSU) for on top of the almost lethal aggravated assault also robbing another man of his possessions and threatening to kill a female bystander if she were to tell the police about what had transpired. The three other defendants also receive relatively short prison sentences for assaulting their three victims. Amazing as it may sound - one of the defendants, the one who had held the house party, had invited the 21-year-old to his party as his friend, but had forgotten all about this friendship after the man had attempted to come between the attackers and their two initial victims. When he later stood before his friend in court, he attempted to apologize for what he had done. With friends like these, who needs enemies?

During the 17-year-old's defence, he appeared more concerned with having gone after the "wrong person" than that he had almost killed someone. A month earlier, at another party, the same man had misidentified other people as "Nazis" as he assaulted them with makeshift weapons, among other things a belt.

Alleged 'Nazis' haven't been the only targets of the left-wing violence; Christians in both the Christian Democratic party and *Livets Ord* have been harassed and attacked as well. And during the 2010 election campaign, the National Democrats have suffered terrorist attacks against themselves and their families, with the stated ultimatum that these attacks will go on until they drop their candidacies; this terrorism seriously jeopardizes the democratic process.

Magnus Söderman, one of the leaders of the Swedish Resistance Movement.

In spite of plenty of posturing and attacks on 'Nazis' who aren't really Nazis, the Marxists are quite reluctant to attack the real ones. *Svenska Motståndsrörelsen*, SMR, the "Swedish Resistance Movement," is the most well-known and also most feared National Socialist organization in Sweden. SMR places high value on street activism, selling their magazine and distributing fliers on public squares with their banners raised. To the SMR, fanaticism is a virtue, though they maintain a code of never attacking civilians. It's often considered the vanguard of the far-right, never backing away from a fight and never abandoning their fellow comrades, and this has earned it a really bad rep in mass media. Here it's instead described in terms such as "the most violent Nazi organization in Sweden." The SMR frequently makes public appearances even though the police usually show up shortly after their arrival to disperse them through whatever legal means they can. Their appearances should constitute excellent opportunity for the "Nazi hunters" to prove their mettle, one would assume.

The times the Marxists have tried it, they've not been very successful. Unlike the unarmed and untrained victims the left-wing terrorists prefer and usually go after, the SMR members are tough cookies to crack. On 1 September 2007, some 20 SMR members had showed up at the Stockholm city centre, split into two groups to sell their magazine, also bringing camcorders to record the event for posterity since they're expecting the usual trouble from the Marxists. First they're put through the routine drill of having the police inspect their magazine to check that it doesn't include anything clearly prosecutable. A little later, a mob of 40 or so terrorists appear and attack one of the outnumbered SMR detachments. The immediate area is turned into a warzone as bottles are thrown as projectiles and fires are lit. The SMR repels the attack, however, and the Marxist mob makes a wild retreat while leaving a couple of stragglers behind. One of these stragglers ends up stabbed with a knife, almost ending his life, though it's not perfectly clear just how that happened.

After swiftly dealing with the stragglers, the SMR detachment pursues the retreating mob until they've fled the scene, returning to their magazine sales afterwards. The stabbed Marxist ends up in a hospital and the doctors notice that if the knife had went in a little to the side, his carotid artery would have been severed, killing him. Now he was left with a severe concussion and a disfigured face along with a dislocated vertebra in his neck. Two men from the SMR detachment are later detained by the police because of the man's injuries, and one of them, Niklas Frost, is somehow charged with attempted murder for an act of self-defence. After the skirmish, Frost and another man had walked around the city with the blood from the stabbed man still on their faces, like modern-day berserkers not bothering to wash it off.

(Footage from a Swedish Resistance Movement video clip)

In the trial, Frost is sentenced to six years in prison in spite of the only evidence being a dubious testimony from one of the members of the attacking party in the confrontation; the other man is sentenced to prison for complicity in attempted murder. Frost himself maintains in his defence that he had indeed taken part in the counter-attack on the Marxists, but that he had not stabbed anyone. Swedish justice usually requires hard evidence for a conviction, testimonies aren't given much value, and six years is an unusually severe sentence for a confrontation of this kind. The SMR declares it a miscarriage of justice and the defendants appeal their verdicts. In Svea Court of Appeal, the charge is changed to attempted manslaughter instead and the sentence is reduced to five years, while the other man is acquitted.

Following this, the SMR attempts to bring public attention to Frost's imprisonment, declaring him a political prisoner wrongfully convicted. On the webpage for the SMR, www.patriot.nu, they've got a section called "imprisoned

372

comrades," which in August of 2010 features six men, three of which have sentences of five years or more listed. Though they're all implicitly presented as political prisoners as far as sentence lengths go, the organization refrains from complaining about hardships, instead providing a means to send messages to them on the inside. Looking at a list of no less than six men imprisoned, with one of them posing with a sniper rifle, along with images of automatic rifles decorating the webpage and local SMR districts being referred to as nests or commandos, you can't help but to get the impression that they signal a message of the sort: "We mean business."

It appears as if their activism, in spite of everything the authorities have done to shut them down, has gained them quite a following. There's a company called Alexa that compiles statistics over Internet traffic at their website on alexa.com. On 15 August 2010, in the middle of the national election campaign, this is how the popularity of the SMR website compared to that of the political parties among Swedish Internet users. (The number is the traffic rank - the lower, the better)

sverigedemokraterna.se   763
(The Sweden Democrats, who entered the parliament this election; Israel- and gay-friendly populist right with Islam being the main focus)

nd.se   941
(The National Democrats, a democratic party to the right of SD, not in the parliament; traditional European far-right)

socialdemokraterna.se   1667
(The Social Democrats; the activity was low before the election, but shot up recently) (1 month +50%)

patriot.nu   2922
(The National Socialist Swedish Resistance Movement; not participating in the democratic process)

info14.com   3052
(National Socialist news site)

moderat.se   3146
(The Moderates, historically conservative but today centrist)

centerpartiet.se   4872
(The Centre party, the former farmer's party)

kristdemokraterna.se   5510
(The Christian Democrats; activity was low here too before the election, but shot up as well) (1 month +120%)

folkpartiet.se   6327
(The Liberal People's party)

svenskarnasparti.se   7108 (as of 10-08-27, not looked up on the 15th)
("Party of the Swedes" - Nationalist party, formerly known as National Socialist Front (NSF) - participating in municipal elections.)

mp.se   7678
(The Green party)

vansterpartiet.se   9773
(The Left party - ex-Communists)

It's quite interesting to note how comparatively little interest there is in the established parties, compared to the far-right. In polls and elections, Swedes tend to keep on voting for the establishment, but when so many are following the activities of the organizations that the establishment attempts to smash, one wonders what this will mean for political stability. How long can the establishment take for granted that Swedes will keep on bending over? It appears as if the spectre of the National Socialist brand does little to dissuade young Swedes from aligning themselves with such organizations. When the political establishment through hate laws and similar anti-democratic

374

measures proves that the constitution isn't worth the paper it's printed on, why should the people then keep on playing along?

The Swedish state is playing with fire, and one day Sweden just might have woken up to a nationalist revolution.

Brief appendix - official exposition on the HMF law

To better give you an idea on the state of free speech today, here follows a number of quotes on the application of the HMF law. Though they aren't official Swedish legislation, this is more or less official commentary taken from *"Brottsbalken: En kommentar,"* summarizing the law and the preparatory work that determines its jurisdiction.

Concerning the wording of the law:

"With the expression disrespect is meant that also other injurious opinions than those that can be considered slander or defamation shall be punishable offences. For criminal responsibility it's enough that a statement about a certain ethnic group is deprecatory to the reputation of the group. Also occurrences that mean that a certain race or ethnic group is ridiculed will probably always fall under the regulation."

Concerning works of art:

"The protection against ridicule is far-reaching. When the ridicule has its basis exclusively in the ethnic group's race, colour of skin, national or ethnic origin or religious creed there can be no doubt about the assessment."

The above was from a discussion that took place before the law included sexual orientation as well, and it's my understanding that the protection against ridicule in works of art is also now extended to homosexuals.

"It was however stated during the preparatory work of the legislation of 1970 that it didn't require that one or more races or ethnic groups were targeted but that liability shall follow even if the object of the criminal act is more general. The regulation could be applied if for example a certain race was praised in a way that all other races must be considered reviled."

So, expressing pride in one's biological or cultural heritage is a "hate crime" for Swedes in their own country. The quoted exposition also explains that the phrase "any other such group of people" in the wording of the law was created in order to cover non-specific groups of people such as for example immigrants in general. It's quite preposterous that Swedish law allows immigrants both to express pride in their own culture, as well as to insult the Swedish people, while doing any of these things is a criminal act for Swedes. I'm amazed at how other Swedes can put up with this law - I sure can't. I propose Swedes suffer from a psychological disorder - a masochistic xenophilia, which is expressed through the abnormal adoration of every little part of alien culture while downgrading one's own; it also manifests itself in a neurotic compulsion to apologize for merely existing.

> "Any requirement that the threat or the expression of disrespect directly refers to the group's race, colour of skin or origin or creed is not established. Also statements, that include insulting accusations of inferior attributes or disparaging conduct yet are only indirectly based on race, colour of skin, origin or creed falls under the regulation. The race or the races it's about don't need to be specifically mentioned for the exposition to be a punishable offence. Also an indirect referral to slurs or other insulting denominations of the race or immigrants in general shall fall under the area of criminal responsibility."

So if you use racial slurs in any circumstance, you may be sent to prison. If anyone wants to become a political offender in Sweden, go to a Swedish city of choice and walk around with a sign saying "jag gillar inte blattar."

> "The regulation on agitation against ethnic group is a crime against the state and not foremost a crime against individuals."

Pay heed to this, anyone who believes the purpose of the hate laws is to protect people - they're rather for banning views! Describing it as a crime against the state puts it in perfect perspective - the censorship is used to stifle criticism of government policy, just as in any other totalitarian state.

"The criminalization doesn't include statements within the completely private sphere. Outside this sphere it's forbidden to disseminate statements that express threats or disrespect against an ethnic group because of race or similar. Dissemination of racist or similar statements within an association is a punishable offence."

"With the expression *disseminate a statement* is meant both making a statement as well as disseminating what one has heard from others. The regulation doesn't only include verbal or written accounts but also for example gestures or representations in images that can't be considered writing."

I dare anyone to find more than ten states in the world today where people enjoy less freedom of speech than Swedes do.

MASS MEDIA

"[...]the Ministry of Truth, whose primary job was not to reconstruct the past but to supply the citizens of Oceania with newspapers, films, textbooks, telescreen programmes, plays, novels with every conceivable kind of information, instruction, or entertainment, from a statue to a slogan, from a lyric poem to a biological treatise, and from a child's spelling-book to a Newspeak dictionary. And the Ministry had not only to supply the multifarious needs of the party, but also to repeat the whole operation at a lower level for the benefit of the proletariat. There was a whole chain of separate departments dealing with proletarian literature, music, drama, and entertainment generally."

George Orwell, "1984"

State involvement in the "free press"

During World War 2, Sweden's official policy was to attempt to stay out of the war, and before it was all over, the state had crossed many barriers in order to do so. One of these barriers was the construction of concentration camps to house individuals who could become inconvenient when the country did its best to placate Germany. The neutrality policy of the state wasn't shared by all elements in society; there were National Socialists who wanted Sweden to enter the war on Germany's side; friends of Britain who wanted Sweden to align with the Western powers; and Communists who desired to overthrow the state and whose sympathies for the Soviet Union brought their loyalty into question.

In 1939, as the war was starting to erupt, Swedish Marxists railed against Germany, attempting to get Sweden involved in the war. One of these Marxists was a man by the name of Ture Nerman, editor-in-chief of a magazine called *Trots allt*, "After all." The Government feared the complications this agitation might have for the relationship with Germany, and in November of that year, Nerman was sentenced to three months in prison over a hodge-podge charge called "defamation of a foreign power." A couple of months later, the government issued a ban on the distribution of *Trots allt*. At the same time, the state started relocating various politically outspoken individuals whose speech might be to Germany's disliking, putting them in concentration camps such as Storsien. Since the records of what went on in these camps were destroyed after the inmates were released, the exact number incarcerated is in dispute - from 600 to several thousand.

The parliament had through a new law approved of the summary relocation of any potential security risks, and Social

Democratic party officials even used their influence in society to denounce competitors in their power struggles, having them relocated as well without proof. After the war, the concentration camps were quickly forgotten in the public discourse, and even today, far from all Swedes are aware of this part of their history.

In 1941, as part of the ministry for foreign affairs, the state also established a censorship department in order to review printed publications before their distribution, making sure that nothing was expressed that would provoke Germany into attacking. Mass media in general was held on a short leash, though German authorities appear to have been pleased - Germany never drew up any plans to invade Sweden.

American "progressives" hail state-funded media as a role model

American printed media is today undergoing a crisis from falling sales. Less and less people buy traditional newspapers where they get editorials shoved down their throats without being able to give any feedback unless they manage to get a letter published. Instead they favour online media and the "blogosphere," as it's called in America today. Media customers have grown accustomed to being able to comment on the reporting and also having a greater selection to pick from. Earlier, what's often derided as the "Mainstream media" would have a strong hold on the perspectives expressed, but in the new world of media, this isn't quite as much so. The everyday man isn't very interested in the subjective portrayal of the world by newspaper editors, and some newspapers are going broke because of it, a natural consequence of the free market when a product doesn't have much of a demand any more.

This mainstream media doesn't see it this way, however; faced with a possible extinction as a cadre of know-it-alls who have taken it upon themselves to "enlighten" the public, some of them are organizing to counter this development. More than anyone else, infamous businessman George Soros, responsible for the financial ruin of many a small people across the world, has after becoming a multi-billionaire devoted himself to setting up a publicly funded "free press" as opposed to the unregulated private business of "corporate media." Earlier he's set up and funded such organizations as the website MoveOn.org - "Democracy in action" and the think tank *Center for American Progress*, and indirectly funded the media watchdog *Media Matters*.

Media Matters has made its task to expose "conservative misinformation," something that should be applauded if media actors are indeed found to be disseminating falsehoods. Their "research" on the website tends to produce short sound bites mostly from conservative talk radio often taken out of context, however, and these short clips seem to have a tendency to actually become misinformation - people who never bother to listen to the media actors themselves tend to get a highly distorted image of them. Perhaps a similar website - newshound.us - puts it best: "We watch FOX so you don't have to." The real intent is to establish negative stereotypes of conservative media so that the visitors of the website never bother to actually listen to this media directly.

Possibly as a result of relying on Media Matters as a source, the Swedish state TV has characterized Rush Limbaugh as a "racist." Well, to be honest - they didn't get his name right, but wrote Russ Limbaugh instead. During the 2008 American presidential election, the commentator on foreign affairs at the state TV, Bo Inge Andersson, answered questions said to have been sent in by viewers. On 21 October 2008, the question posed was: "Can racism make McCain win the election?"[1] Andersson answers by saying that there have been "racist undertones" in

---

1   http://svt.se/2.97345/1.1285934/

McCain's campaign on the part of Sarah Palin and "Russ Limbaugh." Not only did he manage to get Limbaugh's name wrong, he also neglected the fact that Limbaugh wasn't a part of McCain's campaign and that he had even distanced himself from this presidential candidate. Andersson states that he believes Obama will have a hard time winning over certain groups of whites - older voters and blue-collar workers. The idea that racism would affect the election to Obama's disadvantage was repeated several times in the state TV's election coverage. After Obama won, on 5 November 2008 a question for the same commentator was asked: "How do you view that the USA has received its first Afro-American president as relating to a threatening picture surrounding the person of Obama?"[1] This question surely must be made up - I've never in my life heard anyone in Sweden refer to black Americans as Afro-Americans. The terms most frequently used for a black person no matter location are negro, or simply black man/woman.

But, to return to the projects of Soros. In the wake of this drop in sales for the newspapers, new media organizations were launched, one of them being freepress.net. With a gray five-edged star as part of its logo, perhaps an attempt to discretely include the traditional Marxist red star, its motto is: "reform media, transform democracy." In its depiction of the state of mass media in the USA, it's quite alarmist and invites website viewers to join in a call to action. A number of similar sites with the same messages and stories are linked - newpublicmedia.org, stopbigmedia.com and savethenews.org, which has a story that "Journalism is in crisis." In its solutions, it calls for American media to take after the state-funded "independent" media of many European countries in an attempt to save journalism from "corporate media."

So, how independent can the "free press" remain if it ends

---

1   http://svt.se/2.97345/1.1303275/

383

up funded by the government? If the experience from Sweden is of any relevance - not very independent at all.

The Swedish press subsidies - *presstödet*

Since some four decades back, Swedish newspapers can apply for something called press subsidies, *presstöd*, under certain conditions. In 2009, the Swedish state paid out 550 million crowns to printed newspapers and 127 millions to radio- and audio newspapers, or almost 100 million dollars all in all. The exact payouts are available online at the webpage of the Press Subsidies Council at www.presstodsnamnden.se, and the government subsidy per individual newspaper can reach 25 crowns or about $3. Briefly browsing the balance statements of randomly selected newspapers, it appears that quite a few receive no less than half their income from the government. If you also include the lack of a sales tax on newspapers and other tax reductions specifically provided mass media, some of them could be said to be state-financed by about 2/3 of what their budgets had otherwise been.

Initially the press subsidies were launched back in the 1960's, when newspapers were in hard times and it was feared that only the ones who could sustain themselves on advertising would endure - and as a result of anti-capitalist sentiment, the political establishment was concerned that this might mean only right-wing newspapers, which were believed to more easily attract this funding. Hence the state now started funding political media in order to, as this council puts it - "safeguard diversity." What effect might this have had on bias in reporting? Any estimation of whether an inherent bias exists in media is naturally going to be a subjective assessment, with every observer having a different opinion, hence this view will be my subjective one.

Something that aggravated me during the late 1990's and the following decade, as freedom of speech came ever more under attack due to the extension of the HMF law, was that mass media hardly ever criticized the government for indicting these speech offenders. Consistently whenever a publicized trial under the HMF law has taken place, media has taken the side of the state, rarely missing an opportunity to smear the defendant(s) as vicious people unworthy of sympathy. Only fringe media such as *Folket i Bild / Kulturfront* on the left and *Salt* on the right have made a stand for free speech, and have become more marginalized than before as they've done so. In newspapers, you didn't see anyone quoting Voltaire's motto "I disapprove of what you say, but I will defend to the death your right to say it," or attempting to give an honest assessment of the message of the ones on trial. The most newspaper readers were fed with were the short quotes that best depicted the speech offenders as extremists, insinuating that these quotes contained the whole spirit of the message.

During the trial against Åke Green, much was made of the fact that he referred to homosexuality as "a deep cancerous tumour on the entire society," but very few reported that he ended his sermon by reaching out to the homosexuals, saying they ought to be shown "grace and mercy." The newspaper portrayals rather likened his message to Nazism, insinuating that his desire was to exterminate the homosexuals. The media that was funded by the state somehow arrived at the same verdicts about the speech offenders as the state that prosecuted them.

Another area where I've found reporting severely lacking is in the field of the foster care business, the very existence you would never learn of if all you did was read the newspapers. In the USA, it's a commonly discussed opinion that minimum sentencing guidelines in the justice system might be a result of prisons pushing courts to get convicts signed up for as long a sentence as possible; few people are unaware of the potential for abuse of this power, that you should apply the motto of *cui bono* - "who benefits?" Yet the media climate in Sweden is quite homogenous, and though the Swedish foster care system constitutes as large a portion of the Swedish GDP as the American prison system does of its GDP, no newspaper ever hints at that the social services might have other interests in "providing children with care" than the concern for their well-being. As described earlier, the German magazine *Der Spiegel* covered the state of things in Sweden back in 1983, but Swedish media has never produced any such exposition.

Hence in my opinion, American "corporate media" appears to provide better coverage of the issues than the Swedish media whose "diversity is safeguarded" through government funds. Above all, if people want to preserve honest reporting, investigative journalism and media diversity, they have to understand that it falls upon them as individuals to question what they read and hear, rather than to ask for a government body to be their keepers. Calls to action on the part of organizations funded by people who have a stake in the game is not the way to go.

Sveriges Television - the state TV

The Third Reich had a state TV, the Soviet Union had one, and Sweden has one as well, called *Sveriges Television*, Sweden's Television, abbreviated SVT. Though these three states are not identical, their state television media is surprisingly similar. A good insight into the state TV of the German Nazi state can be gained from *Der Spiegel*'s documentary "Television under the Swastika," mostly compiled from old archive footage of what was shown during that period. It featured a large investment into providing the people with a wide array of material - culture, sports and documentaries. The Nazi state utilized television in a systematic manner, supplying the people with the information the state leadership felt was beneficial for the education of the audience. The Third Reich pretty much set the standard for the kind of programming other state televisions would later use, with a model that's still in use in some countries, one of them being Sweden.

Nazi Germany were the pioneers behind the launch of television, but unlike later western TV, it wouldn't be very much about maximizing the entertainment value of the shows, but rather about education and social orientation. The Soviet Union later adopted the same model for its TV - media subjected to the views and the values of the state. The Soviet channels were named numerically - *Programme 1*, *Programme 2*, and so on. The Swedish ones went the same way - *Channel 1* and *Channel 2* initially.

Propaganda on the state TV of all three states is or was constantly present, though not more obvious than to lull the audience into thinking they're watching objective programming. When all they see is the same nature of commentary, how will they ever become aware of the propaganda that's fed to them?

Though Sweden isn't a very large country, the state TV is awarded a hefty budget through taxpayer money. If you own a TV in the country or have any form of device with which you can receive TV transmissions, you're required to pay the TV licence fee, about 2,000 crowns or almost $300 a year. Even if you don't want to watch the state TV, you still have to pay for it. Hell, even if all you have is a computer monitor that's capable of showing the TV feed from the wall jack, that counts too. And let's not forget about computer retailers selling TV cards - they also have to pay the fee. Taxing just about every household makes for a large income; since 2005, the state TV budget has hovered at around four billion crowns a year or a little over half a billion dollars. For comparison, according to the figures yours truly has been able to find, in 2005 both the American TV networks CNN and Fox News had expenditures of around one billion dollars each, hence the state TV in this small country is half the size of these American TV giants, which get their income through attracting viewers - no strong-arming necessary.

During the 80's, in an attempt to preserve the state TV monopoly and shield the Swedish public from Western television, portions of the Social Democrats wanted to ban satellite dishes. In 1980, a statement was made by *Kulturarbetarnas socialdemokratiska förening*, "The Social Democratic Association of Cultural Workers," calling for action to be taken due to their concerns about "the right of the powerful to disseminate views and exploit our minds." Later that decade, during the 1987 party congress, Maj-Britt Theorin expressed herself this way:

> "Give the kids a chance and for the sake of everything good and decent be spared TV commercials. Our party can't keep crouching in the commercial right-wing wave, but must go on an ideological counter-offensive against the exploiters of freedom of speech, no matter in whatever deceptive coat they wrap themselves in."

Yeah... It's not for ourselves we want to ban satellite TV, it's for the children!

Documentaries as education

SVT has been very keen on purchasing the rights for documentaries to show on its channels. On their webpage at www.svt.se, they typically list the documentaries they show, with brief descriptions of them. To quote the webpage:

> "Documentaries on SVT
>
> On SVT you can watch quality documentaries just about every day. Here you'll find all the information about our programs."

There are special shows for domestic reports on Sweden, for reports on international affairs, shows focusing more on the individual opinion makers and so on.

Undoubtedly, the documentaries shown on the SVT play a major role in shaping the thinking of Swedish citizens. It is indeed convenient believing that the state TV is impartial and allow yourself to be spoon-fed with educational material. You can sit down in front of the TV during prime-time hours and learn about the world through what's portrayed as the best attempt of the film makers to cover the world beyond your own domain. But, just how impartial is this programming? Isn't there a risk that the people determining the programming do so to present you with their perspective on things? There are all kinds of documentaries out there, made by major or minor players in the world of film making; both ones made by Hollywood movie studios and the state televisions of various countries, as well as small independent productions. Why does it appear as if topics such as unsatisfactory conditions in American society are covered incessantly, while for example the decline of free speech in Europe isn't even mentioned at all?

Somehow it seems that whenever anyone in the world makes a documentary that's critical about the USA, the Swedish state TV ends up airing it. Though some might accuse me of going out on a conspiracy-minded limb here, could it be the case that the state TV feeds the Swedish audience these documentaries for the specific purpose of distracting people from looking at the faults of their own society?

What follows here is a small portion of the large number of anti-American documentaries shown on the state TV along with how they're described on the webpage.

Bowling for Columbine

Shown on 2 July 2005 at 21:15 as well as on 28 June 2007 at 22:30.

> "Moore plunges into the darkest recesses of American society, where alarm systems, bulletproof vests and guns in the home are commonplace."

> "Both the choice of music and editing are selected in the best way possible to make us stop and think. Quick jumps between disarming humour, ironic presentations of facts, and ghastly depiction of reality. As in the compiled scenes of pictures from surveillance cameras at Columbine high."[1]

Now, is this just me, or does the state TV actually appear to be promoting the movie and not merely describing it?

Fahrenheit 9-11

Shown on 15 June 2006 at 21:00 as well as 17 June at 15:50.

"The outspoken film-maker Michael Moore investigated President Bush's actions after the terrorist attack on the World Trade Centre in New York on September the 11th 2001. And Michael Moore's

---

1   http://svt.se/svt/jsp/Crosslink.jsp?d=61757&a=406803

390

own conclusions on the connections he found between Bush and the wealthy families of Saudi Arabia were embarrassing for supporters of the president during the subsequent election"

"Moore then pulls the lid off the private Pandora's box of the President and reveals the close relations of the Bush clan to the Bin Laden family and the Saudi royal house.

In the documentary, the question is asked whether these strong ties might have contributed to members of the Bin Laden family having been allowed to fly out of USA only days after the 9-11 attacks - without having been interrogated by the FBI."[1]

Michael Moore as producer

Searching for "Michael Moore" on the TV webpage, one gets 66 hits - reviews of all of his movies the last decade; his appearances in media; and reports on projects he's working on. Though his movies Sicko and Capitalism - A Love Story haven't been shown on this TV, the movies have still been discussed on screen.

On 9 September 2009, the state TV interviewed him about his latest production (Capitalism) in Venice and announced its Swedish release date. It was pretty much a sales pitch for the movie, going on for no less than five minutes. In the words of Moore himself, to the interviewer:

"For people in Sweden, to watch this film, this is a window into America. You get to see America, not through CNN's eyes, or your own reporters' eyes, but through my eyes, as an American who sees it a different way."

"I'm trying to convince my fellow Americans to try a different way. I use Sweden of course as an example a lot."

"That's what I want for America."

---

1   http://svt.se/svt/jsp/Crosslink.jsp?d=46074&a=606410

"That's why I'm saying you can't reform or regulate capitalism. It has to be eliminated."[1]

Personally I'm a bit curious as to why he doesn't move here if he loves the country so much while hating the USA. Surely that has to be because he's so altruistic as to let the space occupied by his person (and that's quite a lot of space indeed) be taken by someone more worthy of living in Sweden? And not the 80-85% in taxes he'd pay here with his income? And the fact that the USA is about the only country in the world that will put up with someone like Moore? It's my experience that people with his type of personality typically shout themselves into ever more desperate obscurity in Sweden, unlike what's the case with the life he's been able to make for himself in America.

Jesus Camp

Shown on 3 March 2007 at 21:30 as well as 29 July at 22:10 the same year.

"A growing number of Evangelicals in the USA are convinced that a religious awakening is absolutely necessary for the future of America. To make it possible, they prepare by training children to become future leaders who will pass on their conviction."

"The documentary *Jesus Camp* follows a group of small children to pastor Becky Fisher's summer camp where they learn to become dedicated Christian soldiers in the army of God and are trained to take back the fallen America to Christ. The movie gives a unique insight into the intense training at the camp and how these reborn Christian children are raised to be players in the political future of America."

"Like most children at the camp, he's homeschooled and learns science from a book that connects creationism and science."

"At the camp, the children participate in emotional prayer

---

1   http://svtplay.se/v/1683681/

sessions with sermons against free abortions and are encouraged to turn toward a picture of President Bush and pray for him and his policies."[1]

I'm not so sure most Evangelicals would be happy to be portrayed as training their children to become "soldiers in the army of God."

Outfoxed

Shown on 14 October 2004 at 22:00 as well as 17 October the same year at 14:50.

"Murdoch's murder of journalism"

"Yet there is hardly any more biased reporting than Fox in all of the western TV world."[2]

Oh, really? How about the Swedish state TV?

"The channel has turned into a completely immodest propaganda machine for the right-wing of the American Republican party and for president Bush."

"In *Dokument utifrån* we review Murdoch's journalistic methods or rather his method of killing serious journalism."

"A group of volunteers from all over the USA scrutinized every hour of Fox News' broadcasts and noted examples of prejudice in the coverage. The result is an intensive review of Fox News, showing the falsehood of the TV network's favourite motto: 'Fair and balanced.'"

I wish the media landscape in Sweden was of the nature that would make the same kind of scrutiny of the state TV possible. Unfortunately, there's little in the way of alternative media in the country, and no funding available for such projects.

---

1   http://svt.se/svt/jsp/Crosslink.jsp?d=61757&a=871915

2   http://svt.se/svt/jsp/Crosslink.jsp?d=9603&a=260034

Why we fight

Shown on 31 July 2005 at 21:15.

"Why does the USA go to war? Why does the world's last superpower enter into fight after fight with yet more enemies? What forces are behind it? Which people are in control?

Why we fight was the name of a series of propaganda movies Frank Capra made in 1942 and onwards to encourage American effort during world war 2. In a documentary with the same name, director Eugene Jarecki has used Capra's movies to comment on the apparent military obsession that defines the world's only superpower."[1]

I'd like a documentary on the Swedish state TV titled "Why do we show all of these anti-American movies?"

Che

One of the ever-present icons of the left-wingers is Ernesto "Che" Guevara - Communist revolutionary as well as the infamous executioner of thousands of people during and after Castro's takeover in Cuba, which included Guevara personally taking the lives of political opponents. Indeed, searching the state TV webpage, one gets no less than 30 hits, out of which one is for a short film SVT made in his memory called "Bolivia in Che's footsteps." As described on its webpage:

"But Che was really a revolutionary and here Jorun Collin follows in his footsteps in Bolivia and makes her way on the so called 'Che Guevara route.'"[2]

A longer documentary about Che was the BBC production "Looking for the revolution" from 2007, aired on SVT on 20 July

---

1   http://svt.se/svt/jsp/Crosslink.jsp?d=37437&a=407217

2   http://svtplay.se/v/1369462

2008 at 22:05 as well as on one unspecified date in 2007.[1] As told by the narrator in this documentary:

> "Here is Bolivia, the place where Che Guevara, the most famous revolutionary, died in 1967. My fellow Argentine was captured in the jungle while trying to spark Socialism throughout South America."

> "After Che was executed, his body was tied to a helicopter and flown away, **like a modern Jesus Christ**, dying anew for humanity."

They really must be running out of propaganda material when they actually buy a production where mass murderer Che is compared to Jesus. I had expected them to show more respect for Christianity than to make such a comparison, too. Maybe it was a convenient and straight-forward way for the narrator to summarize what a wonderful man Che was - "This guy was as great as Jesus!" Yet won't that alienate the atheists who hate Jesus? Ah well, not my problem.

On 6 September 2010, it was time again. Though SVT is reluctant to show regular box office movies, it certainly makes exceptions for Che - now it was showing the Argentinian-American movie *The Motorcycle Diaries*. As described on the webpage:

> "*The Motorcycle Diaries* depicts the fascinating journey through South America that the then 23-year-old medical student Ernesto Che Guevara and his comrade Alberto Granada made in the early 1950's."

Coming next... "*Crapper time with* **CHE** - the amazing story of how esteemed revolutionary Ernesto Che Guevara uncovers a capitalist conspiracy while reading newspapers as he's taking a dump."

---

1   http://svt.se/svt/jsp/Crosslink.jsp?d=81516&a=1182082

The night Castro was praised on the Swedish state TV

Communist revolutionary Fidel Castro has always had a special place in the hearts of left-wingers, even ones who don't call themselves Communists. Quite often, mass media is reluctant to even call him a dictator, preferring instead to use his own official title of prime minister or later president. Castro assumed dictatorial power in 1959 after a violent takeover of Cuba, though chose back then to retain the title of prime minister for his office. Even on Wikipedia as of 10 July 2010, the man whom Castro overthrew as leader, Fulgencio Batista, is called a dictator, while Castro isn't. The article only goes as far as saying that "Castro himself has been described as a dictator," as if that's only a disputed notion.

Towards the end of 2006, the state TV was about to pull a stunt that would shock even Swedish viewers. Announcing an intended tribute evening ahead of time, the state TV webpage described it this way on a page that has since then been taken down:

> "On the 2nd of December, Cuba has a dual celebration: Partly Castro's postponed 80th birthday is celebrated, partly the 50th anniversary of La Revolución."

This Saturday night, the state TV ran a four hour long tribute evening with pro-Castro programming and commentary. Starting at 20:00 and ending at 0:10, this was the schedule that night:

"Theme: Fidel Castro" 20:00-20:01

On the 2nd of December, Cuba has a dual celebration: Fidel Castro's delayed 80th birthday and the 50th anniversary of the revolution. Fidel Castro has been at power in Cuba since 1959. Who is he, the man who's survived against all odds and that has seen ten American Presidents come and go?

"History will declare me innocent" 20:01-21:30

Swedish documentary from 1976. The Swedish film-makers Dick Idestam-Almquist, Gaetano Pagano and Anders Ribbsjö were in 1976 given a unique opportunity to follow Fidel Castro on Cuba. He talks about himself, the revolution and his political goals. Now, 30 years later, Dick Idestam-Almqvist returns to the originally almost three hour long movie.

In this part, Castro among other things talks about the Bay of Pigs invasion and other threats Cuba was confronted with after the revolution. We also get to meet him in the cow pasture where he dreams about the Cuban cow."

He dreams about the Cuban cow? I'm almost inclined to make a funny association here... But no, that would be a bit immature.

"Fidel Castro and Cuba" 21:30-21:35

Conversation between Dick Idestam-Almqvist, TV producer, Anja Karlsson Franck, debater, and René Vázquez Díaz, author

"Comandante" 21:35-23:10

American documentary from 2003. Director Oliver Stone meets up with Fidel Castro in a close-up portrait. Castro is allowed to expand his views on the cold war, the Kennedy assassination, Che Guevara, the American blockade and his own life.

"Dear Fidel" 23:10-00:10

"Fidel ruined my life, but it was wonderful.

Marita Lorenz had a love affair with Fidel Castro shortly after the revolution. She was recruited by the CIA to kill him but couldn't do it and was in return forced to fight Communism and the Mafia as a full-time agent. On another assignment she also let her feelings take over and she fell in love with Venezuela's ex-dictator Marcos Péres Jiménez.

In Wilfried Huismann's documentary she talks about a life that's

397

become more eventful than anyone could ever have desired. (Germany 2001)."

The program host this evening had launched the programs by introducing the theme evening with these words:

"On 26 July 1953, the young lawyer Fidel Castro led a guerilla attack against a military installation and thereby he started a revolution that's stuck for almost 50 years and made a beard and a cap highest proletarian fashion throughout the Western world. Hero of the people or dictator or possibly both - that's entirely dependent on whom you ask. But anyway, welcome to a theme evening on Fidel Castro."

The conversation held at 21:30 was non-stop praise of the dictator. These are some of the things the people in the studio said:

"So I experienced the first years, the revolutionary years as... as something that was very happy for me."

"Castro isn't a dictator in the sense the propaganda claims. Like, there is on Cuba a hidden democracy that explains this wonder, that the revolution still lives on and how does this democracy look? It's very, very hard to explain, but it's simply the case that people can decide on a lot of stuff from below."

If the depictions by these people were all you had to base your opinion about Cuba on, you'd think it was paradise on Earth.

Throughout the whole four hour long tribute evening, there was no real criticism uttered against Castro, but instead incessant glorification.

Plenty of complaints are filed against the state TV with the Swedish Broadcasting Commission (*Granskningsnämnden*) because of the tribute evening, though the state TV still maintains it was an objective presentation:

"The point of the theme evenings is that through documentaries and feature films about a topic, a person or some other form of

398

theme elevate different perspectives and narrative forms, contradictory or not. The theme evening on Castro, who's been at power for more than 50 years, focused on the person Fidel Castro. In two of the films he himself was able to speak and it's natural that he in his own rhetoric attempted to give a good portrayal of himself."

"The criticism of the complainants against the episodes and discussions about *History will declare me innocent* focus among other things on that Castro was portrayed as the role model of the time for left-wing movements in different parts of the world. SVT establishes that some parts of the movie were shown to highlight this very perspective and this period of Castro's seat at power."

And this is supposed to be "objective" programming? To balance things out, I propose this to the state TV: Make a four hour theme evening as well in Adolf Hitler's memory. It could focus on the inspiration he was to many Europeans during the 1930's and among other things contain Leni Riefenstahl's 1935 documentary *Triumph of the Will*. Old Waffen-SS volunteers could talk about what Hitler meant for them personally in their lives. Finally, the audience could be given time to learn Hitler's perspective on Jews, Communism, the future of Europe and such matters.

Though the state TV didn't agree that the theme evening was biased, the SBC declared that it was. To quote the so very punitive verdict by the SBC on 16 April 2007:

"THE MATTER

Theme: Fidel Castro, SVT2, 2006-12-02, 20:00-21:00 and 21:15-00:15; question of impartiality

THE VERDICT

The transmission is pronounced guilty. The Swedish Broadcasting Commission feels it violates the impartiality requirement

INJUNCTION

Sveriges Television shall in a suitable way make public the decision of the Swedish Broadcasting Commission."

My my, they make a tribute evening to a dictator, and all that's required by the state TV afterwards is that they declare that the SBC found that the programming wasn't impartial. How about firing the people who organized the tribute evening and the ones who praised Castro?

"Objective reporting"

On 7 August 2009, two months after the murder of American abortion doctor George Tiller, the state TV ran a 6.5 minute long clip on the prime-time news about abortion opponents in the USA. The quoted section below is how the clip was described on the state TV webpage, commentary that was also read aloud in the clip:

"The fight over abortion rights is escalating

The American abortion right is no matter-of-course. Lately the opponents have escalated their strikes all across the country. Only two months ago yet another abortion doctor was shot to death, this time in Kansas. *Aktuellt* travelled to Mississippi and met one of the USA:s most infamous abortion opponents who will use any means in his struggle. Nothing is as incendiary in the USA as the abortion issue. The right to abortion has existed since 1973. Lately the opponents, **the religious right** have escalated their strikes. They do everything they can to shut down clinics or scare away the women. Among the more militant activists is Roy McMillan, one of the most famous abortion opponents in the USA.

- God touched me and told me this was my mission, he says.

McMillan feels among other things that the abortions are a

400

conspiracy against the black race. But in a state where the **Ku Klux Klan** isn't distant history it's hard to take the concern of the white abortion opponents about the black girls fully seriously. It rather hints at **a veiled form of racism**, but this is something McMillan denies. In Jackson, Mississippi, the Baptist church dominates people's lives and the young are exhorted to live in abstinence. The state of Mississippi states that it has fewer abortions than other states - the result is more teenage mums who are forced to live in poverty and squalor."[1]

A textbook example of guilt by (very loose) association, indeed. In spite of the lack of evidence of racism on the part of the activist, with him even carrying a sign that says "Abortion = Black Genocide," the reporter still insinuates that he is actually a racist. And of course when as a Swedish reporter you're covering the American South, naturally you have to bring up the KKK too.

Besides what was written on the webpage, when they reported from a clinic, the reporter's voice-over included these quotes:

> "At the other side of the fence there are doctors and nurses who fight for a woman's right to have abortions. They live under constant threat and siege. Prayer isn't the only weapon in the arsenal of the activists, and several abortion doctors have been shot to death in the USA."

> "The clinic escorts the women. They turn away as they're forced to run gauntlets past the Bible-thumpers."

The same reporter, Eva Elmsäter, covered Iraq after Saddam Hussein's execution as well. To quote:

> "Saddam - feared and admired

> For 23 years Saddam Hussein was Iraq's leader feared and despised for his brutality, but also admired by several[sic] as a

---

1   http://svt.se/2.22584/1.1647631/

strong Arabian leader who dared to challenge the USA and Israel."[1]

Note to this reporter: Learn proper sentence structure - your sentences don't make proper sense without commas.

She was also given the task of reporting on the American presidential election of 2008 on 7 October; this is how she described the TV coverage:

"Objectivity not feasible in American TV media"

"Like a (space) alien on a visit I zap between the channels, fascinated by the spectacle. The TV news resemble entertainment and the program hosts mock the presidential candidates wildly. No objectivity here. For that you'll have to turn to PBS and risk falling asleep."[2]

My my, this reporter is being paid taxpayer money to watch American TV. You think she'd reflect over the objectivity of the Swedish state TV while she's at it. Later that month, the state TV ran a series of shows on the election, presented under the headline **"SVT hits the USA election big."**[3]

"Before the presidential election in the USA, SVT's schedules are packed with interesting shows. In the heavy offering there are a number of current documentaries and movies that dive into American society."

"SVT1 Monday 27 October 22:00 K special: Dixie Chicks shut up and sing

A few years ago, Dixie Chicks were the best selling female artists of all time. But then band member Natalie Maines criticizes

---

1   http://svt.se/2.22889/1.275471/

2   http://svt.se/2.89479/1.1269504/

3   http://www.usaval.se/president/svts-bevakning-av-usa-valet/

402

President Bush at a concert. This has disastrous consequences and the band is banned almost everywhere. An American documentary from 2006 that follows the band during three years when they keep writing music and dare to have children even though they receive death threats."[1]

Now, one can't but help to wonder what relevance this documentary has to the election? The only thing that could be read out of it is that it has some relevance in portraying how the Republicans view free speech. Perhaps the documentary that has no actual relevance to the election whatsoever is also supposed to portray the Republicans as misogynists, who knows? It is however quite curious that the state TV insinuates that American free speech is deficient, when Sweden puts political dissidents and religious preachers in prison. I'm also at a loss as to what criticism Maines' words contained, especially when delivered to a Bush-hating audience: "Just so you know, we're ashamed the president of the United States is from Texas." The word criticism usually implies bringing up some position or action that can be discussed and pointing out its shortcomings, not simply making a personal attack. "The Swedish state TV is extremely biased" is a case of highly warranted criticism, while "the chairman of said state TV rapes small children" would be a case of unsubstantiated defamation. You'd expect media people to recognize the difference.

One could go on and on about highly dubious state TV coverage of America, which is why I'll be quite brief, but this next show was quite alarming too. On 19 August 2009, on the show Kobra, the host interviewed an American journalist for 30 minutes. To quote the show's webpage:

"Lauded journalist about the atrocities in Abu Ghraib and the genocide in Rwanda"

---

1   http://svt.se/svt/jsp/Crosslink.jsp?d=81516&a=1285553

403

Translation notice: The title in Swedish is *Prisad journalist om övergreppen i Abu Ghraib och folkmordets Rwanda*, which literally translates into "... the Rwanda of genocide," grouping together both Abu Ghraib and Rwanda under the term "atrocities." Alas, this would be an awkward sentence in English. The point is that the Swedish wording only makes the word "genocide" a clarification of Rwanda, hence the word could be dropped entirely.

> "The American journalist Philip Gourevitch has written about **two of the most traumatic events of contemporary history** - the atrocities against prisoners by American soldiers in the Iraqi **Abu Ghraib** prison and the genocide in **Rwanda** fifteen years ago. This year Philip Gourevitch's books on Iraq and Rwanda have arrived in Swedish. Kobra's Kristofer Lundström met him in New York, to among other things talk about **what these two events might have in common**."[1]

Now, who can dispute that the almost complete extermination of the Tutsi tribe in Rwanda, with a death toll of 800,000, has something in common with perverts in the US military sexually violating Iraqi prisoners? To analyse the logic left-wing media like the Swedish state TV must be using, I would propose this is how they reason: "When the USA does anything, it's as bad as the worst of the worst committed by any other country in the world, since the USA is the great Satan by default." *Al-mout li Amreeka*?

Yet this wasn't the only time the Kobra show went too far with its anti-American zealotry; as President Bush was leaving office in 2008, an episode called "Kobra on George W Bush" was described with these words: "He's the world's most hated politician, but also God's gift to comedy."[2]

An American that on the other hand received praise was

---

1   http://svt.se/2.106688/1.1610922/

2   http://svt.se/2.93204/1.1295931/

George Clooney, whom Kobra interviewed in early 2006.

"A meeting with Bush-critic George Clooney"

"During the spring he's been in movie theaters in Sweden as a script writer, director and actor in two movies, both of them critical of contemporary USA."

"*Good night and good luck* is the story of how the legendary TV journalist Ed Murrow in the 50's challenged the powerful senator Joe McCarthy and accused him of infringing on civil liberties in his hunt for Communists."

"Syriana is a thriller about the oil industry, this one also with a political message. When American media has shied away from criticizing power, Hollywood has seen a business opportunity.

- Unfortunately, for the last three years, until the Katrina disaster, media has avoided the tough issues, but Clooney feels the movie industry has taken over there somewhat."[1]

---

1   http://svt.se/2.52599/1.605441/

IMMIGRATION

"Jag ger fan i allt
och ta dig nu en sup
och ragla kring på ängarna
i skogens gröna djup

jag ger fan i allt
berusar mig ett tag
om pengarna tar slut
så finns det socialbidrag"

"I don't give a s*** about anything
now drink like a pig
and stagger around on the fields
in the deep green of the forest

I don't give a s*** about anything
get myself intoxicated for a while
if the money runs out
then there's welfare checks"

Eddie Meduza

The journey to Sweden

This is a story of a fictional man named Ibrahim, who decided to escape Sharia law in his Arabian home country and head to the green pastures of a European welfare state, after he witnessed Swedish aid workers erect a hydro power plant near his village.

Ibrahim was standing in his tent when to his surprise he witnessed female workers not wearing a veil of any kind survey the area and apply the building specifications for the intended plant. "What the... do they let women work?" he thinks. "And who taught them how to read building blueprints? Something isn't right here."

As Ibrahim has settled down from this shocking experience, he approaches one of the male workers and asks about their country. "Don't you have your women wear veils the way God instructs us to?" he asks. "No, we consider that oppression of women," the Swedish man responds.

"A veil - oppression of women?" he thinks to himself. "These people must be crazy. They sure seem rich though... wonder how I can get myself a share of that wealth."

Ibrahim approaches the Swedish man again and asks for his name. "I'm called Jöns," he says. "Ok, Jöns, do you have any other projects planned after that power plant is done? We could use some asphalted roads here," Ibrahim says.

"I'm sorry, after this is done we're heading back to Sweden."

"So what will you do then?"

"I'll produce a written report to my female boss and then return to my family who's waiting on me back there.

"A female boss?! These people are clearly committable. Has

their wealth driven them mad?" he thinks to himself. "My tent or life in an advanced society with these lunatics... wonder what would be the best? It sure sucks having to manually pump water out of the well."

Ibrahim addresses Jöns again. "Is there any way for me to come there with you," he asks.

"Well, formally immigration is restricted, but it's pretty easy to be granted asylum if you're a refugee... But that might not be that easy from your country since there's no military conflict here."

"Are there no grounds for granting asylum to me then?"

"Sweden does readily grant asylum to people persecuted for their sexual orientation, which I understand is something that goes on here."

"So if I was the kind of person that did another man up his butt and they didn't like me here because of that, I could be granted asylum?"

"Yeah, we cherish homosexuals. You'd be welcomed with open arms and have all sorts of people accomodate your every need."

"Me... a homosexual? No! There has to be some other way," Ibrahim thinks. "Over in neighbouring Jihadi republic they're at war with the USA... If I tell the Swedes I'm from there I bet they'll believe me... That's it, from now on I'm a citizen of the Jihadi republic!"

Now Ibrahim concocts a story of how he's on the run from the conflict over there and that he because of the American invasion is in need of asylum somewhere. He approaches the Swedish embassy in his own country and tells them he just made it out of the war, and now they buy a plane ticket to Sweden for him and agree to start processing his application for asylum. Upon

408

arriving in Sweden, he's assigned an apartment of his own, which to his astonishment actually has running water and even a colour TV. He doesn't like having it on though, because on nearly all the TV channels, there are lots of women not wearing veils. The Swedish government also pays for all his expenses during the asylum application, and when it's granted, he's entitled to two years of "no questions asked" government support along with voluntary classes in the Swedish language. Ibrahim however prefers staying with his Arabic, and the authorities happily let him manage just fine with that, supplying all the information he needs about participation in Swedish society in his own language.

Ibrahim had almost forgotten his family back home, but now he learns that as an official refugee, he's entitled to have his whole family brought to Sweden, with the government both arranging all the paperwork and also paying for the flight - the official Swedish term is *anhöriginvandring*, immigration of relatives. He learns that Sweden even has a formal law detailing this very entitlement, regulation (1984:936) "on subsidies to refugees for the cost of relatives travelling to Sweden." Ibrahim realizes that the law also gives him the right to apply for having other relatives move here as well and considers bringing his father too. He contemplates the idea for a moment, then decides that Hassan would never stand Sweden with all the unveiled women, so he scratches that idea.

So now, burqa-wearing Aisha and their ten children join him in his 2-room apartment. Soon enough a social worker comes into their home and finds it questionable that they keep so many children in an apartment this size.

Ibrahim thinks to himself. "So this is where my plans end... Guess I shouldn't have brought all ten of them here, Hassan could have kept a couple of them back home. Hmm, wonder which ones I should keep here if I send five home... Which ones do I like the most?"

The social worker is puzzled by Ibrahim being lost in thought. "Hello, have you been listening to me? We need to move your family to a bigger apartment," she says. "A bigger apartment? You'll give us that too?"

"Yeah, I think a 6-room apartment should be suitable for now... Don't worry, I'll sort it all out for you, we'll pay the move there too."

Now Ibrahim's family lives in a luxurious 6-room apartment, and there's little pressure on Ibrahim to earn a living on his own. When he told the employment office he refuses to work with women not wearing veils, they responded that they had understanding for his perspective and let him stay on government support in spite of not working for a living. Soon the social services becomes more involved in family life, and after witnessing Ibrahim instruct his children in the Koran, they take all ten children away to orphanages, where they spend most of their childhood. In a move that makes perfect economic sense, Ibrahim and wife also get to stay in the 6-room apartment while the government pays a large running cost for the foster care of the children. As adults, these children became rapists and bank robbers, but that's another story.

This story is not too atypical for people moving from the third world to Sweden; integration into society has really not worked very well, while the cost to the taxpayers has been enormous - according to some estimates, the yearly net cost of refugee immigration to Sweden is about 10% of the GDP. To the social planners, it has to be said that this can't be seen as anything else than an intended aim, something which will be explained in the coming section.

Social planning meets the intentional creation of an underclass

Since 1980, according to the official statistics of the Migration Board, some 1.2 million permanent residence permits have been granted to a country of some eight million Swedes. Only a tiny fraction of these have been for skilled workers, the vast majority "refugees" or their relatives. When I grew up in the 1980's and early 90's, Sweden still looked quite homogenous, while most Swedish cities today look more or less like New York in their demographic composition - the transformation has been devastating. The United Nations only requires Sweden to receive some 2,000 quota refugees a year, but Sweden has gone far beyond that. The last couple of years, the country has provided asylum or a similar measure to close to 100,000 a year, and extreme problems with financing, social disintegration and crime has followed in the wake of the immigration.

While "refugee" immigration keeps on rising, labour immigration doesn't. In the early 1980's, when this immigration was at its peak, Sweden handed out close to a thousand permanent resident permits to skilled workers, while in 2009, it was a meagre 81. Though many American documentaries praise Swedish society, labour immigration of Americans to Sweden only averages 20 to 30 a year. I personally bet there's at least a thousand Americans that say they're going to move to Sweden for every one actually that does it. Maybe even a million.

Though a country with any instinct of self-preservation can't just hand out welfare payouts to so called "refugees" that flood it, special interests in society can still benefit. The ones that arrive will need the services of the Migration Board - interpreters, refugee accommodations to house them etc, which means work for government employees. And by getting them hooked on welfare and do little to encourage them to seek gainful employment, if any can be had with their limited job skills, it's easy to see what their political perspective will be. Since they're dependent on the government, they usually end up sympathizing with parties that give it a large role. Personally I would never let myself be used in this way, I would vote the other way in mere defiance when I realize that someone has attempted to use me as a pawn in a political game. Statistics from immigrant ghettos do however reveal just how well social planners can create dependent sympathizers.

More than any other city district in Sweden, Rosengård in the southern city of Malmö has made the most headlines. Here, Swedes are not welcome, and often-times both the police and fire fighters find themselves attacked if they attempt to enter the area. The community is defined by an antisocial counter-culture that happily accepts Swedish welfare, but otherwise doesn't bother adapting at all to their host country. There have been numerous riots taking place here, with the immigrant youth using violence as a means of expression whenever they're upset with something or want more handouts. Though immigrants are free to settle wherever they want in the country, with any town wanting to keep them out branded as 'racist,' they've had a tendency to avoid assimilating. Instead they've crammed themselves into city ghettos with much larger families than the apartments they live in are designed for, and reports are coming in of cockroaches returning to Swedish cities, which had been extinct for many decades.

It's quite astonishing to watch the voting tally from these immigrant ghettos and notice just how one-sided the political sympathies are. To quote the 2010 parliamentary election results for a couple of districts of Rosengård:

412

Törnrosen	The Social Democrats 81.54%	The Left Party 5.15%	The Green Party 3.58%	Combined 90.27%
Örtagården V	The Social Democrats 85.26%	The Left Party 2.89%	The Green Party 3.32%	Combined 91.47%
Örtagården Ö	The Social Democrats 83.03%	The Left Party 6.65%	The Green Party 2.06%	Combined 91.74%
Herrgården	The Social Democrats 87.52%	The Left Party 4.61%	The Green Party 0.74%	Combined 92.87%

This last election, the political parties put up election placards in languages such as Arabic and Vietnamese, and the election authorities supply voting information in some 25 languages. You really ask yourself why people who can't read Swedish should be encouraged to vote. I doubt the centrist parties have much reason to attempt to win over this demographic, however, when the far-left parties have their dependents in such a firm grip. Left-wing parties in general in Europe have seen their votes decline the last decade, but the Swedish Social Democrats have obviously found a good counter-measure against the flight of the indigenous population from the party. It's a safe formula luring people here with welfare benefits and intentionally creating ghettos.

The "refugees" come to Sweden in the hope of achieving a better life for themselves, but that's not what the Social Democrats have intended to use them for. They see these immigrants merely as voting cattle, encouraging the formation of ghettos in which life is miserable in order to create a political base for themselves. There's extreme anger among the immigrants due to the life they find themselves having here, yet unfortunately, they don't take it out on the politicians that created the problem. Instead they make it a sport attacking the average Swede - in some cases, outright rape gangs have been formed, hunting down Swedish women and subjecting them to brutal group rapes. Several studies of rape convictions have found that the overwhelming majority of rape offenders are immigrants, most of which come from Muslim countries.

One of the most notorious such rapes that have taken place was the one in *Rissne* in 2000, when seven Arab immigrants had assaulted a 14-year-old girl at an indoors parking lot. All of them join in and rape her in a violent manner, and when they're done with her, they steal her clothes and leave her there. In court behind closed doors, only three of these teenagers are convicted for it, with the act being charged as a case of *gross sexual exploitation*. They're sentenced to care in open forms under the social services while their victim is awarded damages that probably will never be paid. There's an enormous uproar among the public at this atrocity of a verdict, yet the justice system won't budge.

It's no understatement to state that Swedish immigration policies have constituted the worst form of treason, exposing the most vulnerable portion of Swedish society to the worst scum the world has to offer.

Diskrimineringsombudsmannen - Enabling victimization

In 1986, Sweden received a new public authority called *Ombudsmannen mot etnisk diskriminering*, the "Ombudsman against ethnic discrimination." Over the years, this ombudsman has managed some outrageous cases, and today it doesn't only handle ethnic "discrimination," but also "discrimination" on the grounds of disability, equality and sexual orientation.

I refuse to shake a woman's hand

In 2006, a young Muslim immigrant whose anonymity I will respect by referring to him as Alen Malik C., was in an employment measure provided to him by the employment office. At the time, he had no marketable job skills, but the government felt confident in his potential as a welding operator and had decided to grant him training in this profession. After finishing this training, the training provider had set him up with a job interview at the company Melament AB on the 11th of May, for a possible internship. There he would however face complications - the manager at this workplace was a woman, and when she introduced herself, she asked to shake the man's hand. Alen, however, just looked down on the floor and refused to shake her hand, as his religion prohibits him from doing, but didn't tell her why even though she repeatedly reached out her hand.

Crnalic's contact person at the training provider had also followed him to this interview, and after this bad introduction, he had felt it would be hopeless. Later on, he would learn that he didn't get the position, with the employer citing lack of experience and the necessary physical fitness. After the interview, this man drove Alen back to the training provider while they discussed what had happened. Alen expressed the view that there was no need for him to explain why he didn't shake a woman's hand.

Two weeks later, Crnalic is summoned to a meeting at the employment office, where they go through what has happened and how to proceed; they ask if he can go back to the woman and explain to her why he refused to shake her hand, but he refuses. After this, the employment office decides they're going to withdraw his education direction, which will make him lose out on the government benefits he is on at this time. First, though, his handler is in talks with a lawyer at the national employment department to confirm it's justified, which he learns it is, and after that also contacts the department of justice and the department of commerce, all of them agreeing it's the right thing to do. For the decision on the 31st of May, they cite all of Alen's actions.

On the 27th of June, his Swedish adoptive mother Linda files a complaint with the ombudsman for discrimination (DO), asking for damages, where she mentions that Alen is back in his home country of Bosnia at the moment, staying with his father. Linda is a Muslim convert who found Islam after meeting a Swedish convict who had also converted. Along with the formal complaint to the female DO Katri Linna, she also sends a personal letter to the manager at Melament, also a woman. These are excerpts from this letter:

"Here is the letter to the girl:"

"Hi buddy, my name is Linda B C"

"Alen Crnalic', who for a long time has pondered what way to go in life as far as work goes, thought he had found his way when he received his employment training."

"Alen told me the two of you met and that he refused to shake your hand. As a Swedish woman I can understand you felt offended. But buddy listen now to what the reason is.

You know, God has created man weak for the woman, us women know how to do get a man's attention and that's how it should be, that's God's will!"

"So buddy, Alen who is a man in his best years, unmarried, he's touched... and to not awaken his emotions he does what his religion says... don't touch a woman!"

"So buddy don't be offended, he honoured you and respected you as young, beautiful and clean when he in a friendly but firm way chose to decline with disastrous consequences."

The DO now picks up the case and initially decides to sue the employment office for about $20,000. Then next couple of years see plenty of litigation in this case, and finally on 8 February 2010, Alen is awarded 60,000 crowns, or about $8,500. Apart from the discrimination complaint, the DO has added another one picked up along the way; on top of the lost government benefits from the withdrawal of the education direction, he has also lost out on welfare payouts from residing outside the country, and also after returning home when he stepped into the welfare office and was asked to shake a woman's hand. Alen then felt discriminated against and didn't want to return to this office, instead suing for the loss of income that followed this. To quote the DO's complaint:

"Since the officer at the social services attempted to persuade Alen Crnalic to shake the hands of women he felt questioned and subjected to pressure and didn't want to return to the social services in Älmhult."

"Alen Crnalic's net loss then amounts to 35,345 crowns."

On top of this, the DO demands interest on the missing welfare payouts, which made it 60,580 crowns at the time of filing the initial complaint to the court on the 22 May 2008. The court didn't agree to this claim, however.

417

"My disability prevents me from working mornings"

Case HO 1962/2007

"A woman working at a gym in Borås reported to the DO that her employer subjected her to discrimination and harassment because of her disability.

The complainant has a mental disability that makes it hard for her working mornings and before noon. Therefore she had earlier had her hours placed during afternoons and evenings. When a new boss arrived at the gym, he rearranged the schedule so she would be forced to work early sessions.

According to the DO, the investigation supports the notion that the employer has discriminated against the woman through the scheduling. The employer has also not taken necessary support- and accommodation measures to enable the woman to perform her work in spite of her disability.

The DO also feels that the employer through his actions has subjected the complainant to harassment related to disabilities.

The DO has settled out of court with the employer, giving the woman 45,000 crowns($6,500)."

Nothing like the old "I don't want to get out of bed" disability, eh?

Negro balls

As I grew up in Sweden, we had a pastry called *negerbollar*, "Negro balls" in English - a dark round ball covered in white nib sugar topping. Until the 1990's, there were hardly any black people at all in the country and no one had a problem with it, but then it started being deemed "politically incorrect." Efforts were made to change the name of the pastry to *chokladboll*, "chocolate ball," instead, with people using the old name more and more being viewed as racists. As the 21th century arrived, the word didn't see much use, but after a new anti-discrimination law had been introduced in 2003, a case of someone using it was brought to national attention. A bakery in Sjöbo had then still offered the pastry under the name *negerbollar*, and a white woman who passed the store and saw the sign then decided to report the business to the DO mere days after the new law was in effect.

After half a year of deliberation, DO Margareta Wadstein delivered a verdict in January of 2004. Though she states that if the complainant had been able to prove that she was personally offended, it would have been possible to ask for damages from the store, but since this wasn't the case now, no action was made. The DO does however propose that any business that uses the word *negerboll* should be fined 100,000 crowns, or $13,500. She also feels that the word shouldn't be used at all in daily conversation, or the word negro in conjunction with any other word, and also reminds people not to use the word Lapp for Sami people, or Gypsy for Romani.

It sure has its downsides being a white heterosexual male... You can't sue anyone in this country.

THE WEALTH
OF NATIONS

"Sverige, Sverige, hur är det fatt
med vårt gamla land
slita hårt både dag och natt
får vi alle man
priserna, de går upp i ett
lönerna går ner
det finns ingen reson och vett
i allt det som sker

man får slita och ligga i
för sin lilla slant
ändå räcker den aldrig till
alltid likadant
plånboken, den är alltid tom
kan det värre bli
det är dags nu att tänka om,
en ny filosofi"

"Sweden, Sweden, what's the matter
with our old country
toil hard every day and night
all of us have to do
the prices, they keep on rising
the salaries drop
there's no rhyme or reason
to everything that's taking place

you have to toil and put in effort
for your little coin
still it never lasts
always the same way
your wallet is always empty
can it get any worse
it's time to reconsider,
a new philosophy"

Eddie Meduza

Well, at least the wealth of those nations that apply Adam Smith's principles. The ones that don't soon find themselves very lacking in this area. You have to give credit to socialist governments that they can achieve a fairly equal distribution of wealth, but what they are reluctant to tell you is that people in these countries are equal in poverty, not in actual wealth.

420

Money matters

Even though this is 2010 and the political discourse these days are about little else than the need for the government to come bail you out in times of need, there's still something called a personal income - your own money. Until recently, it's been universally assumed that the higher an income you have, the better your life will be. Citizens of the old Communist countries in Eastern Europe afforded little more than food, and for that they often had to stand in line for quite a while - one's personal economy wasn't satisfactory there.

During the post-World War II period, virtually everyone has been aware of the fact that Americans have enjoyed the highest living standard in the world, yet lately, Socialist states in Europe have painted a picture of this wealth only residing in the pockets of the extremely wealthy, with the whole remaining portion of the population being little more than paupers. Left-wing activists invent such indexes as the *Gini coefficient* to give the impression that the middle class is well-off in Socialist societies, indexes that actually reward the societies that don't have any rich people. A country where everyone is equally poor would score very high here. These same activists aren't very happy to show such data as just how much consumption the typical citizen affords, which would be much more relevant. The reason is that even here, the USA beats all of Europe by far. In this upcoming study, only Sweden and the USA will be compared, however.

How deep is your wallet?

To make the comparison more simplistic and overseeable, the following calculation will only involve gainfully employed men. To what extent this is applicable to society as a whole is for the reader to decide. To make the calculation even more simple for yours truly, it will be assumed that the American will live in a state

421

with no state-level income tax, such as Texas.

In 2007, median income for working men was $45,113 in the USA.[1] The same year, the same figure was 336,000 crowns in Sweden. After personal income taxes, the American has $34,120 left while the Swede has 232,680 crowns.

How much private consumption do the two then afford? For this comparison, a coveted prize of many aspiring filmmakers will be used - the Canon XL-2 camcorder.

On Newegg, this camera goes for $3,700, hence the American affords 9.22 of them. The cheapest price to be found in Sweden according to Pricerunner is 46,336, which means that the Swede affords 5.02. In other words, the American affords 83% more camcorders than the Swede, almost twice the amount of private consumption. This might be considered a crude comparison, but many other ones have yielded similar results.

---

1   Source: The American Census Bureau

The British magazine The Economist regularly publishes a purchasing power index called the *Big Mac Index*, which in 2010 found that Sweden was the second most expensive country on the planet, with $6.56 for one burger compared to $3.58 for the USA. Hence, the Swedish burger also cost 83% more.

The *Center for International Comparisons of Production, Income and Prices* (CIC) at the University of Pennsylvania in 2007 published an index entitled "Price Level of Gross Domestic Product" which found that Sweden's prices were 142.78% of the American ones, hence significantly higher. Depending on whatever index one uses, Sweden is among the absolutely most expensive countries on the planet, and any comparison of what earned income means has to take that into account.

The same source also found that Sweden's real GDP per capita adjusted for purchasing power parity was more than 20% below that of the USA's; "Real Gross Domestic Product per Capita Relative to the United States (G-K method, current price)" had Sweden's at 77.35% of the American one.

The country that blew it

Some time around 1970, Sweden was #2 in GDP per capita, only trailing behind the USA. Those days are very much gone - Sweden has fallen a whole lot behind. Between 1950 and 2008, Sweden's real GDP (not adjusted for purchasing power parity) increased by 388%, while the US one increased by 556%. In the CIA World Fact Book of 2009[1], Sweden is at #30 when it comes to GDP per capita adjusted for purchasing power parity, with about half the industrialized world ahead of it. When this author grew

---

1   https://www.cia.gov/library/publications/the-world-factbook/rankorder/2004rank.html?
countryName=Sweden&countryCode=sw&regionCode=eu&rank=30#sw

up, you'd be reminded on a daily basis in school that Sweden was one of the richest countries on the planet, and if it was just a little short of being the richest, it had managed to produce development indexes that "proved" it to be #1. Today Sweden is just barely ahead of the EU median in spite of the expansion the union has gone through. In 2009, Sweden was at $36,600 while the EU median was $32,500.

The same CIA 2009 report found that Sweden through its 5.1% plummet in GDP that year was #187 in the world in economic growth.[1]

---

1   https://www.cia.gov/library/publications/the-world-factbook/geos/sw.html

You get one third, the government gets two thirds

... or the story of Arne and his pay check.

At the end of the month, a blue-collar worker by the name of Arne got curious about the pay check he had just received. Though when he had been hired, he had been told his monthly salary would be 21,500 crowns, his pay checks only amounted to 15,000 with the government keeping the rest in taxes. Noticing his boss not very busy one Friday afternoon, he walks up to him in his office and decides to ask him about why he's left with so much less in income. Shouldn't working-class people such as he get to keep more?

Confronted with the question, his boss Nisse smiles and tells him there's a whole lot more than meets the eye when it comes to taxes. Nisse tells him that in order to keep him hired, Nisse has to pay no less than 32,000 crowns a month, more than twice what Arne gets into his pocket. The visible tax burden put on Arne is only a little less than half of the actual income tax that is deducted from Arne's pay check - the rest is the payroll tax, which while being legally required to pay in order to keep Arne employed, is never visible to him.

"So you mean I get to keep less than half of what I earn," Arne asks.

"Correct," Nisse answers nodding.

"Is there anything more little ignorant ol' me should know about taxes? I seem to be quite clueless on the subject."

"Well, what kind of private consumption do you spend your money on?"

"Is that of relevance to taxes?"

"Yep, there's something called Value-Added Taxes and purchase taxes... The government takes even more from you that way."

"Hmm... There's petrol, of course. And my wife smokes a pack of cigarettes a day. Some weekends we buy some vodka to drink too."

"Let me get my calculator, and let me look up petrol prices."

Nisse gets his calculator out of his desk and enters *www.bensinpris.se* as URL on his web browser. As of 11 October 2010, he finds the cheapest petrol is 11.37 crowns per litre for unleaded petrol.

"Ok, assuming you buy petrol at 11.37 crowns, 6.65 out of that is taxes, or nearly 60%. If you'd purchase petrol with your whole pay check, you'd be handing over 70% of your income all in all to the government."

"70%? That's crazy... I thought that 30% income tax they told me I pay was about all of it."

"It is indeed crazy... It's not this crazy everywhere in the world though. Over in the USA, they pay only a fraction as much as we do for petrol."

"How much does it cost over there?"

Nisse logs on to *www.gasbuddy.com* and checks the prices there. Using the current exchange rate of 6.65 crowns for 1 dollar, Nisse calculates that the cheapest Swedish petrol would amount to $6.47 per gallon in American currency and measurement.

"Ok, looking at these numbers here, I find that petrol costs us a little more than 2.5 times as much as the Americans pay," Nisse says. He continues:

"The cheapest petrol in the USA is $2.526 per gallon today while the cheapest one here is $6.47 in their units. So ours costs more than 250% of theirs."

"I just can't believe it... Our government cons us into paying that much for petrol?"

"Yep... Americans would never stand our prices."

"So how about the cigarettes?"

Nisse looks up the relevant figures.

"Ok, a package of Prince cigarettes costs about 52 crowns, out of which half is purchase taxes."

"Yikes. And my bottle of vodka?"

Nisse gets out a brochure he's got in a desk drawer.

"According to the figures I've got in this brochure here from *Skattebetalarnas förening*, out of the sales price of 229 crowns, roughly 185 is taxes, or a little over 80%."

Arne sighs.

"I sure don't get to keep much of my money," he says.

"That's for sure... They leave you skint."

"So how much taxes all in all does a typical person as I pay?"

"Let's see what the brochure says... Even with your modest salary, you pay about 60% in taxes assuming typical private consumption. A man earning median pay, a little more than you, pays almost two thirds."

"I'm almost glad I don't earn any more then, would stink paying even more than I already do."

Nisse gets an idea.

"Maybe we should freeze your salary the next couple of years and I'll compensate you under the table instead... Then I can pay you more.

"I like the sound of that idea."

This is the reality of making a living in Sweden... Even if

you're a blue-collar worker, the government still takes most of what you earn.

Astrid Lindgren, children's book author asked to pay 102% in taxes

Many people may be familiar with the book characters Pippi Longstocking and her red plaits, or perhaps Karlsson-on-the-roof with the propeller on his back. What might be less familiar to most people outside of Sweden are the troubles the author of these books, Astrid Lindgren, would have to go through with the government in the mid 70's. Though she was never too interested in fame or fortune, even outright frightened at how much money her books were making during this decade from the international sales, what happened in 1976 would overtake even this altruistic-minded human being.

As an internationally renowned author, she was earning a surprisingly large income while being self-employed, which required her to pay both income tax and payroll tax for herself. The tax system wasn't very well set up for her high income, and in 1976 when she did her taxes, she found they added up to a 102% marginal tax rate, making her pay more in taxes than she earned on top of the base level. Satirically, she responded in the most appropriate way an author can - by writing a short semi-fictional story about her plight.

In March of 1976, tabloid Expressen published her story "Pomperipossa in Monismania," in which she described it this way, unofficial translation by me:

"Pomperipossa loved her country, its forests, mountains and lakes and green groves, but not only that but also the people living there. And even the wise men ruling it, oh, she felt they were so wise and therefore she faithfully voted for them every time wise men were going to be elected to govern Monismania. The ones that had now ruled and run things for over 40 years, they had set up such a great society, she thought, no one needed to be poor there, everyone was getting his slice of the welfare cake, and

429

Pomperipossa was happy that she herself had been able to contribute to this baking of cakes.

THERE WAS SOMETHING IN MONISMANIA called the marginal tax rate. That meant that the more money you earned, the greater portion of this money the national tax master wanted to save up for the welfare cake. But more than 80-83% he didn't want to take from anyone, no, because he was reasonable. "Dear Pomperipossa," he said, "something on the order of 17 to 20% you may keep yourself and spend as you like." And Pomperipossa was deeply satisfied with that and lived merry and happy. Still there were in the country a lot of dissatisfied people who banged their shields and dinned about "the high tax rate" as they called it. Pomperipossa never did that, no one in Monismania had never heard her din at all about her contributions to the welfare cake."

Pomperipossa also mentions meeting among others a Russian author who only had to pay 13% taxes on his book sales. Near the end she depicts society's political debate:

"AND POMPERIPOSSA TOOK OUT and reread a short verse, that one of the greatest of Monismania's poets had written:

That you create value, society can't stand
the drivel of bureaucrats you're forced to listen to
You're meant to Castro waging war in Angola lend a hand
or reside in an old men's home and receive therapy do."

Since the parliamentary elections came up later that year, the story and what the tax system had meant for Astrid became a part of the debate. During a session in parliament, Moderate chairman Gösta Bohman read the story aloud to support his criticism of Social Democrat economics. Gunnar Sträng, Social Democrat minister of finance at the time, the man behind the tax system, then responded with an arrogant attack on the beloved author:

"The article is an interesting combination of stimulating literary ability and deep ignorance of the maze of fiscal policy. But we

430

don't expect Astrid Lindgren to manage that."

Astrid was in a radio interview the following day, where she responded to Sträng's comment:

"Yes, he says that 'we don't expect Astrid Lindgren to manage that.' But I expect Gunnar Sträng to manage it! And I don't think it seems as if he counts that much better than I do - what he claims to be miscalculated is if so miscalculated by the National Tax Board, because that's where I got the numbers."

"Gunnar Sträng seems to have learned to tell stories, but he sure can't count! It would be better if we exchanged jobs."

The exchanges between minister Sträng and Astrid Lindgren that followed didn't prove very favourable for voter sympathy for the Social Democrats, and they lost the election for the first time in almost half a century. The Social Democrats did however ensure that no one would have to pay any more than 90% taxes as a consequence of this affair. How gracious of them to let people keep 10% (before VAT and purchase taxes).

Publicly funded addiction treatment

Now there's a great way to spend taxpayer money - to attempt to treat the drug abusers who could quit their abuse at any time if they were really interested. Still, one can't expect individuals to actually tend to their own shortcomings - everything has to be the government's responsibility. The addicts have a "disease," and if you dispute this idea, you're considered ignorant. Sweden's obligations to its adult "victims of society," who have turned to substance abuse, cost a little more than 5.5 billion crowns in 2008[1]. A placement at a treatment centre cost a median 2200 crowns / day in 2007, or roughly $300.[2] The highest costs were in Mönsterås (26,536 crowns/day, $3,600) and Lerum (11,373 crowns/day, $1,560).

Addiction treatment is both an entitlement and a responsibility in Sweden. If you drink too much and aren't interested in treatment, the government can still force you into it under the LVM law. The requirements for commitment are:

"he or she as a consequence of the substance abuse

a) exposes his or her physical or mental health to serious jeopardy,
b) is running the risk of ruining his or her life, or
c) might be expected to seriously injure himself or herself, or some other close relative."

Examples of case b) include if the person risks losing his/her job or failing academic studies. Under the LVM law, though normally a forced commitment requires a court order, a person can be immediately seized at any time if the social welfare council feels a court decision can't be awaited upon. Whoever is subject to

---

1   Jämförelsetal för socialtjänsten 2008, Socialstyrelsen

2   Jämförelsetal för socialtjänsten 2007, Socialstyrelsen

care under the LVM law is forbidden from possessing any kind of drug, including alcohol and anabolic steroids. This is the kind of law that doesn't see much use against well-connected people, but well against the poor.

In the government addiction treatment system, you'd expect the usual intravenous drug users and alcoholics, but in Sweden, other clientele have made use of their right to treatment as well...

I'm addicted to Coca Cola![1]

In 2008, a middle-aged woman who for many years had consumed Coca Cola as well as food in unhealthy quantities decided she was in need of addiction treatment. Her soda consumption had resulted in multiple hospitalizations for adult-onset diabetes and high blood pressure. Deciding to turn her life around, but unable to find the spiritual strength to quit the highly addictive drug Coca Cola on her own, she turned to the social services for help. They're very willing to accommodate her, offering placement at the institutions they've got available for these problems.

She's not interested in the regular addiction treatment, however; she feels that because she's deaf, that treatment won't be of any use to her, since she feels her deafness is a part of the "disease picture." So she appeals to an administrative court to get the treatment at a particular specialist clinic that she wants, but loses here too. Then she turns to the administrative court of appeal, which grants her the right to the requested treatment, citing that her lifestyle is a threat to her health.

Unfortunately I wasn't able to find out whether the woman managed to kick her Coca Cola. I wonder what's next... An obese

---

1

http://www.sydsvenskan.se/malmo/article406792/Kvinna-far-hjalp-mot-laskmissbruk.html

young man demanding treatment for fast food addiction, being offered it but rejecting it because it's "only for heterosexuals," and stating that his homosexuality is a part of his problem?

Mohammed has grasped the essence of life in Sweden

This story is from the National Board of Health and Welfare webpage, where advice is given to government employees on questions of ethics.

http://www.socialstyrelsen.se/etiskafragor/etiskafragestallnin gar/skapersonalhjalpamanattdrickas

"Should staff help a man get drunk?

Half the personal assistants don't want to visit Mohammed. They don't feel it's right helping Mohammed consume whiskey that makes him throw up. They feel the air in his apartment is hazardous to their health because of the non-stop smoking.

Mohammed is a 30-year-old man who 10 years ago suffered a motorcycle accident that left him completely paralysed, he can only move his head. Mohammed is a refugee from Iraq and has no relatives or friends in Sweden but is all alone. He's got an apartment of his own and the municipality is employer for the 11 personal assistants that help him. The assistants work after a schedule.

Mohammed is a chain-smoker and drinks volumes of whiskey. He's perfectly at his senses and makes it perfectly clear he wants to smoke practically non-stop and drink whiskey until he throws up. Mohammed doesn't express any suicidal thoughts.

To be able to smoke and drink whiskey, Mohammed is dependent on the staff holding the cigarette and the whiskey glass (or the drinking straw) and bringing it to his mouth. When Mohammed throws up, the assistants have to suck the vomit out of his throat or he risks suffocating from it.

The personal assistants also spend time with Mohammed by

listening to music or reading books to him."

"When the municipality hires personal assistants for Mohammed, they must inform them that it's about an Iraqi man who doesn't speak Swedish and who smokes and drinks to excess so that they're aware of what awaits them if they're prepared to work with Mohammed. The assistants that will help Mohammed can't feel that he's disgusting for smoking and drinking, but must be tolerant of him. Perhaps the assistants need some nursing training since there may be medical complications when the vomit is sucked out of Mohammed's throat."

"Mohammed decides himself about his life situation and about his desire to smoke and drink whiskey. The personal assistants are hired to help him with what he can't do himself, which is really everything. If Mohammed wants to smoke and drink whiskey, the assistants must help him with that."

"It may also be considered a pressing psychosocial work environment for the assistants when they first help him consume the liquor and then have to do lifesaving efforts to prevent him from suffocating. What responsibility do the personal assistants have if Mohammed would suffocate from his vomit when they've participated in helping him to his liquor?"

"The personal assistants should attempt to convince Mohammed to drink in more moderation and point out to him that it's hard to get the assistants to stay with him when they first have to pour the liquor into him and then suck the vomit from his throat."

Ultimate moocher, thy name is Mohammed.

Somehow I think this story is very symptomatic of life in a Socialist nanny state - the government can't provide you with a dignified life no matter how much resources it's given, but it sure can enable your self-destruction. There just isn't any life to be had, you have to take your refuge in drugs.

Swedish slavery

Though the political discussion in Western countries today might have you thinking otherwise, institutionalized slavery certainly hasn't been confined only to America. Sweden kept indentured servitude supported by law in some form until as late as 1945, when the system of the *statare* was finally abolished. *Statare* were farm workers paid mainly not in cash, but in kind, employed on 1-year contracts with their families living with them on their masters' farms. They did not get to sleep in their master's houses, however, but instead in special rows on the land. The modern Swedish system of slavery lasted for roughly three centuries, slowly coming into institutionalized practice in the 17th century with the enactment of *Tjänstehjonsstadgan*, perhaps best translated as "The indentured servant act," in 1664. *Tjänstehjonsstadgan* concerned itself with the responsibilities of master and servant to each other. The servant could physically admonish his servant if his work effort wasn't satisfactory, while the master was tasked with looking after the health of his servant, and, had he been in service for a long enough time - to sustain him throughout his retirement years.

Initially, this servitude was entered into voluntarily, but during the 18th century, the government of a nation that until two centuries earlier in the beginning of the 16th century had mainly been one of independent farmers, had started concerning itself with residents who didn't conform to what was expected of them. Described in *Legohjonsstadgan* of 1739 as *landstrykare, lösdrivare, lättingar*, perhaps translated as "vagabonds, vagrants and slackers," these were now faced with the duty of every person who didn't support himself to legally report to a farm owner for work, or the authorities could sentence him to forced labour.

In 1723, the status of farm labour took a turn downwards as a national maximum salary was imposed on the indentured servants, who lost more and more of their earlier freedom. The 18th century also saw the introduction of Sweden's first modern set of laws - nine codes of law with names such as *Straffbalken*, "The Punishment Code," *Missgärningsbalken*, "The Malefaction Code," and so on. These tyrannical laws specified loss of life as the punishment for a number of offences, such as decapitation for criticizing the king, his next of heir or the queen; accusing the government of mismanaging its duties without proof; zoophilia; and for mocking God. To quote 1 § 1 of *Missgärningsbalken* from 1734:

"Whoever intentionally, in word or writing, blames and defames GOD, his holy word and the Sacraments; is deprived of life."

For not adhering to religious doctrine, 1 § 3 had this to say:

"If anyone departs from our correct evangelical teaching, and treads into delusion, and if he doesn't let himself be corrected; then he shall be banned from the kingdom"

As late as 1864, when *Strafflagen* replaced *Straffbalken*, new laws were enacted for the same crime - mocking God - though now the penalty had changed from death to a maximum of two years of forced labour, and mocking church services netted you up to six months. It's ironic that today, though this law is long since gone, now you can get up to four years in prison for preaching his word instead. In 1869, a new decree was issued "concerning liability for the one that attempts to influence another to depart from the evangelical Lutheran teaching," which specified a maximum of one year in prison for whoever attempted through force or reward convince someone to change his denomination, as well as for anyone that taught a faith incompatible with the official one to "children who belonged to the Swedish church." The use of the word *belong* in this context makes it clear what meaning the word had in its general use.

438

But to return to the indentured servants - the slaves; in 1833, a new revision of *Tjänstehjonsstadgan* was enacted that would last until 1926, and this law reaffirmed the right of the master to use *husaga*, corporal punishment at home, on his servants. The servants were also required to ask their master for permission to leave the house, and all their belongings had to be placed inside a chest in the master's house. The duty of all people without a legal income to report to farm owners for work was also repeated, and now everyone was also required to inform the authorities about people who weren't employed. The law also provided servant owners with the right to ask the police for assistance in bringing runaway servants back to their farms. The national work duty remained until 1885, but not until 1919 did masters lose the right to bring their servants back with police assistance.

During the later half of the 19th century, the prospect of emigrating to America became very appealing to Sweden's indentured class; though naturally they weren't in good positions to simply get on a boat and move there, they still saved up the means they could to be able to make the journey when the opportunity presented itself. They were attracted by the promises of religious freedom and a much greater prosperity than they could achieve in Sweden. Whether they liked it or not, in their home country they were forced to believe what their ministers told them was "the correct evangelical teaching," and the Swedish church even went as far as to regularly test the scriptural knowledge of its subjects in house interrogations.

There's a famous series of four books by Vilhelm Moberg called *The Emigrants* about a group of Swedes who emigrate to the USA during this era. It wouldn't be too relevant to this section to include a lengthy book review, so I'll keep to simply mentioning that it's highly acclaimed and well researched, though somewhat vulgar in its depiction of the people and their vocabulary. A very substantial portion of the Swedish people emigrated to America, some 1.3 million people all in all between the mid 19th century and the early 20th, comprising a quarter of the population. Until as late as the 1830's, Swedes were not legally allowed to leave their country, and this sudden population loss became a major concern for the government, who saw their work force disappear. The prevalent anti-Americanism you find in Swedish society today just might have originated in the attempts to get people to stay in their country back then.

The country saw substantial political reform towards the end of the 19th century, perhaps the result of more than anything else the emigration to America - these reforms were outright necessary to preserve Sweden as a functional state. The Swedes who left their country were subjected to heavy scorn by both the political establishment as well as clergy, who attempted to convince them that they were being deceived with false promises of a land of milk and honey that just didn't exist. Most of the migration took place after the American civil war; in 1865, some mere 25,000 Swedes had found their way to America, but in 1890, they numbered no less than 800,000. Though generally having been indentured servants in their earlier life, now they became settlers owning and farming their own land, able to choose whatever religious denomination they wanted and even vote in elections. Still in the mid 1800's, few Swedes were eligible to vote, and the gradual extension of suffrage went on until 1945, when it also started including people on government support, who until that point had not been allowed to vote.

It's safe to say that though the proximity of a militaristic Germany most definitely has had its impact on Swedish society through two world wars, more than anything else it has been defined by the existence of the USA, whose influence has swayed the masses to call for political reform in their own country, or simply vote with their feet. Hence it has become a necessary task for the Swedish government to paint a less appealing picture of the

USA, seizing upon anything that will make the country look bad. When the USA took over the occupation of Vietnam from France, Sweden more than any other Western country blasted America for its conduct in the war. To an external observer, this might have been seen as justified criticism, but understanding the political situation in Sweden, one realizes that standing up to the USA was more something to serve domestic needs.

At around year 1900, around 140,000 women worked as maids, roughly 10% of the able-bodied adult population, under contracts at best little better than those of indentured servitude. This employment often had them working 16-hour days every day of the week apart from the time allotted to church service on Sunday. Hence, they had no spare time whatsoever. The ones that made their way over the Atlantic often sought out the same employment in America too, but there they could in the process also prepare a life for themselves as owners of their own homes, which was rarely the case back in Sweden. Their outstanding work ethic also made them very welcome in American society, though the loss of the most ambitious portion of the Swedish work force naturally also meant that the country probably lost a lot of the ambition in its own gene pool.

Some of this archaic legislation on forced labour lasted until 1952: In 1885, building on previous legislation of the same sort, the country introduced "the law on the treatment of vagrants," giving the police the right to detain people who moved from town to town without seeking gainful employment and confine them to special labour camps under government authority.

Hence as late as the early 1940's, these statements were all true in Sweden:

* People on welfare couldn't vote

441

* The indentured servitude of *statare* was still in effect

* The police could put vagrants in forced labour camps

And, as mentioned in an earlier chapter:

* Until 1976, the government could forcibly sterilize people meeting certain conditions.

Alas, how amusing it seems that during these very 1940's, Sweden's greatest social planner - Gunnar Myrdal - went over to the USA to advise American society on how to solve what was known as "the Negro problem" back then, publishing the work "An American dilemma" in 1944. In this work, he charged white Americans with having confined the blacks to their position in society through their condescending attitudes. There's a saying that goes, "it takes one to know one." Myrdal had himself been responsible for introducing forced sterilization into his own society.

Brain drain

The "progress indicators" quoted in the introduction of this book must surely mean that Sweden would never have a problem with the dreaded reality of "brain drain," one would assume? If the country is so great, every well-educated person in the world must be flocking to Sweden to be able to enjoy life in this socialist paradise? And the ones born here who devote a significant portion of their life to academic studies for their intended professions, surely they will appreciate being so fortunate as to enjoy this "the world's most modern country," even if it means sacrificing potential income they could get in other countries and enduring hardship in Sweden, to service the very grateful clientele in this country who would never dream of composing vitriolic rants in public forums about bad services? After all, in a socialist paradise, everything will work perfectly and everyone will sing praises to their compatriots and their most enlightened social planners?

Reality is very far from this.

The area of society that's the most important of all to many people in the western world, perhaps due to them neglecting their own health, is health care. Health care depends on mainly doctors, who through studies have amassed the required knowledge to provide modern health care services. As most people are probably familiar with, health care in Sweden is publicly funded with patients merely paying a token fee for their visits. Private medical practice is permitted, but few people afford going outside the public sector for such services, hence most doctors are employed by the government.

Becoming a doctor is a serious undertaking - the requirements to enter medical school are top grades from high school, or as it would be put in American terms - straight A's. After 5.5 years of studies and 1.5 years of internship as an *AT-*

läkare along with a personal approval by the government, one becomes a licensed medical doctor - a general practitioner. To become a specialist, one can then do another 5 years of studies and yet again be approved by the government to title oneself an *ST-läkare*, employing oneself perhaps as a dentist or an optician. Work as a doctor is generally harder than other professions, with perhaps 80 hour work weeks required which make family life hard, taking its toll both on one's physical and mental well-being. The question is - is the effort worth it?

In the USA, no one would deny that it is. A typical American *family physician* makes about $130k a year, with some as much as $200k, and is in great demand - no concerns about job security, and as far as I can see, the profession appears to be an appealing one with few complaints about this kind of employment. A typical specialist appears to make between $200k and $500k a year, though some make over a million dollars as chief physicians.

Conditions in Sweden are very different.

To quote salary figures from 2005:[1]

The entry level salary for a newly graduated *AT-läkare* was 247,200 crowns per year, or about $34k.

Median pay for *AT-läkare* was 277,200 crowns per year, or $38k. For *ST-läkare* - specialists, 384,000 crowns per year, or $52.6k.

Final pay for specialists ages 60-64 was 450,000 crowns per year, or $61.6k.

Final pay for chief physicians in southern Sweden ages 60-64: 727,200 crowns per year, or $99.6k.

---

1   http://www.sydsvenskan.se/ekonomi/article76370/Lang-utbildning-lonar-sig-inte-alltid.html

Hence a typical doctor makes the equivalent of $40-50k a year in Sweden, to be compared with the estimated mean of $200k in the USA. Confined to work in the public sector, the realistic maximum a Swedish doctor can make is $100k a year no matter what, with no individual salary talks possible, while some American ones make well over a million a year. And as is often the case in socialist countries, there's plenty of suspicion towards well-educated professionals who get blamed for everything under the sun - *läkarhat*, or "hatred of doctors," is a common word in Swedish. Though Swedes can't sue their doctors for malpractice, merely report them to the authorities, there's plenty of vitriol aimed at them on Internet blogs and similar; little is found in the way of appreciation for their services. Just about everyone has their story to share about their dissatisfaction with the health care system. If movies such as Michael Moore's *Sicko* had any basis in reality, people would be saying daily prayers to doctors in socialist countries. Well, maybe Sweden can be excused since it's the most atheistic society in the world.

But to return to more measurable phenomena: Do doctors that graduate stay in Sweden in spite of the much higher salaries in the USA? To make it short: They do not. In 2006, financial magazine *Veckans affärer* interviewed Harriet Wallberg-Henriksson, rector at *Karolinska Institutet*, Sweden's most esteemed medical school and also Sweden's finest university overall. Some 300 people graduate from *Karolinska Institutet* every year, but this article had pessimistic news to report. "Harriet Wallberg-Henriksson estimates that between 70% and 80% of the newly graduated doctors disappear abroad. Some return, but many leave the country for good."

Sweden has a huge problem with *läkarbrist* - doctor shortage. Looking up the word *läkarbrist* on Google, one gets no less than 90,000 hits, quite amazing for a country of about 9 million people, and about 134,000 for *vårdköer* - health care

445

waiting lines. For comparison, a search for the English words "doctor shortage" only gives 70,000 hits. It is obvious that Sweden is suffering a great brain drain from its doctors emigrating to the USA and the better salaries and work conditions there. For another comparison, the word *socionombrist*, shortage of people qualified for social work, only gives nine hits, and five of those are from debate forums or blogs. Perhaps this is an indication of just what a useless profession the one of a social worker is, professionals that no one really wants to have around. On a more serious note, social work is of a different nature than health care. While medical problems are real and a supply that doesn't meet the demand means people will call for more doctors, social workers simply use coercive laws to take children from families to the point needed to meet their quotas. Hence they create their own work, and demand will always be the same as supply.

Work brings freedom?

For most of the last century, the Social Democrats have held power, but since the election in 2006, a centrist government has been in place instead, with the Social Democrats in opposition. Youth unemployment is at an extreme level in today's Sweden - as of 2009, the one up to age 25 was standing at 25% according to Eurostat. So, what is their answer to this problem? In February of 2009, the head of SSU, the Social Democrat youth organization, published a proposal on how to get young people jobs, entitled "Time for the Reinfeldt Government to get the youth jobs instead of worsening *Las*." This proposal focused exclusively on additional measures the government should take to remedy the situation - more spending on education, building more houses and so on. Many critics of Swedish employment policies like to point out the problem that labour laws such as *LAS* mean for the job market, in that companies are wary of hiring new employees. This woman Jytte disagrees, however, believing government can solve it all through active involvement.[1]

So how much of a role does the woman writing this proposal feel the government should have in getting people jobs? Well, the motto introducing the proposal might give a clue: *Arbete ger frihet*, "work brings freedom." Now, where have we seen this slogan before?

----

1   http://www.newsmill.se/artikel/2009/02/27/dags-att-reinfeldt-skaffar-jobb-de-unga-pa-arbetsmarknaden

Perhaps this motto was a Freudian slip, revealing what the true intentions of the Social Democrats are - solve unemployment by putting people to work in concentration camps! The trade union LO even put posters up with this slogan, *arbete ger frihet*, though when critics pointed out just what associations it gave rise to, they quickly pulled the posters down again.

EPILOGUE

Final analysis

"Jag ger fan i allt
och super som ett svin
i fyllans töcken kan
en trasig värld bli ganska fin
jag ger fan i allt
men det är fel ändå
att man ska tvingas supa
för att himlen ska bli blå"

"I don't give a s*** about anything
and drink like a pig
in the haze of drunkenness
a broken world can become pretty nice
I don't give a s*** about anything
but it's still not right
that you're going to have to drink
for the sky to be blue"

/Eddie Meduza

By now, you've hopefully realized that Sweden doesn't function too well as a society, and has to manufacture development indexes that paint the country in a better light. It's my belief that just about all problems Swedish society faces today – an invasion of unskilled workers from the third world; exploding crime rates in spite of more money than ever spent on rehabilitation; complete disintegration of social norms in spite of unprecedented levels of money going to care under the social services; high unemployment (extremely high among the youth) in

449

spite of an employment office that receives 2% of GDP; and the worst indicators of mental health ever among adolescents in spite of the heaviest financing of psychiatry ever.

In 1850, a French economist named Frédéric Bastiat published an essay named "That which is seen and that which is unseen," usually referred to as the "Parable of the broken window," in which he illustrates how politicians might be tempted to produce the appearance of a gain from their policies, which when taking society as a whole into account is actually a loss instead. The parable describes a boy breaking the window of a man's house, which forces him to replace it and in so doing employing the services of craftsmen. Hence it appears that the boy by breaking the window has created a public good and might as well be encouraged to break more in order to get more craftsmen employed. Yet, the fallacy of this parable is that the man's money could have been spent on other things, and the value of the window that is broken isn't taken into account. From the complete perspective of society, as well as the obvious interpretation for anyone watching a window being broken, the use of the man's money is a zero sum affair, while the loss of the window is an actual loss.

Reading the parable today, one is astonished at how Bastiat predicted the development of government, even though it's only during the last couple of decades that governments have been considered wasteful by any large strata of the population. I strongly feel that the temptation to get government to subsidize social and other programs is a motivating force for politicians to, like the boy in the parable, destroy that in society which is indeed functional. To draw on a couple of examples from Swedish society:

* The traditional nuclear family was seen as a source of suffering and social problems. If government stepped in as a

parent instead and employed scientific methods in this matter, it could do a better job than the biological parents. The results of this endeavour are in since a long time - the many broken individuals whose lives have been defined by drug abuse and psychiatric problems due to not getting a proper upbringing with a loving family. But of course, this damage led to even more jobs for government workers in the fields of addiction treatment and psychiatry, neither of which have any records of success to speak of.

* Traditional crime prevention was seen as inhumane and confining the criminals to an unproductive life that didn't let them be what they could be. If society instead attempted to rehabilitate them, it could turn them into contributing members of society. As prison inmates were transferred from traditional prisons to modern institutions of care, costs shot up from the new treatment they received. Alas, this treatment didn't reduce crime rates - instead they started shooting up during the 1970's when the prison system was reformed. Could it have been because staying away from crime wasn't seen any longer as a matter of personal responsibility, but instead of society rehabilitating the inmates in the right way? And the caregivers having no incentive to successfully rehabilitate them, since they'd lose them as clients then, possibly facing unemployment if they all became law-abiding citizens?

* Though for quite some time, unemployment wasn't much of a problem in Sweden, but in the 1990's it started to become one. One could well argue that society up until that point had been given a free ride due to massive American imports and overestimating its own functionality. Nevertheless, as unemployment had become a problem, society provided the employment office with more money for job training and such, and unemployed people were forced to attend the courses they were assigned if they wanted to keep their government money. This naturally meant that they had less time to look for actual jobs,

while society on the other hand rarely had much of an idea about the job market, or who would fit for a certain job. Hence the employment office became an exploding bureaucracy that employed well-connected people to provide the unemployed with "job training" courses, while the actual job skills of these people faded away into obsolescence. The rising unemployment naturally meant jobs for psychiatry as well, when the job seekers became depressed.

Naturally, when government fails in an area, the ones in charge call for more funds, essentially making failure the optimal business plan. The practical application of the broken window fallacy becomes both to identify functional things as broken, and make sure the work that's supposedly aimed at restoring them, rather keeps them broken. Big government is to society what cancer is to the human body - it only devours functional tissue, it can't solve anything or even support itself, but is dependent on healthy tissue upon which it attaches itself like a parasite.

Another way to look at the process is this one: Let's assume for a moment that government employees are altruistic and desire nothing more than to successfully do their jobs. In a hypothetical soon-to-be socialist utopia called Screwupistan, the government hires two people to take care of society's problems. Let's say they work with addiction treatment and that that is something that other people than the addicts themselves can treat. Government worker #1, named Joe, is a skilled person who succeeds at anything he takes upon himself, while worker #2, named Bill, is a failure at everything, never having managed to get anything right in his life. Society's drug abusers are split evenly between the two to treat. Joe manages to get all his addicts to quit drugs during the first year he's employed. The addicts assigned to Bill are all still on drugs by the end of the year on the other hand.

When Screwupistan plans the budget for the next year, they see that Joe doesn't have a workload, there's no need to keep him employed any longer, hence he's fired. Bill on the other hand still has the same work burden on his shoulder, so the government keeps him. By the end of the second year, not a single person in his care has quit drugs either. Out in society, people that formerly saw staying off drugs as something you had to do for your own sake, or you'd risk ending up as a drug addict with a ruined life, now start to feel that they can do drugs when they feel like it since society will take care of them. Hence by the end of year #2, Screwupistan has gained new drug addicts requiring no less than four people in total employed in addiction treatment.

For year #3, the government keeps Bill employed, and also employs his equally clueless twin brother Robert. Like Bill, Robert fails at everything he does, making him perfect for a government position. The government also hires Lisa, who's a good worker who can solve the tasks she's presented with, and on top of that hires Jimmy, who witnessed what happened during year #1 of the government addiction treatment. It's hard to say whether Jimmy can really solve problems, but this doesn't matter, since he's learned that in order to keep a government job, you have to fail at the task or you'll lose the job. By the end of year #3, Lisa has managed to get her addicts off drugs, while the ones assigned to Bill, Robert and Jimmy are all still on them. Joe on the other hand is paying 90% taxes on his job in the private sector to pay for their services. For the next year, Lisa is fired while the extended family of Bill and Robert start to flock to government, using their relatives on the inside as a way in, and plenty of people who would earlier have worked in the private sector in jobs that required you to do them right, started migrating towards government jobs out of convenience. In the end, Screwupistan had nothing left but drug addicts and government workers tasked with treating them. Joe ultimately committed suicide when the government started demanding 99% of his income, and then Screwupistan collapsed.

This is a simplification of the actual process that takes place in government, when you assign it the task of solving problems. Hence, when looking at government as a solution for problems, you can view it in terms of the movie "The Matrix," with the familiar red and blue pills there. The blue pill preserves the illusion under whose influence people in general are deceived about the state of the world, while the red pill wakes you up to reality. It's apparent that government can't solve anything, so what are you going to do about the ever-increasing problems of the Western world? If you take the red pill, you see reality but become depressed since you realize that the world as we know it is disintegrating. With the blue pill, you can tell yourself there's a future in socialism. Ignorance is bliss?

There are however some areas of government where the aims aren't allowed to fail. Socialist governments have always been very strict in keeping people disarmed, and Sweden today is no exception with its vigilant application of the Orwellianly named weapons law. Thought crime, in our 1984 world usually referred to as "hate crimes," is naturally also a prioritized enterprise. In the eyes of the government, everything else in society can fail as long as people are disarmed and unable to speak their minds without being imprisoned. The suppression of weapon ownership and dissent are about the only areas in which the EU according to this author has made actual progress - few people protest these days when European countries sentence people to long prison sentences for having spoken their minds on something without even having caused any conflict.

Sweden is a country where the people have abdicated their sense of justice, morality and truth-finding to the government. The state TV presents an image of Sweden as "the best society in the world," quite often using those very words. People are presented with a streamlined view of the world, conveniently packaged, one that lets the viewer consider himself enlightened, while he can view the rest of the world as backwards. It's a case of collective narcissism, though not founded on actual nationalism, since today's Swedish state is looking for an ethnically diverse population. If the nation had remained homogenous, people would have been able to trust each other enough to form an actual resistance and be able to resist the government's attempts at a rapid change of society.

This collective narcissism instead divides the world into two groups: Winners and losers. You're a 'winner' if you assimilate the views of authority, without even having to educate yourself, do any research or any critical thinking. Simply by watching the state TV and letting it indoctrinate you, you can think of yourself as a 'winner,' able to look down on the 'losers' who aren't willing to submit to this vision. Their backwardness is described as a result of perhaps a bad upbringing, stubbornness, some hidden bigotry or similar. Naturally this can be very appealing for a person who on his own accord wouldn't be able to consider himself a 'winner,' yet who through the eyes of the state TV and connected media can do so. More than any others, Americans are portrayed as the backwards 'losers,' and it often becomes a sign of 'education' that you're well versed in the scandals and shortcomings of American society.

Hence you can become an intellectual, a freedom fighter, the vanguard of everything good and progressive by simply sitting back in your couch and being fed the right views, the only requirement being that you devote yourself to this authority and act as part of a collective in the face of dissenters, people who don't want to be fed the new socialist gospel.

The modern socialist state wants you to view it as your friend, instead of the instruments of oppression states are usually considered. There's a conflict between on the one hand traditional Western thought, stressing the rights of the individual, English common law and its insistence of clearly specified laws that apply to everyone equally. The one that described society as consisting of free individuals. On the other hand, socialism agitates among disaffected populations of society, arguing that the outcome of the traditional Western society isn't fair in the opportunity it provides - that these groups are being ripped off. To overcome their weaknesses as individuals, the disaffected have to surrender their sovereignty to the collective and its leadership, which when the socialists come to power becomes the state. Dissent and individual options are alien to socialist thought - for society to function, the individual has to suppress his tendency to question authority, and the goals of the collective can't be reached if everyone demands to tailor policies to their own needs. Hence the individual has to accept subjugating himself to the state.

To keep power in a democratic system, all the socialist party has to do is to please a large enough portion of the population to gain the continued mandate. Though traditionally in Western thought, every individual in society has been seen as a matter of concern for the public, no one's rights can simply be disregarded; it's a matter of personal responsibility for everyone to be such a watchdog. In a socialist state, when this job falls on the state, all that matters is that 51% of the voting population feels comfortable enough as *subjects* to endorse the socialists. As far as the concern for the minority goes, all the state has to do is address their concerns as *objects* in spite of being actual human beings. As long as the state can pretend it's addressing the concerns of the minority, the majority that voted for the socialists can feel whatever happens to the minority isn't their personal problem. If a member of the minority whose actual concerns aren't addressed approaches a member of the population whose concerns are, the majority person will naturally feel it's the minority person's own fault that he's in whatever predicament he's in - the government addressed his concerns. To the majority person, there really are no such things as human rights - he knows he's not really rightfully entitled to the share of the pie he gains himself through aligning with the party.

The majority can pretend it doesn't oppress the minority since the concerns of both are said to be met - it's just that the majority have an actual say as subjects, while the minority are dealt with as objects. That's one of the problems with representative democracy if it doesn't respect individual rights and lets the state grow too all-encompassing. Rights should be considered belonging to an individual so that he can build himself the life he wants, yet in modern European socialist societies, the concern of the one whose needs aren't met by the policies that satisfied the majority vote has to contend himself with being dealt with as an object at the mercy of an uncooperative government that doesn't respect his basic human rights.

There's also a real danger in having a society founded on secular values, not recognizing a god who created man and endowed him with unalienable rights. Though Western thought generally presupposes natural law, Sweden in particular has endorsed the opposite - legal positivism. This philosophy doesn't recognize any natural rights and permits society to enact whatever laws it likes. The natural consequence of this philosophy is summed up in the three words "might is right" - you only have rights to the extent you can influence policy that affects you. This in spite of all modern societies attesting to just how humane they are - if they're not founded on divine law, they still claim that "secular humanism" will ensure respect for human rights through man's natural ethics.

In Swedish society, traditional institutions such as church and family have been weakened almost to the point of insignificance, and there are few organizational forms people can gather under apart from the ones endorsed by the state - the established parliamentary parties, the gay lobby and such. When the individual is offered little protection, and you don't have church or family to turn to, naturally you will have to look for security in the state. To do this, you can't be a dissident, a so called 'loser,' since the state will then exclude you. To be offered protection, you have to prove your loyalty to the state, that you will not express any dissenting views. This is a kind of fascism.

Media sometimes expresses itself in ways such as "winners don't have the kind of views those people have," when describing dissidents who don't follow the party line. The individual is encouraged to align with authority in order to achieve a higher social standing and be able to look upon himself as a 'winner' and the dissident as a 'loser.'

Though it varies between individuals, just about all men have a certain distaste for merely being a pawn of authority - one likes to think of oneself as a 'rebel.' So how does the system address this problem? By distorting reality - by letting people pretend they're the underdogs while they're really the bullies. Totalitarian societies have always had their eyes on the youth, whose worldviews haven't been cemented yet. Such societies have managed to turn the young into fanatic zealots for the causes of the state by projecting the idea to them that they're the vanguard of change, soldiers in a battle against reaction. The establishment wants the force of this youth harnessed for its own purposes, to secure its political stability. How does it make the youth think they're fighting an important battle? Through revisionist history, portraying the old order as oppressive, the old establishment as evil, and the new rulers as former victims of oppression.

The main enemy of the socialist has always been America, with its unsurpassed liberty, and after World War II, its unsurpassed wealth as well. People around the world have for over a century looked to America as the land of their dreams, which has made establishing socialist societies harder - "why should I toil for the government and its causes here if I could have such a great life over there?" Therefore, socialist movements have had to have as their priority, more than anything else, to look for flaws in American society and undermine the belief in it.

During the time of the Vietnam war, Sweden more than any other Western country lashed out at the USA over its atrocities. Criticism was warranted, of course, but the Swedish Social Democrats exploited the Anti-American sentiment for its own gains. Between WW2 and the Vietnam war, the USA steadily influenced Swedes into demanding more republican reforms, calling for Sweden to become more like America; the old monarchy had to be scrapped. At a time when hope was almost lost for the belief in Swedish socialism due to the success of American society, along came this war, which rallied Western youth against it. Swedish Prime Minister Olof Palme then fully embraced this anti-war movement, even going so far as to compare America to Nazi Germany. Naturally, these actions attracted youth to the Social Democrats, and socialism was saved for the moment.

During the last one or two decades, gay activists have been quite outspoken in America, saying society doesn't do enough for them, saying they're oppressed and such. Even by the mid 1990's, gay rights was hardly a concern at all in Sweden - people who practised this lifestyle had no reason at all to not be content. Yet as America started to do some soul-searching and believe that maybe it wasn't such a great society, Sweden seized the day and hit full throttle when it came to gay rights - I believe I've covered it fairly well in this book. This was yet again something the Swedish state could exploit in order to present itself as 'good' and the USA as 'bad.' The Iraq war naturally came in handy too, with the bad reputation it gave America.

By slamming the USA over this, Sweden could yet again rally the youth, making them think they're fighting for change while they're really being used by the Swedish establishment, turning their backs on traditional Western thought. All this youth learns is that the country that's more than any other has stood for freedom, is really only about bashing homosexuals and searching the globe for enemies to fight. The youth rarely gains a more traditional and timeless perspective. Hence the socialists makes the youth think they're fighting to break new grounds in liberty, while they're really being exploited by the state in advancing socialism.

Socialists, in the 'winner' vs 'loser' manner, portray people as more refined if they let their views be shaped by the state through dubious use of science - or rather pseudo-science - as opposed to the crude people that stick with views that have stood the test of time. To be a refined person, you're supposed to view a criminal as a "victim of society," and rehabilitation as the humane way to deal with the problem. Calling for punishment is supposedly crude, not to mention endorsing the death penalty. To be able to see yourself as a 'winner,' you have to embrace the policies of the establishment, and their policies are due to the use of Bastiat's broken window fallacy ones that don't work. It's a bit of a trade: The state wants to profit through destroying society, then being able to charge the taxpayers money for restoring it. To get support for these destructive policies, the state regards individuals that embrace them as more refined, hence these people become 'winners' by supporting the policies of destruction.

Sweden has a government agency called *Forum för levande historia*, "Forum for living history," whose stated goal is the following:

> "Forum for living history is tasked with being a national forum that will further the work on democracy, tolerance and human rights with its foundation in the holocaust."

It's essentially an agency for influencing of public opinion, where the government defines what should be matters of concern. It goes without saying that this agency is quite selective in what it instructs about, and it takes away from the individual the responsibility to make up his own mind on ethics and what to learn from history. Curiously absent from the historical atrocities described on the website for this agency is any mention of the many Swedish children that were taken from their parents and placed into orphanages. Perhaps because society still today does just that, and the real (though not admitted) purpose of this agency isn't to criticize policies practised today.

The Swedish state has throughout the 20th century fiercely fought attempts by non-socialist reformers to clearly define the limitations on state power and establish the rights of the individual. People have been expected to be naive about the use of governmental power, concepts such as the "common good" have validated its call for dominance over society. Olof Palme more than any other politician popularized soft totalitarianism through slogans such as "the people are the government," and "everything is politics." As I've covered in this book, this philosophy has led to great tragedy and suffering. It's time man learns from the failed socialist experiments for good.

When Communism fell two decades ago, they tore down the Berlin wall and the statues of society's leaders. When will Sweden tear down the statue of the infallible welfare state?

Acknowledgements and inspiration

All the translations of law texts (except in a few noted cases such as the Penal Code) and printed works have been made by me personally, hence they are to be considered unofficial. Since the book was intended for an international audience, I've strived for using official documents that are available over the Internet as sources for this book. I've attempted to avoid using any information that isn't easy to verify, and even a layman reader should find it fairly easy looking up all the sources. For the case vignettes described in the book, I've used relevant publicly available media as personal sources, although without bothering the reader with just where some piece of soft information was found. Though I've personally gone to great lengths to verify information I've made use of and rejected it if has seemed the least bit dubious, it simply doesn't matter where I read that a certain person did something insignificant at a given time. The overwhelming backbone of these case vignettes does however consist of official government accounts, though in some cases I've had to fill them up with the personal accounts of the described people.

For law and case citations, *www.notisum.se* and *www.lagen.nu* have been used along with Swedish government websites, referenced as footnotes. A good portion of the material for the chapter on the government as parent was taken from the Nordic Committee for Human Rights website - *www.nkmr.org* - and I must pay tribute to the great work Ruby Harrold-Claesson, Siv Westerberg and the others at the NCHR have done over the years. While the state TV and established mass media has elevated assorted dimwits to the level of gurus and let them both comment on events in media as well as provide feedback on legislation in circulation, the freedom fighters of the NCHR have been virtually

462

ignored by the establishment, though word has made it to the people whose rights the state have trampled. I can however tell that our oppressive government here in Sweden has felt their presence as a thorn in its side every time it assumes it's got free reins to do as it pleases, finding them exploring the legal venues available to stop it and the media venues to highlight it.

I must also acknowledge the work of magazines such as *Folket i bild / Kulturfront* and *Salt* for standing up for freedom of speech and criticizing the application of the HMF law, when the climate in mass media and the political establishment has been one of intense persecution of not only dissidents, but also the ones who support their right to speak. Undoubtedly, these reporters and writers would have had more personal financial success had they aligned themselves with the state and joined the rest of media in endorsing censorship, but thankfully even in this Sodom of a society, there are still people with principles. It is this authors opinion that a free society simply can't have laws such as HMF and LVU, laws that only belong in a totalitarian state, which it's my hope that the reader will now have come to realize Sweden is.

The last person whose life work I will here acknowledge is that of Eddie Meduza. Though he passed away in 2002, his memory still lives on. This man is known for two things - both his vulgar and banal songs mostly focused on genitalia and various forms of sexuality, often only involving one person - but also his defiance towards society's norms, standing up as an individualist in spite of being ostracised by the cultural establishment. Meduza's attitude towards Swedish society and government has been a great inspiration to this author, especially when mass media keeps flooding you with reports on how great contemporary Sweden supposedly is, when you personally know that it's not.

Review questions

Some readers might ask themselves the question, "did I really learn anything from this book?" Well, if you're one of them, here are a number of questions through which you can test your knowledge of the madhouse that is Sweden, with answers on the following pages.

1) Which of the two countries was the last to abolish slavery, Sweden or the USA?

2) Which of the two countries has a higher rate of violent crime?

3) In which of the two countries does the average person enjoy a higher living standard?

4) Which of the two countries has been the only one to be able to attract labour immigration the last four decades?

5) In which of the two countries do citizens enjoy the greatest civil liberties?

6) Which of the two countries has committed the most atrocities against its own citizens?

7) Which of the two countries has the greatest amount of state meddling in the free press?

8) Which of the two countries has criticized the other the most?

9) Which of the two countries has had the most celebrities say they're going to leave the country unless their favourite presidential candidate is elected?

10) Which of the two countries has the best climate?

Answers:

1) Sweden, in 1945; the USA did in 1865.

2) Sweden, about twice as high.

3) A man earning median income in the USA affords about twice as high private consumption as one in Sweden.

4) The USA; Sweden has only been able to attract welfare moochers since 1970. Lots of people want to move to the USA, including many Europeans, but they can't due to immigration laws.

5) The USA; freedom of speech, freedom of religion, the recognition of natural rights etc, things that are largely missing in Swedish society.

6) Sweden; the largest portion of the population of any country forcibly sterilized. Job exclusion on a scale that puts America's McCarthyism to shame.

7) Sweden; severe restrictions on the freedom of the press; state payouts to newspapers; and during World War II, direct censorship of media to ensure that no anti-German sentiment was expressed, for fear of Germany attacking Sweden.

8) Sweden; almost incessant negative reporting on American society going on for decades, describing the USA as an economic prison, as a country of violent religious fanatics, as well as comparisons between Nazi Germany and the USA by a former prime minister. About the only criticism from the USA against Sweden was when Olof Palme compared the bombing of Vietnam to the holocaust, which made American state officials point out just what state Sweden crawled before during World War II.

9) The USA. As far as this author has found out, while several American celebrities have vowed to leave their country, no Swedish celebrities have done so.

10) Sweden, of course - at least the northern part with its traditionally cold winters. The state of Alaska is equal to Sweden in this regard, however. The spirit of the state of Texas truly seems great with the outlook on life people have there - but alas, the climate is much too hot.

INDEX

www.ingramcontent.com/pod-product-compliance
Lightning Source LLC
Chambersburg PA
CBHW080602270326
41928CB00016B/2897